Kilian McDonnell, O.S.B.

The Baptism of Jesus in the Jordan

The Trinitarian and Cosmic Order of Salvation

A Michael Glazier Book

THE LITURGICAL PRESS
Collegeville, Minnesota

A Michael Glazier Book published by The Liturgical Press.

Cover design by Frank Kacmarcik, Obl.S.B. Manuscript illumination, "Baptism of Jesus," Der Landgrafenpsalter, 13th century, State Library of Württemberg, Germany.

Library of Congress Cataloging-in-Publication Data

McDonnell, Kilian.
    The Baptism of Jesus in the Jordan : the trinitarian and cosmic order of salvation / Kilian McDonnell.
       p.   cm.
    "A Michael Glazier book."
    Includes bibliographical references and index.
    ISBN 0-8146-5307-3
    1. Jesus Christ—Baptism. 2. Bible. N.T. Gospels—Criticism, interpretation, etc. 3. Trinity. 4. Baptism—History—Early church, ca. 30–600. 5. Baptism. 6. Baptism (Liturgy) 7. Baptism--Catholic Church. 8. Catholic Church—Doctrines. I. Title.
BT350.M33 1996
232.9'5—dc20
                                        96-8000
                                           CIP

Contents

Introduction

For years Jesus' baptism in the Jordan has engaged my interest. That the Synoptics all mention it, and the Fourth Gospel gives a report of it, would indicate an event of some importance. One is surprised that the baptism of Jesus has not prompted more serious scholarly attention.[1] This volume looks at a series of themes. This is not a work in historical theology; I am a systematic theologian working with historical texts. The small chapter on the biblical materials is meant only to serve as an introduction to the themes that arise in the post-biblical period, and is not considered an adequate exegetical presentation.

Of principal interest is how the early post-biblical period appropriated the biblical evidence. What were the theological preoccupations of the authors of that period? What themes did they elaborate?

The mystery is approached with a view to its trinitarian content. This early triadic teaching is not yet the more precise trinitarian teaching of the Cappadocian settlement in the fourth

---

[1] Among the major studies are J. Bornemann, *Die Taufe Christi durch Johannes in der dogmatischen Beurteilung der christlichen Theologen der vier ersten Jahrhunderte* (Leipzig: Hinrich, 1896); J. Kosnetter, *Die Taufe Jesu: Exegetische und religionsgeschichtliche Studien* (Vienna: Mayer, 1936); F. Lentzen-Deis, *Die Taufe Jesu nach den Synoptikern* (Frankfurt am Main: Knecht, 1970); D. A. Bertrand, *Le Baptême de Jésus: Histoire de l'exégèse aux deux premiers siècles* (Tübingen: Mohr [Siebeck], 1973). D. Vigne, *Christ au Jordain: Le Baptême de Jésus dans la Tradition Judéo-Chrétienne* (Paris: Gabalda, 1992).

century. Given this *caveat*, it is proper to speak of trinitarian thought before the fourth-century controversies. The Trinity did not spring full blown only in the age of Athanasius and the Cappadocians.

Also, I have attempted to pull out of the texts the cosmic dimensions of the baptism in the early texts. This constitutes a thread through the book. The cosmic meaning of Jesus' baptism should not be isolated from the incarnation and the paschal mysteries.

No consistent use exists of "the baptism of Christ" or "baptism of the Lord" or "the baptism of Jesus." Though there is a difference, they are sometimes used interchangeably by the same author. I have tried to be sensitive to gender issues in my own text, but have left the use of the masculine unchanged in documents I am quoting.

The circular logic of symbolic language means that a certain amount of repetition is implicit in the texts. Occasionally, I have, by necessity, repeated the same text in different chapters. This seems demanded by the differing contexts. Also, I have identified the different documents more than once—again, to help understand the contexts.

Though this is a systematic work rather than a historical one, I have tried to keep to the chronological order, sometimes violating it for systematic reasons.

I hope I can demonstrate that the baptism of Jesus is a major mystery in the life of the early Church.

Chapter One

The Beginning of the Gospel: The Scriptures

John the Baptist belongs to a broad movement in Palestine and Syria in which baptism was practiced by a number of religions —ancient oriental, Jewish, and Christian—beginning in the mid-second century B.C.E. and lasting until about 300 C.E.[1] Early Christianity was profoundly marked by the baptist movement. Jesus stood in continuity with that branch of the baptist movement which John the Baptist represented. One can believe that John baptized his first disciples in the Jordan, and after the baptism of Jesus, some of the Baptist's followers became followers of Jesus (John 1:35-42); but there was no wholesale abandonment of John by his followers to join a greater prophet. Luke notes that twenty years later John still had disciples in Ephesus (Acts 19:3). Herod had a certain justification in saying that Jesus was a new John the Baptist, a remark recorded by all the Synoptics (Mark 6:16; Matt 14:2; Luke 9:9). Jesus, indeed, took over the baptist inheritance.

Nonetheless, there is a consistent attempt by the four Gospels to undercut the continuing rivalry between the followers of John and those of Jesus by repeated insistence that John was

[1] J. Thomas, *Le Mouvement Baptiste en Palestine et Syrie (150 av. J.-C.–300 ap. J.-C.)* (Gembloux: Catholic University of Louvain, 1935).

only a herald identifying his greater successor.[2] The Spirit descends and remains on Jesus, showing that he is the one promised by John, the one who will baptize in/with the Holy Spirit (Mark 1:8). In the Judaism of the time, to receive the spirit almost always meant prophetic inspiration.[3]

As to the purity of the tradition that Mark hands on, we are not sure that the Markan version is without retouching.[4] Mark, the only independent witness to the baptism among the Synoptics—Matthew and Luke depend on him—arranges this material to demonstrate Jesus' superiority to John. If Jesus stands in the inheritance of John, much more is he heir to the Old Testament prophecies, which themselves explain why Jesus is superior.[5] Mark associates the Baptist with Malachi, Isaiah, and Elijah, and he goes out of his way to relate the baptism of Jesus to imagery of the crossing of the Red Sea by Moses.[6] The rending of the heavens is the instrument of a theophany, attested already in Judaism.[7] The heavenly voice proclaims that Jesus is God's Son in an expansion of the words of Psalm 2:7, "You are my Son, the Beloved." The words in Mark are addressed to Jesus, not to the onlookers; Jesus is informed of his status for the first time.[8] These are the words Yahweh

[2] M. E. Enslin, "John and Jesus," *Zeitschrift für die Neutestamentliche Wissenschaft und die Kunde der älteren Kirche* 66 (1975) 10; R. E. Brown, *The Gospel According to John I–XII* (Garden City: Doubleday, 1966) 65; C. K. Barrett, *The Gospel According to St. John,* 2nd ed. (Philadelphia: Westminster, 1978) 171.

[3] H. L. Strack and P. Billerbeck, *Das Evangelium nach Markus, Lukas and Johannes und die Apostelgeschichte* (Munich: C. H. Beck, 1924) 2:127.

[4] S. Légasse, "Le baptême de Jésus et le baptême chrétien," in *Studium Biblicum Franciscanum* 27 (1977) 56.

[5] J. P. Meier, *A Marginal Jew: Rethinking the Historical Jesus,* 2 vols. (New York: Doubleday, 1991) 106. All references are to vol. 1.

[6] A. Stock, *The Method and Message of Mark* (Wilmington: Glazier, 1989) 47.

[7] The call of the messianic high priest has both the splitting open of the heavens and the voice of the Father as from Abraham to Isaac in *The Testament of Levi* 18:6. *The Testament of Judah* 24:2, 3 speaks of the Messiah in similar terms. *The Old Testament Pseudepigrapha,* J. H. Charlesworth, ed., 2 vols. (Garden City: Doubleday, 1983) 1:795, 801.

[8] J. Meier, *Matthew* (Wilmington: Glazier, 1980) 28.

addresses to the Davidic king on the day of his enthronement. The words of Psalm 2:7 and the symbolic "anointing" with the Spirit suggest that this Son is also the promised Davidic Messiah. The phrase "with you I am well pleased" comes from Isaiah 42:1, making Jesus the Servant of Yahweh, the mysterious transcendent figure whom God endows with the spirit to reestablish the covenant community by his sacrificial and atoning death, vindicated by his resurrection. The superiority of Jesus is stressed. "You," not John, are "my Son"; "you," not John, are the beloved of the Father; "you," not John, are the Messiah; "you," not John, are the Servant of Yahweh.[9]

Yet the case must not be overstated. When Jesus is asked the basis of his authority (Mark 11:27-33; Matt 21:23-27; Luke 20:1-8), his counter-question, whether the baptism of John came from heaven or from men, should not be taken simply as a dodge. Rather, if taken seriously, it means "My authority rests on John's baptism" or, more expansively, "My authority rests on what happened when I was baptized by John."[10] Though baptism must have meant something different to Jesus, he always acknowledged the value of John's baptism (Mark 11:30-33; Matt 21:32; Luke 7:29-30).[11]

The Boundary Event

Very likely there was a period of overlap between John and Jesus's time, but weighty evidence suggests that it cannot have been very long, and that "a break" came between the two. Their central messages are quite different: while John believed that eschatology was at hand, Jesus believed that the shift in eons had already taken place. The sign that the kingdom was already present in him was the presence of the Spirit working in and through him in words, healings, and exorcisms. In this

---

[9] Meier, A Marginal Jew, 1:106, 107.

[10] J. Jeremias, New Testament Theology (New York: Scribner, 1971) 56. J.D.G. Dunn thinks that Jeremias may press his point "over-confidently," but grants that some such inference is justified. Jesus and the Spirit (Philadelphia: Westminster, 1975) 64.

[11] R. Schnackenburg, The Gospel According to St. John, 3 vols. (New York: Herder and Herder/Crossroad, 1968–1982) 1:411.

view the Spirit is the decisive factor.[12] John baptizes in water; Jesus baptizes in/with the Holy Spirit. Indeed, the distinction between water baptism and Spirit baptism seems to be decisive.[13]

But the Jordan may represent an even more basic break between John and Jesus. John P. Meier points out that Jesus came to the Jordan an unknown quantity, a carpenter from Nazareth, without fame, an anonymous face in the crowd. When he began his public ministry, immediately after the baptism and temptation, both his family and neighbors were astonished, embarrassed, and affronted. Nothing in his personal history could account for his sudden entrance into a ministry to the whole of Israel. The sole historically verifiable bridge between the two phases of his life is his baptism. This boundary event at least means that Jesus sees himself as a member of that chosen, beloved, but sinful Israel that John the Baptist threatens with divine judgment. By accepting baptism at the hands of the Baptist, Jesus recognizes that this baptism is the divinely appointed means of passage from the sinful Israel to the Israel promised salvation on the day of judgment.[14]

Beyond that, there is a decisive transformation of the Baptist's message of repentance. The significance of this event at the Jordan, which belongs "indubitably" to the life of the historical Jesus, is that Jesus began with "the same burning expectation of the End as the Baptist, and that he therefore had himself 'sealed' from the imminent judgment of wrath and incorporated [himself] into the holy remnant of the people of God."[15] But when Jesus, newly sealed against God's anger, walks away from the Jordan and proclaims repentance, there is a departure from John's message. No longer is repentance primarily a protection against the wrath of God; it is a gift of grace and mercy.[16] The difference is unambiguous. The baptism is, therefore, a

[12] Dunn, *Jesus and the Spirit*, 64.

[13] E. Haenchen, *John 1* (Philadelphia: Fortress, 1984) 154.

[14] Meier, *A Marginal Jew*, 1:108–111.

[15] E. Käsemann, "On the Subject of Primitive Christian Apocalyptic," *New Testament Questions of Today* (Philadelphia: Fortress, 1969) 112; Haenchen, *John 1*, 148.

[16] Ibid., 113.

bridge-burning event—the boundary cannot be recrossed—representing a radically new orientation in the life of Jesus.

Should the Event Be Psychologized?

The baptism of Jesus is recorded with some specificity by the Synoptics (Matt 3:13-17; Mark 1:9-11; Luke 3:21, 22). Whatever differences among the Synoptics, they agree on three phenomena: the splitting of the heavens, the Spirit descending upon Jesus, and the voice speaking from the heavens declaring him the beloved Son. Only after the Spirit has descended on him (or into him) does he engage in ministry. All the strata of the Gospels agree on this, including the Fourth Gospel (Mark 1:10; Matt 3:16; Luke 3:22; John 1:32-51), and possibly Q, another sign of the boundary quality of the baptism. Further, the Synoptics all agree (Mark 1:12; Matt 4:1; Luke 4:1) that after being anointed with the Spirit at the Jordan, the Spirit leads Jesus into the desert to be tempted—Mark has the forceful expression "he drove him out" or "he expelled him"—the temptation being understood as preliminary to his ministry.[17]

Does the theophany first recorded in Mark reflect some inner vision, some interior experience that Jesus had? Contemporary exegetes are reluctant to psychologize the text. Very likely the text represents less Jesus' inner experience and more the necessity of the early community to establish Jesus' identity at the very beginning of the Gospel. Built into the definition of his identity is the answer to the question of Jesus' subordination to John because he received his baptism.

One has to be open to the possibility that Jesus was aware of his role as Servant of God even before his baptism. In this case his motive for coming forward for baptism would have been to manifest himself as the one who was to take upon himself the sins of all (Mark 10:45; Matt 20:28; John 1:29). At the very least, it seems clear that when Jesus went down into the waters of the Jordan, he was conscious that he was fulfilling the will of God. Further, he recognized that John was a true prophet, that his preaching and his baptism was "from heaven" (Mark 11:30).

[17] J.D.G. Dunn, *Christology in the Making* (Philadelphia: Westminster, 1980) 138–139.

In other words, Jesus saw John's mission as a fulfillment of the will of God and a preparation for his own messianic mission.[18]

Mark is the first to present the tradition. Matthew transforms Mark's account with some help from Q. In Mark, Jesus has a vision and he hears a voice addressed to him. This is a more private affair. Matthew turns Jesus' private vision into a public epiphany. Here the opening of the heavens is narrated as an observable event. To all present the voice from heaven proclaims "This is my son."[19] Later, Mark records the words of Jesus joining his baptism to his death (10:38, 39), a theme that appears also in Luke (12:50).

Matthew introduces a dialogue between John the Baptist and Jesus. John objects to baptizing Jesus, an objection Jesus overrules in the name of "all righteousness" (3:15). As Meier observes, in this case "righteousness" seems to mean the saving activity of God. Matthew is obviously engaging in theological reflection on the meaning of Jesus' baptism. Matthew also moves the source of Jesus' sonship back to the virginal conception. For this reason it is not necessary to inform Jesus that he is the Son at his baptism, as though this would be new knowledge. For this reason Matthew directs to others the message *"This* is my beloved Son." The allusion to Psalm 2:7 is more obscure in Matthew. But the reference to God's chosen servant, on whom God bestows his spirit (Isa 42:1), is clearer than in Mark.[20]

The Universalizing Content

In the original Greek, Luke's account of the baptism (Luke 3:21, 22) is disposed of in one long sentence. Luke has already identified Jesus as Savior, Lord, and Messiah (Luke 2:11) and has named him "Son" (Luke 1:32, 35). But in the baptismal narrative, he omits identifying Jesus as coming from Nazareth and leaves out mention of the Jordan. But he adds two details: Jesus is depicted as praying when the heavens open up—thus touch-

---

[18] J. Blinzler, "Baptism of Jesus," *Sacramentum Verbi: An Encyclopedia of Biblical Theology,* J. B. Bauer, ed., 3 vols. (New York: Herder and Herder, 1970) 1:62, 63.

[19] Meier, *Matthew,* 26.

[20] Ibid., 28.

ing on Jesus' inner experience—and the Spirit descends in the form of a dove.

Luke seems to reduce subordinating themes by leaving out any reference to John the Baptist in his baptismal narrative. Luke almost removes John from the scene: the reader does not see John acting on Jesus. He also omits John's hesitation to baptize Jesus. Luke's account is neither as private as Mark's nor as public as Matthew's. But by having Jesus praying, Luke provides the reader, ostensibly through the descent of the Spirit and the audition of the voice, with an empowerment and a declaration of sonship taking place during prayer, as in the transfiguration narrative (Luke 9:28-36).[21]

Luke's narrative tells of Jesus' baptism preceding his Galilean ministry, whereas the transfiguration story precedes his journey to Jerusalem and his death. In both cases a significant phase of Jesus' ministry begins with a declaration of sonship and, according to Joseph A. Fitzmyer, a unique relationship to the Father.[22] Finally, Luke follows the baptism with a genealogy that traces Jesus' lineage past Abraham all the way back to Adam, thus retrieving the note of universality he sounded in 3:6 (. . . "all flesh shall see the salvation of God"). By placing the genealogy immediately after the baptism, Luke indicates that his status has less to do with a human ancestry and more with the status as God's son established in the power of the Spirit.[23]

The Spirit Remains on the Pre-Existent Son

The verses in the Fourth Gospel very likely represent traditional material, but from sources independent of Mark (and therefore of the other Synoptics).[24] Though there is no direct report of Jesus' baptism in the Fourth Gospel, John does allude to the tradition obliquely (John 1:29-34).[25] The evangelist, seemingly not

[21] L. T. Johnson, *The Gospel of Luke* (Collegeville: The Liturgical Press, 1991) 71.

[22] J. A. Fitzmyer, *The Gospel According to Luke I–IX* (Garden City: Doubleday, 1981) 482, 483.

[23] Johnson, *The Gospel of Luke*, 72.

[24] Brown, *The Gospel According to John I–XII*, 66.

[25] Meier, *A Marginal Jew*, 1:102, says "the event of the baptism is simply suppressed."

interested in historical detail, focuses on theological meaning, recording "the mature Christian reflection" of the community.[26]

The context for this sidewise glance at the baptism of Jesus is a deputation of Jewish authorities approaching the Baptist to investigate his intentions and claims. In response, the Baptist sums up his mission as one witnessing to a mightier one, standing in their midst yet unknown, who is to come after him. Later the Baptist clarifies with the declaration that Jesus is the Lamb of God, the one equipped with the Spirit who can baptize with the Holy Spirit, he being the Elect of God. In narrative form he sums up the content of the Prologue.[27]

The relation to the prologue is important. Whether or not Meier is correct in saying "the event of the baptism is simply suppressed,"[28] the indirect narrative does not have the same function of identifying who Jesus is for the reader. Already in the prologue Jesus has been identified for the reader as the eternal Son of God (John 1:1, 18). Pre-existence is already established. In the indirect report of the baptism of Jesus, there is a theophany directed to the Baptist (contrary to Mark 1:9, 10), identifying Jesus for the Baptist (the reader of the Fourth Gospel already knows who Jesus is). In the Synoptics it is assumed that John the Baptist knew Jesus before the baptism (Matt 3:13, 14; Luke 1:41, 44), but in the Fourth Gospel the Baptist expressly says "I myself did not know him" (John 1:31). Previous to the Jordan event, God had revealed to the Baptist that "he on whom you see the Spirit descend and remain is the one who baptizes with the Holy Spirit" (John 1:33). So John testifies first to a revelation, and then to a theophany, namely, he saw the Spirit in fact descending and remaining on Jesus. Therefore the Baptist declares: "And I myself have seen and have testified that this is the Son of God" (John 1:34).

In the Synoptics it is the voice from heaven declaring Jesus to be the Son of God; here it is the Baptist, though the evangelist

[26] Schnackenburg, *The Gospel According to St. John,* 1:297.

[27] Barrett, *The Gospel According to St. John,* 170.

[28] *A Marginal Jew,* 1:102. R. Bultmann says "it would be wrong to conclude from this that Jesus' baptism was an embarrassment for the Evangelist, so that he passes over it as quickly as possible." *The Gospel of John* (Philadelphia: Westminster, 1971) 94.

is not adverse to having a voice from heaven give direct testimony (John 12:38).[29] While the Jordan event in this Gospel is neither to identify Jesus to the reader (he has already been informed) nor to John (he has previously received a revelation), there is a further specification of his identity: because the Spirit has descended on him, and remained on him, he will baptize with the Holy Spirit.

The evangelist may be countering the claims of the Baptist's disciples, who claim that their master is superior to Jesus because priority in time means priority in dignity. Though preexistence can have a number of meanings, the Baptist's disclaimer "He existed before me" (John 1:15) may mean preexistence in the Christian sense, that is, existing before the beginning of time, as we know it. If priority is decisive, then, even in this "temporal" sense Jesus is superior to the Baptist. To put such a declaration in the mouth of the Baptist is matter of the greatest daring.[30]

To strengthen his case against the sectarians, the evangelist removes any aspect of the baptism of Jesus that might elevate the position of the Baptist.[31] For example, to de-emphasize the Baptist, the fourth evangelist no longer equates him with Elijah, as the Synoptics had done.

Christian iconography often presents Jesus as standing in the river with the Baptist pouring water over him from his cupped hand or some shell. This is hardly true to the text (Mark 1:9; Matt 3:16; Luke 3:21), where the Greek means "undergo immersions" or "immerse oneself." Mark goes back to the tradition which implies that Jesus immersed himself.[32] Though baptism by immersion has largely been lost in the Church, with some recent retrievals, it has nonetheless remained the ideal because the sign is clearer.[33]

---

[29] Brown, *The Gospel According to John I-XII,* 65.

[30] Schnackenburg, *The Gospel According to St. John,* 302.

[31] Brown, *The Gospel According to John I-XII,* 65.

[32] Jeremias, *New Testament Theology,* 51.

[33] In *The Rite of Christian Initiation of Adults,* 32, immersion is mentioned first in the appropriate ways of administering the baptism.

What, if any, is the messianic character of the baptism? In the Synoptics the whole event is about the identity of Jesus. Or as Ernst Haenchen puts it, "who he really is."[34] Who is he? The answer of the text of Mark is: the Son of the God endowed with the Spirit. The whole of what is to follow must be seen in the light of this event. The splitting of the heavens connotes an act of power such as only God can perform, and indicates that the Spirit which descends on Jesus is no less than God's Spirit. That the Spirit descends on Jesus is a reference to Isaiah: "The spirit of the LORD shall rest on him" (Isa 11:2), indicating the messianic role that Jesus is assuming. The long drought of the Spirit is over, and the silence of God's voice is ended: "You are my Son, the Beloved; with you I am well pleased" (Mark 1:11).[35] Mark seems to combine the idea of messianic son with that of the Servant.

Matthew identifies Jesus as the Messiah in the first verse of his Gospel as a way of introducing the genealogy, the only time he uses the formulation "Jesus Christ (Messiah)" (1:1). In Matthew the Baptist's messianic witness (3:11-17) leads immediately to the baptism of Jesus. Mark and Luke also see John's role as primarily the precursor to the Messiah. Though the Baptist's disciples see him as a kind of messiah, John points away from himself to Jesus, the one who will "baptize you with the Holy Spirit" (Mark 1:8), which introduces Jesus' baptism. Luke has already told us that Jesus is Savior, Lord, and Messiah (2:11) and presents John as "more than a prophet" (7:26), the one who announces that "one who is more powerful than I is coming" (3:16), the messianic person who baptizes with the Holy Spirit.[36] John is no ordinary prophet, because by proclaiming

[34] *Der Weg Jesu* (Berlin: de Gruyter, 1968) 52.

[35] E. Schweizer, *The Good News According to Mark* (Richmond: John Knox, 1970) 41.

[36] R. Bultmann contends that the baptism of Jesus represents "Jesus' consecration as messiah." *The History of the Synoptic Tradition* (New York: Harper & Row, 1972) 248. Fitzmyer, *The Gospel According to Luke I–IX*, 466, 480, rejects that position. Fitzmyer holds that "neither the descent of the Spirit upon Jesus, nor the recognition of him as 'Son,' nor the implication of his being Yahweh's Servant connote a messianic function." Even if nei-

Jesus, he inaugurates the eschaton. In all four Gospels the witness of John immediately precedes Jesus baptism.

If the question is what kind of a messiah Jesus will be, Luke, through the baptism and the genealogy, which should be read together, would answer "a prophetic messiah."[37] A connection exists between the descending of the Spirit and the voice declaring that Jesus is the Son of God. Jesus is addressed as the Son of God in virtue of his installation as Messiah; one cannot receive the messianic role without the personal endowment of the Spirit. As in the birth narratives, the Spirit is the creative power of God that constitutes the inauguration of the messianic age.[38] The endowment with the Spirit is more than just a sign that the eschatological area has begun in Jesus. The descending of the Spirit is also the sign that he is equipped with power for that messianic role (Mark 1:8, 12; Matt 12:18, 28). Luke probably understands the baptism of Jesus as a messianic designation. Luke's formula "God anointed Jesus of Nazareth with the Holy Spirit and with power" (Acts 10:38) very likely refers to his baptism, joining the messianic anointing with the coming of the Holy Spirit and power at the Jordan.

Though great theological constructions should not be built upon a single word, the fourth evangelist says twice that the descending Spirit "remained" on Jesus (1:32, 33; cf. Mark 1:10; similarly, Matt 3:16). That Yahweh will put the Spirit on Isaiah's Servant of God (42:1) and that the Spirit will rest on the future Davidic king was already in the tradition. This characterizes Jesus as God's unique instrument, both Servant of God and Messiah. Jesus, therefore, fully and permanently possesses the Spirit, and can impart that Spirit after the resurrection (John 20:22) out of his own fullness. Through prophetic illumination

---

ther son nor Servant is necessarily messianic, Luke has already identified Jesus as "Messiah" (Luke 2:11). Fitzmyer does admit that in Acts 10:37, 38, Luke, when reflecting back and making a résumé of Jesus' ministry, interprets Jesus' baptism as a messianic anointing. "God anointed him with the Holy Spirit and with power," ibid. 480. There does not seem to be sufficient evidence for rejecting Bultmann's position.

[37] Johnson, *The Gospel of Luke*, 70.

[38] C. K. Barrett, *The Holy Spirit and the Gospel Tradition* (London: SPCK, 1947) 44, 45.

the Baptist recognizes Jesus as the Son/Elect of God (John 1:34).[39] On the lips of the Baptist (as on the lips of Nathanael [John 1:49] and Martha [John 11:27]) this would be understood primarily in a messianic sense, even though the evangelist meant it also to be taken in the higher sense of "metaphysical" Son of God (John 20:31).[40] Only by interior illumination did the Baptist recognize Jesus as the Messiah in the descent of the Spirit.

The Baptist points to Jesus as "the Lamb of God" (John 1:29). Though there is no solid evidence that the Baptist thought that the one who would come after him would suffer and die, the evangelist did think so. The fourth evangelist seems to intend the Lamb of God to refer to the Suffering Servant and the paschal lamb.[41] In the baptismal event, therefore, the evangelist has the Baptist acknowledging Jesus as eternal Son/Elect, Servant of Yahweh, Messiah, unique bearer of the Spirit, and the Lamb who atones vicariously—a breathtaking christological synthesis.

Backward Christology

Mark lets the readers know that at the baptism Jesus was already the Son of God, yet during his lifetime Jesus never openly reveals his glorious identity to the disciples, very likely because, in Mark's judgment, they were not able to comprehend such a transcendent figure.[42] In Mark the mystery is fully revealed only after the death of Jesus: "Truly this was God's Son" (Mark 15:39), says the pagan centurion. Mark insists that Jesus was already the Son of God and Messiah during his life-

---

[39] Schnackenburg, *The Gospel According to St. John,* 1:305, holds that although "Son" is given in the majority of manuscripts, "Elect" is "undoubtedly to be preferred" both on grounds of the manuscripts and intrinsic reasons. "The Elect" seems to be a variation of "beloved" (Matt 3:17).

[40] Ibid., 306.

[41] Brown, *The Gospel According to John I–XII,* 60, 61, 63. But Schnackenburg, *The Gospel According to St. John,* 300, does not think that Lamb of God is explained by the latter two titles alone.

[42] *The Birth of the Messiah: A Commentary on the Infancy Narratives in Matthew and Luke* (Garden City: Doubleday, 1977) 30–31.

time, but this was known neither by the disciples nor the public. The unique character of Jesus' sonship is indicated by the adjective "beloved."[43]

In Matthew and Luke the view of Mark is compromised.[44] At least in an initial way, the disciples begin to penetrate the mystery of Jesus' identity during his public life. Mark has no confession of Jesus as God's Son in places one would expect them, though they are found in Matthew (Matt 14:33 with Mark 6:51, 52, and Matt 16:16 with Mark 8:29). In the Fourth Gospel Jesus speaks without hesitation as a pre-existent divine figure (8:58; 10:30; 19:9; 17:5).

According to Raymond E. Brown, in both the Synoptics and the Fourth Gospel, the identity of Jesus gets pushed back from resurrection to the baptism of Jesus, and then beyond.[45] In the pre-Gospel period, as witnessed to by Paul and Acts, it was the resurrection that first prompted the divine proclamation of Jesus' identity. When God raised Jesus from the dead and elevated him to God's right hand, God made him Lord, Messiah, and Son of God (Acts 2:32, 36; 5:31; 13:32, 33; Rom 1:3, 4; Phil 2:8, 9). In the words of the pre-Pauline hymn: "The gospel concerning his Son, who was descended from David according to the flesh and was declared to be Son of God with power according to the Spirit of holiness by resurrection from the dead, Jesus Christ our Lord" (Rom 1:3, 4).

In the beginning of Christian reflection, it was God's raising Jesus from the dead that provided new information about the identity of Jesus. The resurrection presented a new point of departure for theological reflection concerning who Jesus is. The pre-resurrection convictions have to be re-thought in order to incorporate the meaning of the risen Christ. But the identity was not to be fully determined by the resurrection. As they further consider the public life of Jesus (of which the baptism of Jesus is the entrance) they think of the significance of the miracles he worked, the good news he proclaims. This pushes

---

[43] Schweizer, *The Good News According to Mark*, 41.
[44] Brown, *The Birth of the Messiah*, 31.
[45] Ibid., 29–32, 133–143.

the reflection of Jesus' identity back to the baptism, the beginning of his public life.

Yet Jesus, who cured the sick, raised the dead, and walked on the water, came from somewhere. He had a pre-history before his baptism and public life. Identity is pushed back to the infancy accounts, to annunciation and conception. Further reflection made persons wonder whether the infancy accounts fully account for the identity of Jesus. In the Johannine Prologue, the identity of Jesus is pressed back beyond conception to the pre-existence before creation.[46]

Brown's backward development of christology consists in regressive theologizing of three themes: a divine proclamation of identity, the begetting of God's Son, and the agency of the Holy Spirit (Rom 1:3, 4). Brown notes "how consistent the christological language has remained in this development, a language involving divine revelation, and the designation of Jesus as related to God, and the action of the Holy Spirit."[47] This retreat is therefore from resurrection back to the baptism of Jesus, and from there to the annunciation and conception, and from there back to pre-existence.[48] In the decisive question of identity, the answer is found in resurrection, baptism, conception, and pre-existence, four major staging points of Jesus' existence.

In Brown's view the begetting of Jesus as God's Son is figurative when attached to the resurrection and the baptism, but when the complex of Davidic sonship and divine sonship is moved back to the conception of Jesus, it takes on a more realistic sense.[49]

---

[46] R. Brown does not think that Matthew and Luke manifest any knowledge of pre-existence. *The Birth of the Messiah*, 31, n. 17.

[47] Ibid., 135.

[48] In the Orthodox tradition the transfiguration would be added. They understand the cloud of light to be an external sign of the descent of the Holy Spirit. R. Ware, *The Orthodox Way* (London: Mowbray, 1979) 123. In this interpretation the transfiguration manifests the same three elements: the heavens open, the Spirit descends, and the voice of the Father identifies the Son.

[49] *The Birth of the Messiah*, 137.

Chapter Two

Sinlessness and Liturgy

Very early some importance must have been placed on the baptism of Jesus. For Mark it is the beginning of the Gospel. Luke has Jesus in the synagogue at Nazareth recalling his anointing with the Spirit at the Jordan (Luke 4:16-21).[1] No replacement for Judas was considered if he had not been with the disciples from the time of Jesus' baptism (Acts 1:22). In a very short summary of the good news, Peter includes Jesus' baptism (Acts 10:38). The persistence of this embarrassing event in the biblical tradition led Johannes Bornemann in the last century and Vincent Taylor and Fritzleo Lentzen-Deis in this century to contend that it belongs to the earliest strata of New Testament witness.[2] Günther Bornkamm, Hans Conzelmann, and Ernst Käsemann, among others, hold that it belongs to the undoubted events of the historical Jesus.[3] For contemporary theologians it is the

[1] Fitzmyer, *The Gospel According to Luke I–IX,* 529.

[2] Bornemann, *Die Taufe Christi,* 4; V. Taylor, *The Gospel According to St. Mark,* 2nd ed. (New York: St. Martin, 1966) 158, 159; Lentzen-Deis, *Die Taufe Jesu,* 27.

[3] Bornkamm, *Jesus of Nazareth* (New York: Harper & Row, 1960) 54; Conzelmann, *Jesus* (Philadelphia: Fortress, 1973) 31; Käsemann, "On the Subject of Primitive Christian Apocalyptic," *New Testament Questions Today,* 112. The fact is historical but the form is legendary. A. Legault, holds that the text of Mark is without the doctrinal baggage of Matt 3:14, 15, and without Luke's additions. Jesus is presented without an explanation, "a striking

starting point of any historical reconstruction.[4] Yet one can be allowed some surprise. Why is the sinless One having himself baptized in this well-attested event?

Mark has a bold account of the baptism, "theologically naive and unembarrassed."[5] Would it be possible that his account became a source of confusion to the early Church? Could the sinless Jesus really receive a baptism for the repentance of sins? Could this be the reason why Matthew omits Mark's reference to "a baptism of repentance for the forgiveness of sins" (1:4) and inserts the dialogue between John and Jesus, a dialogue that may arise out of the bewilderment caused by Jesus' submission to John for baptism? Some could interpret this as an admission of personal sin and of John's superiority. Before the tradition was committed to writing, it was already cause for embarrassment, as recorded by Matthew, whose account is controlled by the need to justify it.[6]

Matthew's Apologetic Answer

Matthew is the only Synoptic who displays some embarrassment at the baptism. He alone stresses Jesus' intention to be

---

argument in favor of historicity." "Le baptême de Jésus," in *Sciences Ecclesiastiques* 13 (1961) 153; Bultmann maintains that the baptism is historical, but in form "a faith legend." *The History of the Synoptic Tradition*, 247. M. Goguel contends the baptism is "an established fact," but the accounts are not therefore historical. *Jesus and the Origins of Christianity*, 2 vols. (New York: Harper, 1960) 2:270; H. G. Marsh holds that it is "one of the best attested facts of His life." *The Origin and Significance of the New Testament Baptism* (Manchester: Manchester University, 1941) 101; See also E. Schweizer, *Das Evangelium nach Markus* (Göttingen: Vandenhoeck & Ruprecht, 1979) 15. D. J. Harrington maintains that it is "among the most certain historical facts in the Gospel tradition," in *The Gospel of Matthew* (Collegeville: The Liturgical Press, 1991) 63. Among those who doubt its historicity is E. Meyer, who believes that the event is mythological because historical narration begins only after Jesus' baptism. *Ursprung und Anfänge des Christentums*, 3 vols. (Stuttgart: Gotta, 1921) 1:83, 84.

[4] Meier, *A Marginal Jew*, 1:100.
[5] B. T. Viviano, "The Gospel According to Matthew," in *The New Jerome Biblical Commentary* (Englewood Cliffs: Prentice Hall, 1990) 637.
[6] R. L. Wilken, "The Interpretation of the Baptism of Jesus in the Later Fathers," in *Studia Patristica* 11, pt. 2 (1974) 268.

baptized.[7] His dialogue emphasizes Jesus' superiority and has Jesus supply the reason for the baptism: . . . "to fulfill all righteousness" (Matt 3:15). The reason is still enigmatic. Righteousness or justice (diakaiosyne) is a major theme of Matthew and in such a context generally means doing perfectly what is just and makes just because one is obedient to the will of God. In this context righteousness could mean the baptism of the superior, Jesus, by the inferior, John, because it is the will of God that Jesus show solidarity with the people.[8] The baptism Jesus receives is neither a private matter taking place in private, nor is it simply about individual sin and individual forgiveness. The baptism of Jesus is related not only to his own righteousness, but to that of the whole people. The baptism of Jesus is his "yes" to John's program of the restoration of Israel.[9] Jesus wishes to associate himself with John's message and his ministry, and perhaps initially as his disciple, though the latter cannot be demonstrated. By his baptism Jesus identifies with the eschatological people John is assembling.

Matthew interpolates a dialogue between John the Baptist and Jesus: "I need to be baptized by you, and do you come to me?" the Baptist says. Jesus responds: "Let it be so now" (Matt 3:14, 15). The apocryphal Gospel of the Ebionites (first half of the second century) elaborates on that tradition by having the Baptist, on seeing a great light and hearing the voice of the Father, throw himself down before Jesus and say "I beseech thee, Lord, baptize thou me."[10] This piece of dialogue, along with the Matthaean dialogue, might be seen as an apologetic answer of the early Christian community to pagan objections that Jesus was subordinate to John or in need of baptism because of sin. Even so, this does not exclude the possibility that

[7] G. M. Burge, The Anointed Community: The Holy Spirit in the Johannine Tradition (Grand Rapids: Eerdmans, 1987) 50.
[8] O. Cullmann, Baptism in the New Testament (London: SCM, 1950) 18.
[9] R. T. France, "Jesus the Baptist?" in Jesus of Nazareth: Lord and Christ: Essays on the Historical Jesus and New Testament Christology (Grand Rapids: Eerdmans, 1994) 104; W. G. Kümmel, The Theology of the New Testament (Nashville: Abingdon, 1973) 31.
[10] New Testament Apocrypha, J. H. Charlesworth et al., eds., 2 vols., rev. ed. (Louisville: Westminster/John Knox, 1991) 1:169.

the dialogue in Matthew preserves a genuine saying of Jesus uttered on some other occasion about the need "to fulfill all righteousness."[11]

Also one should emphasize the "all." Then it seems to mean concretely that Jesus will bring forgiveness. This is in keeping with his character of the Servant of God who suffers for all the others. What is entirely new is that Jesus *at the same time* is the Messiah and the Suffering Servant, a conception impossible for Judaism. Suffering is never ascribed to the Messiah in Judaism, while Jesus will continue to make the link between the two. Indeed, the Jordan event reaches out to the future death on the cross when all baptism will find its fulfillment.[12]

The Fourth Gospel's Indirect Report

The Fourth Gospel somewhat avoids the problem of Jesus' sinlessness by omitting a direct account of Jesus' baptism and inserting rather an indirect report recorded in the tradition.

Whether the fourth evangelist "feels the embarrassment of the baptism so acutely that he fails to mention it at all" is a matter of conjecture.[13] If the fourth evangelist had any hesitations, the tradition of Jesus' baptism was so strong that he could not wholly omit it. One might want to suppose that the high christology of the Fourth Gospel prompted the evangelist to downplay an event that had raised questions from the earliest days about Jesus' sinlessness. Or perhaps he simply did not want to give a handle to the sectarians who claimed the Baptist's superiority over Jesus.[14]

But the question of Jesus' sinlessness needs to be approached at a different level. If this is seen as a historical question, one notes immediately that many sins, as purely internal acts, are not historically verifiable. Sin is a theological category—infidelity

[11] A. Descamps, *Les Justes et la Justice dans les Évangiles et le Christianisme Primitif hormis la Doctrine Proprement Paulinienne* (Gembloux: Catholic University of Louvain, 1950) 119.

[12] Cullmann, *Baptism in the New Testament*, 18, 19.

[13] Viviano, "The Gospel According to Matthew," in *The New Jerome Biblical Commentary*, 637.

[14] Brown, *The Gospel According to John I–IX*, 64, 65.

to the covenant—not primarily a historical issue, open to scientific verification.[15] Nonetheless Jesus, as we have seen, may have considered himself a sinner because he belonged to a sinful people. Ezra, in confessing the apostasy of Israel, was not a personal participant in that sin, but he belonged to sinful Israel (Ezra 9:6, 7, 10, 11, 5; Neh 9:36, 37).[16] The baptism of Jesus, of itself, does not solve the question of personal sin.

What gives credence to the historicity of the event of Jesus' baptism is the realization that the early Christian community would not fabricate an event that would cause so many difficulties and demands explanation.[17]

How Embarrassing!

A look at the exegetical tradition of the first two centuries shows that the baptism continues to be a source of embarrassment. It was widely discussed in all the currents of theological reflection, without doubt partly because of the problems it posed.[18] That the baptism of Christ continued to be problematic is seen in Ignatius of Antioch (ca. 35–ca. 107), who mentions the baptism of Jesus Christ twice—but otherwise does not emphasize the importance of Christian baptism—on both occasions is moved to justify it, once by saying that he was baptized in order to sanctify the waters, and then by saying he was baptized to fulfill all justification.[19] Justin Martyr (ca. 100–ca. 165) also feels the necessity of a justification.[20] The discussion con-

---

[15] Meier, *A Marginal Jew*, 1:112–116.

[16] Ibid., 114.

[17] Légasse, "Le baptême de Jésus et le baptême chrétien," 53, n. 8.

[18] Paul was not greatly interested in the events of Jesus' historical life, save for his death and resurrection, and showed no interest in Jesus' baptism; the Apostolic Fathers are preoccupied with pastoral rather than exegetical problems; the Apologists rarely consider the historical acts of Jesus, and in this case, the baptism might prove an embarrassment. Bertrand, *Le Baptême de Jésus*, 134. Still, Bertrand is certainly mistaken when he writes that "[Jesus'] baptism was not of primordial importance in the theological systems of antiquity," ibid., 135. At least in the early post-biblical era it was of great importance.

[19] *Ephesians* 18:2; *Smyrnaeans* 1:1; SC 10:74, 132.

[20] *Dialogue with Trypho* 88; PG 6:686, 687.

tinues further in the patristic period.[21] In a fourth-century fictitious debate between a Mesopotamian bishop, Archelaus (otherwise unknown), and one Turbo, a disciple of Mani, the Manichaean tries to trap Bishop Archelaus on the baptism of Christ:

Mani: "Baptism is given for the remission of sins."
Archelaus: "Yes."
Mani: "Therefore Christ sinned, because he was baptized."
Archelaus: "Far be it . . ."

Then Archelaus explains that both the birth of Christ and his baptism were for the sake of others who are sinners, the standard position in the early Church.[22]

In a text attributed to Melito of Sardis (d. ca. 190) by responsible scholars—but not indisputable—the early bishop is clearly in a defensive position regarding the propriety of Christ's baptism. If you stand on the edge of the ocean, "the sun's swimming pool," you will see that the sun, the moon, and the stars bathe and are baptized in the sea.[23] If the creaturely sun is baptized in the sea, why not the "Sun out of the Heaven" in the Jordan?[24] Melito sidesteps the scandal of the sinless one receiving baptism, and gives the cosmic justification of the baptism of Christ, namely, if the cosmos is baptized, why not the Christ? I will return to Melito's argument when I present a more lengthy treatment of the cosmic dimensions of Christ's baptism.

---

[21] H. Braun, "Entscheidende Motive in den Berichten über die Taufe Jesu von Markus bis Justin," in Zeitschrift für Theologie und Kirche 50 (1953) 39–43; F. Hahn, "Analysis of the Transfiguration and Baptismal Narratives," in The Titles of Jesus in Christology: Their History in Early Christianity (New York: World, 1969) 334–346.

[22] Acts of the Disputation of Archelaus with Mani 50; PG 10:1516. Wilken, "The Interpretation of the Baptism of Jesus in the Later Fathers," in Studia Patristica 268. Vigne contends that the issue in this dialogue is not the sinfulness of Jesus, but the importance of baptism in regard to the polemics that Mani had with the baptists, in particular with the Elkesaite milieu. Christ au Jourdain, 161.

[23] Fragment 8b, Melito of Sardis, On Pascha and Fragments, S.G. Hall, ed. (Oxford: Clarendon, 1979) 73.

[24] Ibid.

An apocryphal *Gospel of the Hebrews,* coming from Jewish Christian communities in Palestine or Syria probably sometime toward the end of the first century, contains a relevant passage. It seems to have been inspired by Matthew's Gospel (not in the canonical Greek text) but in a pre-canonical Aramaic form.[25] In this text Mary and the brothers of Jesus invite him to go with them, saying: "John the Baptist baptizes for the remission of sin. Let us go and be baptized by him. But he responded, 'What sin have I committed that I should go to him for baptism? Unless perhaps what I am saying is a matter of ignorance.'"[26] This text, preserved for us by Jerome (ca. 342–420) in his *Against Pelagius,* seems more about the motive for baptism than about baptism itself. If Jesus is hesitant about receiving baptism because of sin committed, he may not exclude being baptized for another reason. Or the reference to ignorance may mean that he may be laboring under an illusion when he says that he is without sin. Whatever the sense, the text is a witness to the continuing embarrassment of the early Christians concerning the baptism of Jesus—and in a text honored by Jerome.[27] Walter Bauer believes that *The Gospel of the Hebrews* supposes that John's baptism did not effect forgiveness of sins, in contrast to the baptism Jesus himself institutes, which did.[28]

A treatise *On Rebaptism,* coming from a third-century milieu, and attributed to Cyprian (d. 258), cites a now lost apocryphal work entitled *The Preaching of Paul,* where Jesus Christ admits to sin and has his mother again urging baptism at the hands of John. Pseudo-Cyprian says that in *The Preaching of Paul* "you will find Jesus acknowledging his own proper sin—he who absolutely committed no sin—compelled *(esse compulsum)* by his mother Mary to receive the baptism of John."[29] But Pseudo-

[25] Vigne, *Christ au Jourdain,* 26.

[26] Jerome, *Against Pelagius* 3:2; PL 23:570, 571. *New Testament Apocrypha,* W. Schneemelcher and R. McL. Wilson, eds. (Louisville: Westminster/Knox, 1991) 1:160.

[27] Vigne, *Christ au Jourdain,* 143, 145.

[28] *Das Leben Jesu im Zeitalter der neutestamentlichen Apokryphen* (Tübingen: Mohr [Siebeck], 1909) 111. Some confusion exists between *The Gospel of the Nazareans* and *The Gospel of the Hebrews.* See Vigne, *Christ au Jourdain,* 28, 29.

[29] *On Rebaptism* 17; CSEL 3/3:90.

Cyprian complains that the book contains "absurd, improper, and fictitious" material.[30] Not a trustworthy source, but at least evidence that the issue of Jesus' sinlessness was still alive.

Cyril of Alexandria (d. 444) says that Christ was indeed sanctified: "Having become man he was under obligation to receive the Spirit." For this reason he received baptism. But his baptism was of a different order: "Because he knew, and knows, no sin, the Spirit will dwell in him from this time forward; [the Spirit] will rest on him as on the first fruits of the race, and its second root."[31] The sanctification, however, touches only his humanity, that is, his flesh. Likewise, the Gnostic solution was to separate the question of purification from that of culpability. Christ had no sin on his conscience, but he bore sin in his body.[32] At the beginning of the fourth century, Lactantius (b. ca. 250) repeats the same idea. Christ himself was without sin, but he is baptized because of "the sins of the flesh or human nature which he was bearing."[33]

A Datum of Faith

The early Christian tradition is convinced of the sinlessness of Jesus Christ as a datum of the faith. It is inviolable. Origen (ca. 185–ca. 254) and Ephrem (ca. 306–ca. 373) try to keep the sinlessness of Jesus intact without surrendering the nature of John's baptism, namely, that it was a baptism of repentance for sins. Origen specifies: "Every soul which puts on a human body has its stains. You ought to know that Jesus was also soiled, and this of his own free will, because he had taken on a human body."[34] Basing himself on his reading of Job 14:4, which he reads as saying "no one is exempt from stain," Origen further specifies that "stain" really means "sin." Here the sinfulness is not acquired by a sinful act but by the assumption of a sinful nature. The Son could not have taken on the

---

[30] Ibid.

[31] Cyril of Alexandria, *Dialogues on the Trinity* 5:591; SC 246:23.

[32] Vigne, *Christ au Jourdain*, 163.

[33] *The Divine Institutes* 4:15; CSEL 19:329, 330.

[34] Origen, *Homilies on Luke* 14:4, SC 87:221; Vigne, *Christ au Jourdain*, 156.

full humanity and escape the sin tainting that nature. Therefore by assuming a sinful nature, Jesus, by a free voluntary act, assumed sin.

Ephrem had a similar position that was specifically related to baptism. "If Jesus had not put on the flesh, why did he approach baptism?"[35] Before sin there is flesh. Jesus comes to John because soiled human nature demanded cleansing. Jesus was drawn to baptism not because of personal sin but because of the sin of nature. Ephrem continues: "The divine nature has no need of baptism. . . . But he put on the flesh . . . and [therefore] he approached baptism in order to render testimony to his [authentic] humanity."[36] Genuine humanity demands baptism. Baptism would have no meaning if Jesus did not possess a nature that was fully and truly human.[37] If Jesus had not put on our poverty, he would not have approached the Jordan.

Earlier, Melito of Sardis had reflected on the relationship of Jesus' baptism to his physical maturity. After saying that one and the same being is both "God and perfect man,"[38] he goes on to demonstrate his view. Christ proved his manhood in "the thirty seasons before the baptism."[39] Indeed, during the period preceding his baptism, "he hid the signs of his godhead because of his fleshly immaturity."[40] Not until his manhood was perfectly developed was he baptized; only then did he reveal his perfect godhead. Perfect godhead demands perfect manhood. Between 300 and 317, Lactantius returns to the theme of Christ's maturity, his sinlessness, and his baptism. John baptizes Christ "as soon as he [Christ] began his manhood."[41]

When John resists Jesus' request for baptism, Ephrem has Jesus Christ going beyond insisting by word of mouth. No, "our savior took the right hand of John and put it on his [Jesus'] head," asking that all justice be fulfilled.[42] By his bap-

[35] Ephrem, *Commentary on the Diatessaron* 4:1; SC 121:93.

[36] Ibid., 4:1; SC 121:93. Vigne, *Christ au Jourdain*, 156, 157.

[37] L. Leloir, *Doctrines et Méthodes de S. Éphrem d'après son Commentaire de l'Évangile Concordant* (Louvain: Catholic University, 1961) 30; CSCO 220:30.

[38] Fragment 6; Melito of Sardis, *On Pascha and Fragments* (Hall) 71.

[39] Ibid.

[40] Ibid.

[41] *The Divine Institutes* 4:15; CSEL 19:329, 330.

[42] Ephrem, *Commentary on the Diatessaron* 4:2, SC 121:94.

tism he takes on himself the justice of the Old Testament in order to receive "the perfection of the anointing," so that he could give that anointing "fully and integrally to his disciples."[43] The function of the anointing is that it be shared with those who believe in him. By his baptism Jesus Christ also puts an end to John's baptism. In Ephrem's graphic phrase, "by his baptism he destroyed John's."[44] In his own baptism, Christ manifests "the true baptism,"[45] or in other words, "Christ, himself, is the beginning of the New Testament."[46]

Not Baptized for His Own Sins

Almost the unanimous witness of the early authors is that Jesus Christ was baptized not for his own sins but for our purification. Justin Martyr and Clement of Alexandria (ca. 150–ca. 215) can represent this tradition. Justin, at this early date, the middle of the second century, already has an extensive section in the *Dialogue with Trypho* on the baptism of Jesus Christ, an indication of its significance even though, as we shall see later, he has his reasons for not giving it too much importance.

"We know," he contends, "that he did not approach the river because he needed either the baptism or the Spirit who came down upon him in the shape of a dove."[47] Four times he denies that Jesus had any need for the anointing of the Spirit.[48] Two reasons are given: first, he possessed the Spirit and the gifts of the Spirit since his birth; secondly, as the Christ/God he has no absolute necessity of such great mysteries as the incarnation and the crucifixion—how could the baptism have been necessary?[49] Why did the Spirit descend on him? He is baptized "for the sake of the human race, each having sinned individually."[50] The descent of the Spirit on Christ did not establish his dignity as "the Christ" (Anointed One) but only manifests that

[43] Ibid.
[44] Ibid.
[45] Ibid., 4:1; SC 121:93.
[46] Ibid., 4:2; SC 121:94.
[47] Justin, *Dialogue with Trypho* 88; PG 6:684.
[48] Ibid., 87, 88; PG 6:681–688.
[49] Ibid., 88; PG 6:685–688.
[50] Ibid., 88; PG 6:684.

dignity to humanity. The Jordan event is a manifestation of the identity of Christ.

Justin believes that the prophetic gifts, poured out in such abundance on the prophets of the Old Testament, have totally ceased among the Jews but begin again to dwell in Christ, in whom the new economy takes its beginning. Justin is precise on this point. The reason why the Spirit rests on Jesus and imparts the full abundance of the gifts to him at his baptism is that such gifts "come to an end with him [as the termination of the old dispensation] so that there would be no more prophets among your [Jewish] people as of old."[51] The baptism of Jesus by John the Baptist constitutes the last act of the last of the Old Testament prophets. A door closes definitively. These gifts that no longer exist among the Jews, says Justin, are now evident in the lives of Christians. A new door opens.[52] "From the fact that even to this day the gifts of prophecy exist among us Christians, you should realize that the gifts that had resided among your [Jewish] people have now been transferred to us."[53] Therefore, because the baptism of Jesus purifies and imparts the Spirit, these gifts, once the pride of the Jewish people, are now extant among the Christians. "You can see among us both women and men who have charisms from the Spirit of God."[54]

The Early Liturgical Witness

In a number of ways the baptism of Jesus had theological weight. In spite of the small scandal, it belonged to the early tradition.[55] Mark's interest is obviously not biographical, because he tells us nothing about Jesus' origins, though he makes the baptism the beginning of the preaching of the kingdom, and therefore of considerable theological importance.[56] Luke has Peter twice give a certain precedence to the baptism of Jesus (Acts 1:22; 10:38). The baptism of Jesus, even while it causes

[51] Ibid., 87; PG 6:683.

[52] Bertrand, Le Baptême de Jésus, 93.

[53] Dialogue with Trypho 82; PG 6:669.

[54] Ibid., 88; PG 6:685.

[55] Taylor, The Gospel According to Mark, 158, 159.

[56] R. E. Brown, An Adult at Christmas (Collegeville: The Liturgical Press, 1988) 7.

problems, recognized from the beginning, is acknowledged as belonging by right to New Testament witness.

The religious substance which the baptism of Jesus carries, a kind of priority, seems to be reflected in the liturgical practice that is enshrined in the Synoptics. J. Daniélou, in an article Raymond Brown has called "extremely important," has shown that the Synoptics, in general, and Mark, in particular, arranged the ensemble of Christ's life according to the liturgical cycle of the year.[57] This began with the preaching of John the Baptist and the baptism of Jesus. In conformity with the ancient sacerdotal calendar—the Jewish year—which the earliest Jewish Christians followed liturgically, the Synoptics began the year at the end of September. John, in contrast, follows not the Jewish liturgical calendar but the Jewish legal calendar, so that the baptism of Jesus, which began the liturgical year, came immediately after Easter. In the calendars followed by the Synoptics and John, the baptism of Jesus opened the liturgical year. Among orthodox and heterodox groups, the year begins at the Jordan.[58]

In the immediate post-biblical period, the weight attached to Jesus' baptism is evidenced already in the *regula fidei* of Ignatius of Antioch in two of his letters (Ephes 18:2; Smyrn 1:12) though baptism does not have a large role in Ignatius.[59] Also, Melito of Sardis mentions the Jordan event in a context that did not demand it, and expands on its cosmic meaning, as demonstrated below.[60] As we shall see in more detail, both Justin Martyr and Clement of Alexandria give significant attention to Jesus' baptism, Clement more than Justin. Quite properly the baptism of Jesus represents a liturgical mystery of the first order. This is seen in the later, but still quite early, Syrian witness, where the baptism of Jesus takes place on the first day of creation, Adam

---

[57] J. Daniélou, "Les quatre-temps de septembre et la fête des tabernacles," in *La Maison Dieu* 46 (1956) 121, 124–127. Brown, *The Gospel According to John I–XII*, 326.

[58] Daniélou, "Les quatre-temps de septembre et la fête des tabernacles," 127.

[59] *Ephesians* 18:2; *Smyrnaeans* 1:1; SC 10:72, 74, 132. Bertrand thinks, mistakenly in my view, that Ignatius "clearly tends to diminish the importance" of Jesus' baptism, ibid., 135.

[60] Melito of Sardis, *On Pascha and Fragments* (Hall) 82, 83.

and Christ being fused in one person.[61] The importance the early Church assigned to the mystery is demonstrated in its becoming the dominant model for Christian baptism, a point to which we shall return more extensively.

The earliest liturgical celebration is that of Easter, but we have no texts, and therefore do not know how they formulated the celebration. It is highly unlikely that they adopted the categories of Romans 6:4. Such a choice would have left some echo in the other early non-liturgical texts. As we shall see, except for a brief flourish of interest in Origen, it is not until well into the fourth century that attention was turned to the Pauline theology of Romans. The celebration of Easter predates that of the baptism of Jesus. However, the origins of the feast of Epiphany witness to the primary weight of the Jordan event. Very likely the liturgical feast of Epiphany, which is the celebration of the baptism of Jesus, is anterior to the feast of Christmas, noted already by Bornemann in the last century.[62] This priority must have a theological grounding. It seems its origins are Egyptian.[63] The first mention of a liturgical feast is in Clement of Alexandria, who notes that this was a feast also celebrated by the Gnostic followers of Basilides,[64] who would have a special

[61] S. Brock, "Clothing Metaphors as a Means of Theological Expression in Syriac Tradition," in *Studies in Syrian Christianity: History, Literature, and Theology* (Brookfield: Variorum, 1992) XI:21; Brock, "Baptismal Themes in the Writings of Jacob of Serugh," in *Symposium Syriacum 1976* (Orientalia Christiana Analecta 205) (Rome: Pontifical Oriental Institute, 1978) 328. Brock, to whom I am indebted in these pages, has identified the pertinent baptismal texts of Jacob of Serugh in these two articles. See also G. Winkler's review of A. Mouhanna, *Les Rites de l'Initiation dans l'Église Maronite* (Rome: Pontifical Oriental Institute, 1980) in *Oriens Christianus* 65 (1981) 199, 200.

[62] *Die Taufe Christi*, 2; C. Mohrmann, "Epiphania," in *Études sur le Latin des Chrétiens*, 4 vols. (Rome: Edizioni di Storia e Letteratura, 1958–1977) 1:255.

[63] For the discussion concerning the feast of the baptism of Jesus as having its ultimate origin in an Egyptian festival of the Nile, see T. J. Talley, *The Origins of the Liturgical Year* (New York: Pueblo, 1986) 105–117; also J. F. Coakley, "Typology and the Birthday of Christ on 6 January," in *V Symposium Syriacum 1988* (Orientalia Christiana Analecta 236) (Rome: Oriental Institute, 1990) 247–256.

[64] *Stromata* 1, 21, 145; SC 30:150. See Mohrmann, "Épiphania," *Études sur le Latin des Chrétiens*, 1:255; T. J. Talley, "The Baptism of Jesus on January 6," in *The Origins of the Liturgical Year*, 121–129.

interest because they believed Jesus received his humanity at the Jordan. On the vigil of the feast of the baptism of Jesus, the followers of Basilides would pass the night in readings.

Even though the authorship is in doubt, the *Canons of Athanasius*, from the second half of the fourth century, indicate that the feast did not remain with the sectarians.[65] The feast of Epiphany is the oldest feast of which we have evidence, with the exception of Easter and its cycle. Epiphany, as the feast of the baptism of Jesus, goes back to the first years of the second century. A tradition attributed to Polycarp (ca. 69–ca. 155), which is probably authentic, confirms this early date of the feast.[66] In Syria (and Armenia), where the baptism of Jesus would play a role unequaled in either the Latin or Greek traditions, the feast is not known until the second half of the third century.[67] By the time of Ephrem it was the greatest feast in Syria.[68] In the West there is no trace of the feast until the fourth century.[69] It is in Gaul, in 361, that we have the first attestation in the West.

The baptism of Jesus represents, then, a first-order liturgical mystery. The religious substance of the Jordan event carries a kind of liturgical priority. When the Church, during its earliest years, took the mystery of Jesus' own baptism as the paradigm for Christian baptism, it was, in part, reflecting a liturgical tradition rooted probably in the New Testament witness.

[65] *Canons of Athanasius* 16 in Arabic text, and 66 in the Coptic text; *The Canons of Athanasius of Alexandria*, W. Riedel and W. E. Crum, eds. (London: Williams and Norgate, 1904) 27, 131. For questions of authorship and authenticity see Talley, *The Origins of the Liturgical Year*, 121, 122.

[66] Vigne, *Christ au Jourdain*, 69–72, 90, 91.

[67] B. Botte, *Les Origines de la Noël et de l'Épiphanie* (Louvain: Abbaye du Mont César, 1932) 21.

[68] B. Luykx, "Epiphany," in *Liturgische Woordenboek*, L. Brinkhoff et al., eds., 2 vols. (Roermond: Romen, 1958–1962) 1:689.

[69] H. Leclercq, "Épiphanie," *Dictionnaire d'Archéologie Chrétienne et de Liturgie* 5, pt. 1:197.

Chapter Three

An Article of the Creed and the Ordo of Salvation

Care needs to be taken when speaking about credal formulas in the earliest materials. In the New Testament, no creed or confession or formula of faith, in their proper meaning, can be found, with the possible exception of phrases as "Jesus is Lord." The history of the study of New Testament credal statements shows that most scholars came to the conclusion that "there were no fixed formulae in the New Testament, at best, only sayings with a tendency to fixed forms."[1] What we do possess is a common body of doctrine, determined in its broad outline, regarded by all as the possession of no one individual but by the Church as a whole. As the teaching became more formalized, it fell into more or less conventional patterns. Though the structure tended to harden, the language could still remain somewhat open and fluid.[2]

---

[1] I. Havener, *The Credal Formulae of the New Testament: A History of the Scholarly Research and a Contribution to the On-Going Study*, (Ph.D. dissertation, Ludwig-Maximilians University, Munich: 1976) 74.

[2] J.N.D. Kelly, *Early Christian Creeds*, 3rd ed. (London: Longman, 1972) 23, 24.

When one finds in Ignatius of Antioch this patterning of language, "a formalized kerygma," it has a quasi-credal character.[3] The appearance of the baptism of Jesus in two of these quasi-credal formulations is especially significant in Ignatius.[4] In the whole of his corpus, baptism is mentioned only four times,[5] twice having to do with the baptism of Jesus. In contrast to other early authors, he does not seem to have placed much emphasis on baptism, as was noted. In fact, he is the sole apostolic father who gives more attention to the Eucharist than to baptism.[6] So when he twice places the baptism of Jesus within a quasi-credal formulation, it has added significance. Very likely he was using a wording that was already somewhat traditional,[7] and an ecclesial confession.[8]

Let us look at the text from his *Ephesians:* "For our God, Jesus the Christ, was carried in the womb of Mary according to God's plan—of the seed of David and of the Holy Spirit—who was born and baptized that by his suffering he might purify the water."[9] Ignatius seems to have recourse to this credal formulation as a way of defending his teaching. The bishop appears to be isolating some essential mysteries in the life of Jesus: not

---

[3] *Ephesians* 18:2; *Smyrnaeans* 1:1, 2; SC 10:72, 74, 132; H. Schlier, *Religionsgeschichtliche Untersuchungen zu den Ignatiusbriefen* (Giessen: Topelmann, 1929) 43; W. R. Schoedel and H. Koester, eds., *Commentary on the Letters of Ignatius of Antioch* (Philadelphia: Fortress, 1985) 84, 220, 221. Hereafter cited as Schoedel and Koester.

[4] Another formulation seems not to have a credal character, but here the baptism of Jesus is omitted: "The virginity of Mary and her giving birth eluded the ruler of this age, likewise also the death of the Lord—three mysteries of a cry [proclaimed loudly] which were done in the stillness of God." *Ephesians* 19:1; SC 10:74.

[5] Besides the *Ephesians* 18:2 and *Smyrnaeans* 1:1 texts, baptism is referred to in *Polycarp* 6:2 and *Smyrnaeans* 8:2.

[6] A. Benoit, *Le Baptême Chrétien au Second Siècle* (Paris: University Press of France, 1953) 59.

[7] O. Cullmann, *Les Premières Confessions de Foi Chrétiennes* (Paris: University Press of France, 1948) 24.

[8] H. W. Bartsch, *Gnostisches Gut und Gemeindetradition bei Ignatius von Antiochien* (Gütersloh: Bertelsmann, 1940) 137.

[9] *Ephesians* 18:2; SC 10:72.

only conception by the power of the Spirit but a period of gestation in the womb of Mary, as also baptism in the Jordan, and death. What is also remarkable is the reason for Jesus' baptism, the purifying of the water, probably a reference to pure water for Christian baptism. Christ is baptized to prepare and sanctify the water, now rendered worthy, for the baptism of Christians. This theme will surface again in the tradition, especially among the Syrians.[10]

Ignatius' *Smyrnaeans* text is longer, but I give it in full: "I perceived that you are settled in immovable faith, having been nailed, as it were, on the cross of the Lord Jesus Christ both in flesh and spirit, and established in love by the blood of Christ, convinced as to our Lord [that he is] truly of the family of David according to the flesh, Son of God according to the will and power of God, truly born of a virgin, baptized by John that all righteousness might be fulfilled by him, truly nailed for us in the flesh under Pontius Pilate and Herod the tetrarch—from the fruit of which are we, from his divinely blessed passion—that he might raise an ensign to the ages through his resurrection to his saints and believers whether among the Jews or among the Gentiles in the one body of his church."[11] The repetition of "truly" would indicate an anti-docetic concern. Again Ignatius enumerates the chief mysteries of Jesus' life: a descendant of the house of David, born of a virgin, Son of God, baptized in the Jordan, died and rose. The appearance of almost the same elements in both passages suggests that Ignatius is giving here the *regula fidei* or confession of faith in use in the church.[12]

[10] Tertullian, *On Baptism* 4:4; SC 35:70; Clement of Alexandria, *The Teacher* 6:3; SC 70:158; Ephrem, *Hymns on Epiphany* 10:2; CSCO 187:166. The Epiphany hymns are attributed to Ephrem but are very likely slightly later. Schlier, *Religionsgeschichtliche Untersuchungen zu den Ignatiusbriefen*, 44–48. For the same theme in Jacob of Serugh, see Brock, "Baptismal Themes in the Writings of Jacob of Serugh," in *Symposium Syriacum 1976*, 326, 327. The same idea is found in the Chaldean Breviary. See Brock, *Spirituality in the Syriac Tradition* (Kerala [India]: St. Ephrem Ecumenical Research Institute, 1989) 62; idem, *Holy Spirit in the Syrian Baptismal Tradition* (Kerala [India], no publisher given, 1979) 76.

[11] *Smyrnaeans* 1:1, 2; SC 10:132, 134.

[12] Schlier, *Religionsgeschichtliche Untersuchungen zu den Ignatiusbriefen*, 43–48.

In contrast to the *Ephesians* formulation, where the reason for the baptism of Jesus was to purify the water, in *Smyrnaeans* Ignatius quotes the justification found only in Matthew 3:13, namely, "that all righteousness might be fulfilled." The two explanations seem to be an answer to the scandal of his being baptized at all. If he sanctifies the waters and fulfills all justice, these would be sufficient reasons for his descending into the waters of the Jordan. Ignatius does not try to harmonize the two different reasons for Jesus' baptism in the two epistles. The baptism features significantly in both credal formulations.

Since Ignatius is here citing Matthew's account of the baptism, one can note the special relationship Antioch has to Matthew. This Gospel is the one Ignatius knows best.[13] The most viable hypothesis is that Matthew was composed at Antioch between the years 80 and 90.[14] This is supported by the special attention Matthew gives to Peter, who had sojourned there for some time. G. Downey thinks that Matthew 16:18 ("You are Peter, and upon this rock I will build my church") is recording an Antiochene tradition from the earliest days of Christianity in the city, and is the basis of Antioch's jurisdictional supremacy over Jerusalem.[15] In three places Ignatius cites material found only in Matthew.[16]

In two other texts, in *Trallians* and *Magnesians*, where at first glance one might expect the baptism of Jesus to be mentioned, it is not found.[17] The absence of the baptism of Jesus in these

[13] G. Downey, *A History of Antioch in Syria from Seleucus to the Arab Conquest* (Princeton: Princeton University, 1961) 282. J. Meier proposes a three-stage early history of ecclesiastical Antioch: "the first generation, the church of Barnabas, Paul, Peter, and James (roughly 40–70 B.C.E.); the second generation, the church of Matthew (roughly 70–100); and the third generation, the church of Ignatius (after 100)." R. E. Brown, J. P. Meier, *Antioch and Rome* (New York: Paulist, 1983) 27.

[14] Ibid.

[15] *A History of Antioch*, 283.

[16] *Smyrnaeans* 1:2 ("that all righteousness might be fulfilled in him"—Matt 3:15); *Polycarp* 2:2 ("be wise as serpents and innocent as doves"—Matt 10:16); *Ephesians* 19:2, 3 (an expansion of themes from Matt 1 and 2). Brown and Meier, *Antioch and Rome*, 24.

[17] "Be deaf, then, when someone speaks to you apart from Jesus Christ, of the family of David, of Mary, who was truly born, both ate and drank,

texts, which also have a quasi-credal character, may be due to Ignatius' polemic against Judaizers. To deny the birth, death, and resurrection of Jesus is to fall into Gnostic Docetism. In an anti-docetic passage there would be less reason to mention the baptism of Jesus. Also, Ignatius sees the denial of the birth, death, and resurrection as implying Judaizing tendencies.[18] If this is true, then the absence of the baptism of Jesus would be unremarkable. The Judaizers were not especially preoccupied with the baptism of Jesus.

The texts of *Ephesians* and *Smyrnaeans* do appear to contain elements of a confession of faith. But as André Benoit notes, the confession of faith is not yet fixed in the manner of later times.[19]

The Authority of Antioch?

Ignatius is bishop of Antioch. Does Antioch have any preeminence that demands special respect for its theological heritage? In the secular order, the cities of first rank in the East were Alexandria, Seleucia, and Antioch, ''the beautiful city of the Greeks,'' as Isaac of Antioch calls the latter. As an administrative, military, and trade center, it exceeds the importance of Jerusalem. Up into the fourth century it was often the residence of the emperor.

As regards Christian antiquity, the Church of Antioch was probably established in the 30s by Jewish Christians belonging to the Hellenists, who undertook the mission without imposing

---

was truly persecuted under Pontius Pilate, was truly crucified and died, as heavenly, earthly, and sub-earthly things looked on, who was also truly raised from the dead, his Father having raised him, in whose likeness his Father will also raise us up who believe in him through Jesus Christ.'' *Trallians* 9:1, 2; SC 10:100, 102. ''(I write) these things, my beloved, not because I know that some of you are so disposed, but as one less than you, I wish to forewarn you not to get caught on the hooks of vain opinion but to be convinced of the birth, and of the suffering, and of the resurrection which took place in the time and rule of Pontius Pilate.'' *Magnesians* 11; SC 10:88.

[18] Schoedel and Koester, *Commentary on the Letters of Ignatius of Antioch*, 129.

[19] Benoit, *Le Baptême Chrétien au Second Siècle*, 59–61.

circumcision on the converts.[20] The Church at Antioch
represented one of the oldest Christian communities outside of
Palestine.[21] For the general history of the universal Church during the first four centuries, Antioch played a role of greater significance than Jerusalem. The mission to Antioch made possible
the spread of Christianity to a substantial number of people
who were not Jews, people of diverse backgrounds. Antioch
was the original center of Gentile Christianity, the city from
which missionaries went out to the Greek world.[22] In part, this
was due to Peter's stay before he went on to Rome. According
to Acts 15, the first council, deliberating a Gentile problem, met
in Antioch. In 325 the Council of Nicaea gave it second place
after Alexandria. Only at the end of the fourth and the beginning of the fifth centuries did Antioch give way to Constantinople and Jerusalem in religious influence.

No one can be surprised that Ignatius, living in two linguistic
environments, a Greek bishop with a Semitic (Syrian) mentality, writes in Greek. Antioch, a Greek *polis*, was capital of a
Syriac-speaking country—or more precisely Antioch was the
capital of the diocese of the Orient. Probably Ignatius was bilin-
gual.[23] As a city near the Mediterranean, it was dominated by
Greek culture. Ignatius himself was succeeded in the episcopal
chair by a series of Greek-speaking bishops up to the end of
the third century (Theophilus, Serapion, Paul of Samosata).
Within the city both Greek and Syriac were spoken, with Greek
prevailing; but once one passed the gates of Antioch into the
country, the language was Syriac.[24] As the metropolitan see of
Syria, Antioch dominated the Syrian rite.[25] Very likely by the

[20] Brown and Meier, *Antioch and Rome*, 28–44.

[21] Downey, *A History of Antioch* 187, 275.

[22] Ibid., 287, 304.

[23] G. Grant, "The Odes of Solomon and the Church of Antioch," in
Journal of Biblical Literature 63 (1944) 373.

[24] G. Bardy, *La Question des Langues dans l'Église Ancienne* (Paris:
Beauchesne, 1948) 18, 19; B. M. Metzger, *The Early Versions of the New Testament* (Oxford: Clarendon, 1977) 5.

[25] H. M. Riley, *Christian Initiation* (Washington, D.C.: The Catholic University of America, 1974) 16. A somewhat similar situation obtained in
fourth-century Jerusalem. Though Cyril of Jerusalem was Greek-speaking,

latter half of the second century, there would have been a Syriac version of the Scriptures. Other Christian literature may have been available earlier.[26] But the obscurity of the sources for the earliest period is suggested by want of Syriac texts that can safely be dated earlier than the fourth century.[27]

So, very early (Ignatius' death is set at approximately 107) a writer living in Antioch, acquainted with both Greek and Syriac cultures, not given to emphasizing the baptism of Christians, twice mentions the baptism of Jesus in a quasi-credal formulation, one baptismal text being a citation found only in Matthew. The baptism of Jesus seems to have quasi-credal stature in one of the earliest writings outside the biblical corpus issuing from a center of secular and religious importance. The quasi-credal importance given to the baptism of Jesus does not seem a peripheral theological conviction.

The Syrian Pedigree

Early in this century Adolph Harnack noted that the baptism of Jesus was not taken into the Old Roman Creed, originally a Greek text[28] whose pedigree can be traced with some confidence to the closing decades of the second century. This creed was of great importance, being the direct ancestors of all other local creeds in the West, and having influence even in the East. The Apostles' Creed itself is among its descendants.[29] Daniel Vigne goes further and records that the baptism is absent from all the creeds, except one in Pseudo-Athanasius, which reads in part: "Concerning the Holy Spirit we believe that the Spirit is divine, the Spirit is holy, the Spirit is perfect, the Paraclete,

---

the basic rite of initiation was probably the old Syrian rite, which he modified. E. J. Cutrone, "Cyril's Mystagogical Catecheses and the Evolution of the Jerusalem Anaphora," in *Orientalia Christiana Periodica* 44 (1978) 53, 54.

[26] Metzger, *The Early Versions of the New Testament*, 8.

[27] S. Brock, "The Syrian Tradition," in *The Study of Spirituality*, C. Jones, G. Wainright, and E. Yarnold, eds. (Oxford: Oxford University, 1986) 203.

[28] *Beiträge zur Einleitung in das Neue Testament*, 7 vols., (Leipzig: Hinrich, 1906–1916) vol. 2: *Sprüche und Reden Jesu: Die zweite Quelle des Matthäus und Lukas*, 216.

[29] Kelly, *Early Christian Creeds*, 101.

who has spoken in the Law, the Prophets, and the Apostles, and who descended on the Jordan."[30]

Gabriele Winkler, on the other hand, contends that the baptism of Jesus was an essential article of faith in the early Armenian (and Syriac) creeds. The fact that the first evangelizers of Armenia came from Syria, accounts for the derivation of the Armenian liturgy from Syriac sources, even to the use of the same liturgical terminology. Do we have here the handing on of an early Syrian tradition, going back to the earliest days of Christianity, attested to in the quasi-credal formulas of Ignatius, formulations that were probably already old when he wrote his letters?

If this tradition has been preserved in the Armenian and Syrian sources, it would be helpful to know something about the stature of these cultures, especially of Syriac, which so greatly influenced Aramaic Christian texts.

In its origins the Syriac tradition was Palestinian and Aramaic.[31] What is especially significant is that originally the gospel was preached in Aramaic to the Syriac-speaking people, though, in the beginning, the available text of the Scriptures was in Greek. What language Jesus spoke has never been definitively established,[32] though the supposition is that as a Galilean rabbi he very likely spoke Hebrew and the Galilean dialect of Aramaic. Behind the Greek Gospels are the teaching and sayings of Jesus, probably in the Palestinian Aramaic tradition.[33]

---

[30] Pseudo-Athanasius, *The Teaching of 318 Holy Fathers Who Were at Nicaea, Giving a Teaching on the Trinity Which Is Holy, Marvelous, and Salvific;* PG 28:1638. Vigne, *Christ au Jourdain,* 106. Inexplicably, Vigne does not mention the important work of G. Winkler, though he refers to Syrian sources and cites Sebastian Brock.

[31] Brock, *The Holy Spirit in the Syrian Baptismal Tradition,* 1; idem, *Spirituality in the Syriac Tradition,* 1–4; idem, "Early Syriac Asceticism," in *Syriac Perspectives on Late Antiquity* (London: Variorum, 1984) 1:1–19; A. Voöbus, *The History of Asceticism in the Syrian Orient,* CSCO 184:197.

[32] C. Rabin, "Hebrew and Aramaic in the First Century," in *People in the First Century,* 2 vols., S. Safrai and M. Stern, eds. (Philadelphia: Fortress, 1976) 2:1033.

[33] M. Black, *An Aramaic Approach to the Gospels and Acts* (Oxford: Clarendon, 1967) 16.

Syriac is a dialect of Aramaic, or, more precisely, is Late
Aramaic. It was thought to have little impact beyond the con-
fines of Palestine. The contrary is true. From the sixth to the
third centuries of the pre-Christian era, Aramaic was one of the
great languages of the East. From the Euphrates to the Nile, it
was the international language of government, culture, and
commerce, even in countries where there was no native
Aramaic culture. Possibly during or after the Babylonian Exile,
it became the language of the Jews. As a result of the conquests
of Alexander the Great, Greek attained a dominance throughout
the civilized world. Nonetheless, Aramaic was neither displaced
among the Jews of Palestine and Babylon nor among the Semitic
peoples in Syria and Mesopotamia. Greek was studied and
used also in Syria and Mesopotamia, but Syriac, or Late
Aramaic, was still the dominant written and spoken language.[34]

The first evangelizers in Armenia were Syrians from Edessa
and Nisibis, who brought with them Syrian theology and liturgy.
So successful were the missionaries that Armenia was the first
kingdom to officially adopt Christianity. The new religion and
its persecution by the Sassanids fostered a strong nationalistic
spirit. On the testimony of a chronicle ascribed to the fictitious
Agathangelos, the conversion of Armenia is due to the labors of
an Armenian, St. Gregory the Illuminator (ca. 240–332), credited
with royal lineage. As an exile in Cappadocia toward the end of
the third century, he was brought up Christian. He received
theological training at Caesarea in Cappadocia, where he also
received episcopal ordination. After his return to Armenia, he
gathered Armenian co-workers, some trained in Hellenistic culture, while others came under Syrian influence. Both cultures
were important in Armenia, though at one point, under Persian
domination, Greek books were banned and burned, but were
later re-introduced. The period of Greek proscription and Syriac
cultural ascendancy, together with the activities of the early
Syriac missionaries, accounts in part for the Syriac impact on
Armenian religious culture. A dramatic point in the Christian
history of Armenia is the conversion of the king, in 294, by St.
Gregory.[35]

[34] Ibid., 15.
[35] Ibid., 155; G. Winkler, *Das Armenische Initiationsrituale: Entwicklungs-*

So the traditions concerning the baptism of Jesus were preserved in Syriac, a major Semitic eastern language, a dialect of the language that Jesus probably spoke. The Syrians mediated the traditions to the Armenians.

"We Believe in the One Who Descended into the Jordan"

The Armenian credal text Winkler has isolated reads: "We also believe in the Holy Spirit, uncreated and perfect, who spoke in the law, the prophets, and the gospels, who descended into the Jordan, and proclaimed the Sent One, and dwelt in the saints."[36] The "Sent One" is the proclamation of Jesus as the Messiah, the one sent by the Father at his baptism. Based partly on the presence of the Jordan event in the *regula fidei* of Ignatius of Antioch, and other evidence from the early Church (including a later reference to the baptism of Jesus in the credal formulation

---

geschichtliche und liturgievergleichende Untersuchung der Quellen des 3. bis 10. Jahrhunderts (Rome: Oriental Institute, 1982) 54–62.

[36] Quoted in Winkler, "Eine bemerkenswerte Stelle im armenischen Glaubensbekenntnis: Credimus et in Sanctum Spiritum qui descendit in Jordanem et proclamavit missum," *Oriens Christianus* 63 (1979) 130–162; idem, "A Remarkable Shift in the 4th Century Creeds: An Analysis of the Armenian, Syriac, and Greek Evidence," in *Studia Patristica* 17, pt. 3 (1982) 1396–1401. In place of "and proclaimed the Sent One," some variants have "and proclaimed in the apostles." But in both versions, the constant is the reference to the Jordan. See Winkler's critical evaluation. See also W. Cramer's further specifications of Winkler's research in "Der Heilige Geist und die Taufe Jesu im armenischen Glaubensbekenntnis," in *Oriens Christianus* 65 (1981) 40–61.

A reference not to the baptism of Jesus but to Christian baptism as an article of the Creed, is found in the *Apostolic Constitutions* 336:100. The text reads in part: "I believe also in the baptism in the Holy Spirit, that is to say, the Paraclete, who acts in all the saints since the beginning, and afterwards, he has likewise been sent to the Apostles by the Father, according to the promise of our Savior and Lord, Jesus Christ, and after the Apostles, to all those in the holy, catholic, and apostolic church who believe." The reference "to all the saints since the beginning" seems to include the saints of the Old Testament. This is a significant corrective to the inclination of theology to take Pentecost as the entry into history of the spirit/Spirit, depriving the whole of the Old Testament of the power of God in act.

of Melito of Sardis [d. ca. 190],[37] and in Theodore of Mopsuestia's [ca. 350–428] creed[38]), Winkler believes that its presence in the Armenian creed represents an ancient stratum, and is, indeed, the oldest and purest tradition.[39] Though the Armenian formulation is the oldest, it is supported by very early Syriac credal texts and anaphoras.[40]

The later tradition saw the baptism of Jesus as among the primary truths taught to catechumens. In the *regula fidei* of Philoxenus (ca. 440–523), one of the leading thinkers and authors of the nascent Monophysite church, he recounts the chief mysteries of the Word of God, among which he relates the incarnation of the Word, infancy years, his obedience to his parents and John the Baptist, the baptism of Jesus, his being led into the desert, his death and resurrection.[41] After finishing his recitation, Philoxenus adds: "Such are the first doctrines which one usually communicates to those who present themselves to become disciples."[42] The baptism of the Word of God is among

[37] *Fragment* 15; Melito of Sardis, *On Pascha and Fragments* (Hall) 73.

[38] *Symbol des Theodorus von Mopsuestia; A. Hahn, Bibliotek der Symbole und Glaubensregeln der Alten Kirche* (Hildesheim: Olms, 1962) 307.

[39] Winkler, "A Remarkable Shift in the 4th Century Creeds: An Analysis of the Armenian, Syriac, and Greek Evidence," 1398. This formula was used in the baptismal rite and in the eucharistic liturgy. A baptismal formula retained in the 1961 Jerusalem ritual (Mastoc) reads: "We believe in the all holy trinity, in the Father and the Son and the Holy Spirit, the announcement of Gabriel, the birth of Christ, the baptism, the suffering. . . ." A variant baptismal confession in form of a question is that of the Catholicos Nerses Snorhali (in office between 1166–1173) reads: "Do you believe in the incarnation of Christ . . . who was also baptized by John in the Jordan, and was witnessed to by the Father and the Spirit." A credal formula used in the Armenian Prayer of the Hours reads: "We believe [that] our Lord Jesus Christ, having gone about the Earth, after thirty years came to Baptism: [that] the Father bore witness: 'This is my Beloved Son,' and the Holy Ghost like a dove came down. . . ." Photocopies of the Armenian text and translations are in Winkler, "Eine bemerkenswerte Stelle," 131, 132, 153, 155.

[40] Winkler, "A Remarkable Shift in the 4th Century Creeds: An Analysis of the Armenian, Syriac, and Greek Evidence," 1398, 1399.

[41] *Commentary on the Johannine Prologue* 64; CSCO 381:158.

[42] Ibid., CSCO 381:159. In another passage having the character of a *regula fidei*, Philoxenus sees the baptism as the point from which Jesus is "the first born and the new man." *Fragments of the Commentary on Matthew and*

the chief mysteries the catechist presents to the catechumens. In other places, when he reviews the chief mysteries of the Word of God after the manner of a *regula fidei*, he includes the baptism in the Jordan.[43]

A late manuscript from 1216 shows better the larger theological framework. The baptismal candidate is asked about belief in the Trinity, incarnation, baptism, crucifixion and the three days in the tomb, the holy resurrection, the divine ascension, the sitting at the right hand of the Father, and the Parousia.[44] Here, again, the baptism of Jesus is ranged with the chief mysteries of the faith.

Winkler, whom I am summarizing here, points to Syrian anaphoras where what is normative is the descent of the Spirit on Jesus in the Jordan, not the coming down of the Spirit on Mary at the incarnation. Because of the parallelism between the descent of the Spirit on Mary, effecting the conception of Jesus, and the descent of the Spirit on the bread, making it the Body of Christ, one would expect that the descent of the Spirit at the incarnation would better serve the eucharistic moment than the descent of the Spirit on Jesus at the Jordan. However the text is silent on Spirit at the conception of Jesus.[45] This, in conjunction

---

Luke 8; CSCO 393:5. See A. Grillmeier, "*Die Taufe Christi und die Taufe der Christen*. Zur Tauftheologie des Philoxenus von Mabbug und ihre Bedeutung für die christliche Spiritualität," *Fides Sacramenti: Sacramentum Fidei*, Festschrift for P. Smulders, H. J. Auf der Maur et al., eds. (Assen: Van Gorcum, 1981) 139–142.

[43] *Fragments of the Commentary on Matthew and Luke* 2; CSCO 393:2. "Therefore he who was made man is (in company) with the Father, Son; and in the virgin, embryo; and in the world, man; and under the law, circumcised (man); and from baptism, the first-born and the new man; and on the cross, man of sorrows and knowing sufferings; and in the grave, dead (man); and in Sheol, visitor of the souls; and in Paradise, heritage-giver; and after, he rose, according to the order of the angels and *the first-fruits of the sleeping;* and where *he was taken up*, king of glory; and (in company) with the Father, *God all in all* and *all and in all Christ*. Ibid., 9; CSCO 393:5. See also *Commentary on the Johannine Prologue* 2; CSCO 381:3.

[44] Winkler, "Eine bemerkenswerte Stelle," 154.

[45] "Have mercy upon us, God the Father almighty, and send upon us and upon these gifts . . . thine Holy Spirit, the Lord and life-giver, who shareth thy throne, God and Father, and shareth the kingdom with the Son, who is of one substance and coeternal, who spoke in the law and the

with the appearance of the baptism in the creed, seems to support the contention that the Jordan event was rightly included in the creed, and represents an ancient strata.

Whether one is citing the creeds used in the baptismal rite or the eucharistic liturgy or the Prayer of the Hours, the baptism of Jesus is a consistent and constitutive element. The role of the Spirit at the Jordan, Winkler concludes, is therefore the primary, creative, norming manifestation of the Spirit.[46]

Adoptionists and Arians as Abusers of Jesus' Baptism

Except in the Armenian Church, the baptism of Jesus as a constitutive element in the creeds did not survive the christological controversies. Because of Adoptionism, which held that Jesus received his divine sonship and became the Christ, or anointed one, at his baptism, there are protests that touch the theology of Jesus' baptism. Sebastian Brock, whom I am following here, calls attention to the position of Jacob of Serugh (ca. 451–521), who says that the Holy Spirit did not appear at the Jordan to sanctify either Jesus or the water but merely to bear witness. The proof: the Spirit appeared only *after* Christ ascended out of the water.[47] The Syriac breviary, the *Fenquitho*, even gives a polemical view of the Jordan event: "Who will dare to say, and not tremble, that Our Lord received the Holy Spirit when he

---

prophets and thy new testament, who descended in the likeness of a dove, upon our Lord Jesus Christ in the river Jordan, who descended upon thy holy apostles in the likeness of fiery tongues . . . that coming down he may make of this bread the life-giving body . . . of our Lord, for the confirmation of thy holy church . . . delivering it from all heresy." Ibid., 161.

[46] "A Remarkable Shift in the 4th Century Creeds," 1399.

[47] *Homiliae Selectae Mar-Jacobi Sarugensis*, P. Bedjan, ed., 5 vols. (Leipzig: Harrassowitz, 1905–1910) 1:159. Hereafter cited as Bedjan. These volumes contain the Syriac text but no translation. Many of the texts of Jacob of Serugh have never been translated. Excerpts used here of the untranslated texts relating to the present theme are given in S. Brock, "Baptismal Themes in the Writings of Jacob of Serugh," in *Symposium Syriacum 1976,* 327, and in Brock, "Clothing Metaphors," *Studies in Syriac Christianity* II:11–38. I thank Columba Stewart for verifying the texts cited here and in other chapters.

was baptized in the Jordan."[48] To say that the Christ received the Spirit at the Jordan would call into question his constitutive reception of the Spirit at his conception.

The Arians also use Jesus' baptism as a club. Both Athanasius (ca. 296–373) and Cyril of Alexandria respond to the Arian taunts about Jesus' need of the Spirit, a want some said was incompatible with claims to divinity. Athanasius explains that the eternal Word was not lacking something, but "when the Lord, as man, was washed in the Jordan, it was we who were washed in Him and by Him."[49] Christ, as man, is not washed for himself, but for us. Cyril notes that when the Arians read of the baptism of Jesus, they give "a big laugh" because Christ "receives what he did not have."[50] Unyielding, Cyril gives the Spirit a decisive role in the economy, with the baptism of Jesus as the point of departure, the new beginning,[51] a point to which I shall return.

While the baptism of Jesus did lend itself to heterodox christologies that called into question the divinity of Jesus, it is clear from both Ignatius of Antioch and Ephrem that, on the contrary, early authors used it as a way of speaking of the divine origins of Jesus.[52] The Jordan event is not necessarily Adoptionistic. Had it been essentially tainted with Adoptionism, it would never have been enshrined in any orthodox creed.

Jesus First Revealed Who He Is at the Jordan: Justin

Justin Martyr is in a bind. He feels constrained to talk about baptism, but he cannot make too much of it, as he has attacked the Jews for their exterior rites.[53] How can he, then, comfortably talk about the exterior rites of Christians? This must have affected the way he spoke of the Jordan event. His approach to

---

[48] Text in S. Brock, *Holy Spirit in the Syrian Baptismal Tradition*, 78.

[49] *Against the Arians* 1:47; PG 26:109.

[50] *Commentary on John* 2:1.

[51] Wilken, "The Baptism of Jesus in the Later Fathers," in *Studia Patristica*, 271.

[52] Grillmeier, "Die Taufe Christi," in *Fides Sacramenti: Sacramentum Fidei*, 174.

[53] Benoit, *Le Baptême au Second Siècle*, 142, 143.

the Jordan event is that of a polemicist, so the presentation is slightly skewed. In fact his exposition is made in a digression.[54]

Justin emphasizes Christ's reception of the Spirit at his baptism.[55] Immediately, Justin is in trouble. If it is true that Christ received the Spirit at the hand of John at the Jordan, what about Christ being conceived of the Holy Spirit? Why is Christ receiving the Spirit at his baptism if he was already conceived by the Spirit from the beginning—later this is also the problematic of Jacob of Serugh, among others. Justin's answer: Christ fulfilled the mysteries of his birth and his crucifixion, as well as his baptism, "solely for the sake of man."[56] Evidently this was, even for Justin, not completely satisfying. So he gives a second reason why he received the Spirit at the Jordan. At his baptism the heavens open and the voice of the Father says "You are my Son, the Beloved; today I have begotten you" (see Ps 2:7). Justin is using the Lukan variant, which turns the Jordan experience into a birth event, but without giving it an Adoptionistic interpretation.

For Justin, therefore, the baptism of Jesus is the messianic manifestation of who this person is, a messianic sign given to the Church. Also unmistakably clear is the relationship between Christ receiving the Spirit at his baptism and Christians receiving the Spirit at theirs. Just as one can find evidence of this in the gifts of the Spirit manifest in the lives of Christian men and women, so also in the life of Christ, and this even before his baptism in the Jordan, ostensibly because he was conceived by the power of the Spirit. "As soon as he was born, he possessed his powers."[57] Before the Jordan event, people discerned in his birth only the son of Joseph, but he nevertheless gave proofs that he was the Son of God and "exercised appropriate powers at each stage of growth."[58] Even in the crucifixion, he gave proofs so that others could discern that he was the Christ.

In a word, Justin is attempting to show that at birth, at the baptism, and finally at the crucifixion, through the signs of

---

[54] Bertrand, *Le Baptême de Jésus*, 97.
[55] *Dialogue with Trypho* 88; PG 6:685.
[56] Ibid.
[57] Ibid.
[58] Ibid.

power and his true identity, Christ was demonstrating the plan of salvation. However, in the mysteries that reveal the identity of the Christ, the baptism has a certain precedence because it was at the Jordan that humankind "first realized who he was,"[59] more precisely, the Messiah. The Jordan event is the first sign. In the historical perspective of Justin, the baptism stands in the tradition of the great pneumatological events of the Old Testament, and is the first pneumatological event *as sign* of the New. "Theologically the baptism of Christ is the point of convergence, the exact-center of the pneumatological manifestations of the past and of the future."[60] This is true even though the baptism of Christ does not play a large role in Justin's theology.[61] In this, he resembles Ignatius of Antioch.

Hilary—Jesus Fully Realizes the Mystery of Salvation

Hilary of Poitiers (ca. 315–367) also relates Christ's baptism to the plan of salvation. Here the economy is revealed. He says that in his baptism Christ "fully realized the mysteries of human salvation."[62] Indeed, "the order of the heavenly hidden mystery is expressed" in the baptism of Christ *(ordo etiam in eo arcani caelestis exprimitur)*.[63] "Order" here means the plan of salvation, the divine economy. Hilary details the order. "Through the testimony of the vision and the voice," through the opening of the heavens and the visible descent of the Spirit, through the Father's word attesting Christ's divine sonship, "we learn . . . that according to what is fully realized in Christ, the Spirit . . . rushes down upon us *(involare)* so that we might bathe in the anointing of heavenly glory, and, as attested by the voice of the Father, become children of God by adoption. For the truth has prefigured in the very reality of the facts, and the image of the mystery *(sacramenti imaginem)* has thus been prefigured for us."[64] The

---

[59] Ibid., PG 6:688.
[60] Bertrand, *Le Baptême de Jésus*, 136. See also page 97.
[61] Benoit, *Le Baptême Chrétien au Second Siècle*, 183.
[62] Hilary, *On Matthew* 2:5; SC 254:110.
[63] Ibid.
[64] Hilary, *On Matthew* 2:5: SC 254:110. J. Doignon suggests that Hilary is dependent here on Tertullian, *On Baptism* 8, in "La Scène Évangélique du

baptism of Christ is proleptic, and is both order and image of our baptism and of the Christian life.[65]

The Armenian text from the end of the fifth century, *The Teaching of St. Gregory*, teaches that the baptism of Christ is "the divine image of salvation" that all are to imitate.[66] But the image is more than the naked rite of baptism; it is, as shall be seen below, the order of the whole economy of salvation, which is cosmic in its scope. The baptism shows itself to be the cause of our salvation.[67]

Jordan: Icon of the Trinitarian Identity

The Jordan establishes the principle of identity. With some frequency the Spirit alone identifies who Jesus is. Ephrem wants the singular way in which the Spirit rested on Jesus, passing over the others who were baptized by John on the same day, to be the decisive factor in naming Jesus Messiah: "The Spirit broke through the heights . . . and he abandoned the others and let himself rest only on one."[68] Jacob of Serugh (ca. 451–521) uses the whole Trinity to define the Christ: "At the time of the Epiphany of the Son [in the Jordan], the Trinity appeared at the

---

Baptême de Jésus Commentée par Lactance (*Diuinae institutiones*, 4, 15) et Hilaire de Poitiers (In Matthaeum 2, 5–6)," *Epektasis:* Mélanges patristiques offerts au Cardinal Jean Daniélou (Paris: Beauchesne, 1972) 71, n. 62.

[65] A possible parallel is Optatus of Milevis (fl. 370), who writes that the descent into the water before the anointing "initiates and orders the mysteries, providing in full measure for the baptized." What follows is "the order of the mystery." *Against Parmenian the Dontatist* 4:7; CSEL 26:113. This could refer either to the mysteries within the sacrament of baptism or to the larger order of salvation.

[66] 413; *The Teaching of St. Gregory: An Early Armenian Catechism*, R. W. Thomson, ed. (Cambridge: Harvard University, 1970) 89. Hereafter cited as Thomson.

[67] Vigne, *Christ au Jourdain*, 155.

[68] *Hymns of Epiphany* 6:1; CSCO 187:147. Ephrem says something similar in his *Commentary on the Diatessaron* (Armenian version): "Although many were baptized on that day long ago, the Spirit descended on only One, and [on only One did he] rest." CSCO 145:34. G. Winkler, "Ein Bedeutsamer Zusammenhang Zwischen der Erkenntnis und Ruhe in Mt 11, 27–29 un dem Ruhen des Geistes auf Jesus am Jordan: Eine Analyse zur Geist-Christologie in Syrischen und Armenischen Quellen," *Muséon* 96 (1983) 298.

Jordan."[69] But Jacob also wants to establish the Spirit as the principle of identity, while avoiding the suggestion that the Spirit's role was a sanctifying one, again a polemical note.[70] The Spirit came "to indicate [him], and not to sanctify."[71] The Spirit acts as the "the finger" of the Father, pointing to the Son.[72] In Ephrem this showing of the Son by the Spirit descending on Jesus is directed to Christian baptism "because through his baptism the Spirit is given."[73] By reason of the Jordan event, and through it, the Spirit is imparted to others who believe in Jesus.

The Father, too, has a special role in identifying Jesus by naming him the Son. Already in Justin Martyr it was through both the descent of the Spirit and at the same instant a voice out of the heavens declaring who the Christ is that the naming is done.[74]

In one of the Armenian creeds, as well as in the *Teaching of St. Gregory*, and in Philoxenus, both the Father and the Spirit bear witness to Christ's identity, thus providing for the two witnesses demanded by Jewish law.[75]

The baptism as a trinitarian event is developed with special insight in the *Teaching of St. Gregory*. Here the mutual knowing and mutual showing of the Father, Son, and Spirit are the center of the Jordan event. Christ "was first understood and known as the true Son of God [at his baptism] by the voice of his Father and the descent of the Spirit over him."[76] For the *Teaching of St. Gregory*, as for Justin Martyr, it is at the Jordan

---

[69] *Homily on Epiphany* 33, PO 43:565.

[70] S. Brock, "The Epiklesis in the Antiochene Baptismal Ordines," in *Symposium Syriacum 1972* (Orientalia Christiana Analecta, 1972) (Rome: Pontifical Oriental Institute, 1974) 205.

[71] Bedjan, 1:185.

[72] Ibid.

[73] *Commentary on the Diatessaron* (Armenian version) 4:3; CSCO 145:35.

[74] *Dialogue with Trypho* 88, PG 6:689.

[75] *The Key of Truth: A Manual of the Paulician Church of Armenia*, F. C. Conybeare, ed. (Oxford: Clarendon, 1898) 159; Winkler, "Eine bemerkenswerte Stelle," 155. *The Teaching of St. Gregory* 416; Thomson, 90. Philoxenus, *Fragments of the Commentary on Matthew and Luke* 11; CSCO 393:9, 10. Brock, "Baptismal Themes in the Writings of Jacob of Serugh," in *Symposium Syriacum 1976*, 327, n. 12.

[76] *Teaching of St. Gregory* 416; Thomson, 90.

event that his contemporaries first realized who the Christ is. "He came to baptism and at the baptism was made known to all."[77] How was Christ made known? First by the Baptist,[78] then by the Spirit,[79] and finally by the Father.[80] This is in keeping with the trinitarian perspective of the *Teaching of St. Gregory*, which begins and ends with the Trinity.[81]

Revelation of the Consubstantial Mystery

In the *Teaching of St. Gregory*, the double witness of the Father and the Spirit reveal "the consubstantial mystery of the power of the coming of the Son."[82] The specific content of this consubstantial mystery is the Word who was with God and was God from the beginning. Because no one knows the Son except the Father, the Father witnesses by voice from heaven that the Son is the eternal Word. Referring to the Father, the eternal Word says "When he was, I then was," in this way demonstrating the consubstantial unity of the Trinity "acting together in establishing and united in renewing."[83] For thirty years the Son "moved silently and unseen" among his contemporaries; "then he came to baptism, and at the baptism was made known to all" as the Word of God who tents among us.[84] The baptism of Christ is the revelation of his identity as trinitarian communion. In Ephrem this revelation is made even to the human senses: "The Father to the hearing, by means of the divine voice and the proclamation, the Son to the touch, and the Spirit to the sight, in the bodily form of the dove."[85] The Father

---

[77] Ibid., 417; Thomson, 90.
[78] Ibid.
[79] Ibid., 418; Thomson, 91.
[80] Ibid., 421; Thomson, 92.
[81] Ibid., 259, 715; Thomson, 12, 41, 182.
[82] Ibid., 421; Thomson, 92.
[83] Ibid., 420; Thomson, 91.
[84] Ibid., 417; Thomson, 90.
[85] *Hymns on Faith* 51:7; CSCO 155:136. Jacob of Serugh has a similar formulation: "The trinity was revealed by three senses: the Father by the voice, the Son by the touch, and the Spirit by sight. The Father spoke, the Son was baptized, and the Spirit was seen. . . . The hearing was filled by the Father, the touch by the son, and the sight by the Spirit. . . . One single

is heard to proclaim the divine Sonship at the Jordan, the Son is touched (ostensibly by John the Baptist), and the Spirit is seen to descend on Jesus.

According to the *Teaching of St. Gregory*, after Christ is revealed as the Word, the Son, "standing in our midst, shows the Father and the Spirit to the world."[86] The Son revealed reveals the Father and the Spirit. Not a private experience, the baptism is turned outward to the salvation of all, to mission. Toward that concrete end, the revelation of the Father is not an abstract word but is demonstration of "the glory of the Father in himself [Christ]."[87] To see Christ is to see the glory of the Father.[88] The Spirit revealed Christ as the one who is without sin—righteous and holy.[89] By his baptism Christ orders all "to imitate the divine image of salvation."[90] That image includes the movement through the Spirit back to the Father. The goal of Christian baptism is "to become pleasing to the Father."[91] The Spirit, therefore, comes down on the Son to teach us how to attain the Father, so that the Son might "reveal salvation to all."[92] The baptism of Jesus sets the pattern for the whole trinitarian economy. The rhythm of salvation from the Father to the Father is here revealed.

For Philoxenus the trinitarian dimensions of the baptism of Jesus are "the ineffable mystery, an incomprehensible act, a deed unfathomed by the mind."[93] Each of the persons of the Trinity lays open the trinitarian mystery: "I recognize the Trinity in the Jordan: the Father who speaks, the Son who is baptized;

God was heard, touched and seen. Three persons were recognized, proclaimed, and adored." *Homily on the Epiphany* 35; PO 43:565, 567.

[86] 425; Thomson, 93.

[87] Ibid., 426; Thomson, 93.

[88] The knowledge of the Father in the context of the baptism in the Jordan is found in the Persian version of the Diatessaron as well as in the Armenian catechesis of baptism. G. Winkler, "Ein Bedeutsamer Zusammenhang," 313.

[89] *The Teaching of St. Gregory* 418; Thomson, 91.

[90] Ibid., 410; Thomson, 88.

[91] Ibid., 420; Thomson, 91.

[92] Ibid.

[93] *Fragments of the Commentary on Matthew and Luke* 12; CSCO 393:16.

and the Holy Spirit who shows."[94] Here, as in Justin Martyr, the mystery of the Jordan is related to the incarnation and to the cross: "One of the Trinity was in the womb; one of the Trinity was in the baptism; one of the Trinity on the Cross."[95] All who enter that mystery through Christian baptism "are born of baptism, that is, of the Trinity."[96] To be born of baptism is to be born of the Trinity. Those who imitate Jesus' baptism, says Philoxenus, embrace the whole human/divine spectrum. Such communion in the Jordan event restores one's true, integral humanity ("everyone not born of it is not reckoned a man"), at one end of the spectrum; at the other end, Christian baptism places one on the road, on the "return" to the Trinity, the source, the beginning and goal of the Christian life.[97]

These accents return in Severus of Antioch (ca. 465–538), who uses a rite essentially Syrian in character. Severus, too, sees the Jordan event as revealing the Trinity. "With the eyes of the mind I [seem to] see the river Jordan being lifted upwards in floods not of water but of light, pouring the knowledge of the Holy Trinity into our souls."[98] The Jordan is the locus of the trinitarian knowledge of God.

[94] *Letter to Emperor Zeno on the Embodiment and Incarnation of God the Word;* text in A. A. Vaschalde, *Three Letters of Philoxenus, Bishop of Mabbôg (485–519),* (Ph.D. dissertation, The Catholic University of America, 1902) 123.
[95] Ibid.
[96] *Fragments of the Commentary on Matthew and Luke* 11; CSCO.
[97] Ibid. Also 12; CSCO 393:16.
[98] *Hymn on the Epiphany* 24; PO 6:65.

Chapter Four

The Cosmic Baptism

From the earliest years authors perceived that the baptism of
Jesus is not an isolated act of private piety. Neither the messianic import nor the entrance into the public life exhausts its
significance. The meaning is also cosmic.

In the text attributed to Melito of Sardis, the author uses not
only his rhetorical skills, but his considerable acquaintance with
philosophical vocabulary and astronomical writings.[1] These
themes, as well as the bathing of the sun, moon, and stars in
the ocean, are already the common treasure of Stoic philosophy, and were used in the Stoic exegesis of Homer.[2] Melito
uses this vocabulary for his own soteriological purposes.

Speaking of the lights above he says: "If you wish to observe
the heavenly bodies being baptized, make haste now to the

[1] R. M. Grant, "Melito of Sardis on Baptism," in *Vigiliae Christianae* 4
(1950) 33. The early author, possibly at the end of the second century, hints
at the cosmic overtones of Jesus' baptism, but with a twist.
Some authors argue from the baptism of Jesus to cosmic meaning.
Melito, however, argues the other way around. Because the cosmos is baptized, it is proper for Christ to be baptized. He speaks first of the baptism
of various elements: in the forging of metals they are dipped in water,
earth is bathed in the rain, Egypt is renewed by the flooding of the Nile,
the air itself is bathed in raindrops.

[2] F. J. Dölger, *Sol salutis, Gebet und Gesang in christlichen Altertum*
(Münster: Aschendorff, 1920); Grant, "Melito of Sardis on Baptism," 35.

Ocean, and there I will show you a strange sight."[3] If you look there you will see "the heavenly bodies being baptized." At the end of the day they "make haste now to the Ocean," there to go down into the waters, into "the outspread sea, and boundless main, and infinite deep, and immeasurable Ocean, and pure water."[4] The sun sinks into the sea, and when it has been "bathed in symbolic baptism," it comes up exultantly from the waters, rising as a new sun, "purified from the bath."[5] What the sun does, so do the stars and the moon: "they bathe in the sun's swimming pool like good disciples."[6] "By this baptism, sun, moon, and stars are soaking up pure brilliance."[7] If the baptism of Jesus needs justification, this is the cosmic rationale.

If sun, together with the sun's disciples, that is, the moon and stars, are baptized in the water, should it be a matter of surprise that Christ, "the king of heavens and creation's captain, . . . a Sun out of heaven," should "bathe in the Jordan."[8] The creaturely sun sinks into the ocean, but is not quenched. Rather having "driven off the nocturnal darkness and begotten bright day," it rises as "a new sun."[9] As the sun rises exultantly from the waters, so also Christ, "creation's captain, Sun of uprising," emerges from the waters and appears "both to the dead in Hades and to mortals in the world."[10] If the heavens and the earth are baptized, why not the King of the Universe? The cosmic triumph of Jesus' baptism leads to the cosmic triumph of his resurrection manifested both to those in Sheol and to believers.[11]

---

[3] Fragment 8b; Melito of Sardis, *On Pascha and Fragments* (Hall) 72. For a review of the research on authenticity, see ibid., xxx, xxxi.

[4] Ibid.

[5] Ibid.

[6] Ibid.

[7] Ibid.

[8] Ibid.

[9] Ibid.

[10] Ibid.

[11] Theophilus of Antioch makes a similar cosmic argument for the resurrection of Jesus based on the monthly resurrection of the moon. *To Autolycus* 1:13; SC 20:86, 88. Clement of Rome likewise follows the same argument. *To the Corinthians* 1:24; SC 167:142.

Melito argues from the cosmic baptism of sun, moon, and stars to the baptism of Christ, but the logic is really determined by the Jordan event.[12] His intent is basically polemical.

The Gospel of the Hebrews

The cosmic ramifications of the baptism are more indirect in one of the earliest apocryphal texts, *The Gospel of the Hebrews*, cited by both Ignatius of Antioch,[13] and Clement of·Alexandria.[14] The text was highly esteemed by ancient authors of reputation. None of the early authors who cite it suggested that it was unorthodox in teaching. Ignatius of Antioch quotes it, apparently without problems. Clement does not doubt that it belongs to the real history of Jesus.[15] Jerome always considered it orthodox and, in fact, says that he "recently translated it into both Greek and Latin" from a manuscript he found in the library in Caesarea.[16] Not determined is whether he translated a part or the full text. The complete text has been lost, though the Hebrew text existed in the fourth century in Caesarea; and there was a Greek translation, of dubious value in Jerome's mind, now also lost. Excerpts have been preserved, especially by Jerome, who also notes that it was "often used" *(saepe utitur)* by Origen.[17]

The Gospel of the Hebrews was not written in an obscure language. As we have seen, Aramaic was the *lingua franca*, indeed the chancery language, for a time in a large part of southeastern Asia after about 300 B.C.E. As Gabriele Winkler points out, *The Gospel of the Hebrews* is apparently the oldest and most important representative of the Syrian type of the gospel.

---

[12] In fragment 6 (*On Pascha and Fragments* [Hall]) 68, 70, having the incarnation as its theme, he justifies the baptism of Jesus as the first manifestation of his divinity.

[13] *Smyrnaeans* 3:2; SC 10:134. See G. Bardy, "Saint Jérôme et l'évangile selon des Hébreux," *Mélanges de Science Religieuse* 13 (1946) 13.

[14] *Stromata* 9; PG 8:981.

[15] Bauer, *Das Leben Jesu*, 2.

[16] *On Illustrious Men* 2; PG 23:611, 613.

[17] Jerome, *On Illustrious Men* 2, 3; PL 23:613, 614. G. Bardy has studied all the citations of *The Gospel of the Hebrews* in Jerome in "Jérôme et l'évangile selon les Hébreux."

Though reserve is always in place when dealing with the apocryphal writings, Daniel Vigne is quite correct to remind us that to say "apocryphal" is not to say "lie."[18] As regards dating, there would be little support for Walter Bauer's view that *The Gospel of the Hebrews* may predate the canonical Gospels.[19] Yet it is very early; toward the end of the first century according to Louis Leloir,[20] the first half of the second century according to Wilhelm Schneemelcher.[21]

Jerome has a special reason for quoting the text in his *Commentary on Isaiah*, which he began in 408. He is commenting on Isaiah 11:1, 2: "A shoot shall come out from the stem of Jesse. . . . The spirit of the LORD shall rest upon him, the spirit of wisdom and understanding. . . . Jerome here quotes the text of *The Gospel of the Hebrews*: "And it came to pass when the Lord was come up out of the water, the whole fount of the Holy Spirit descended upon him and rested on him and said to him: 'My Son, in all the prophets was I waiting for you that you should come and I might rest in you. For you are my rest; you are my firstbegotten Son who reigns for ever.' "[22]

How does Jerome interpret the quotation? Jerome quotes part of the text twice, but in slightly different form.[23] The differences are a matter of accent. First, "there descended on him the whole source [fountain] of the Holy Spirit." Jerome interprets this to mean that the Spirit of the Lord rested upon him in the Jordan because in him the whole plenitude of the divinity was pleased to dwell bodily (Col 2:9). That is, the Spirit did not rest on Jesus partially, as in the other saints, but with the full weight of the divinity, with the complete measure of the divine power.[24] The second, larger quotation reads, in part, "there descended on him the source (fountain) of the whole Spirit."[25] Possibly this form wishes to emphasize less the plenitude of the

18 *Christ au Jourdain*, 44.
19 Ibid., 1.
20 *Le Témoignage d'Éphrem sur le Diatessaron*, 107.
21 *New Testament Apocrypha*, 1:176.
22 *Commentary on Isaiah* 4:11; PL 24:144.
23 Vigne, *Christ au Jourdain*, 170.
24 *Commentary on Isaiah* 4:11; PG 24:144.
25 Ibid., PG 24:145.

fountain (the secondary image) and more the plenitude of the Spirit (the primary referent of the fountain). According to Jerome this means that the Spirit has in Jesus not only fullness but "an eternal dwelling, and will not depart to return again" *(aeterna habitatione permansit: non ut avolaret et rursum ad eum descenderet).*[26] After naming again the "gifts" of the Spirit in Isaiah 11:2, he remarks that though the names of the seven gifts (Jerome calls them "virtues") of the Spirit are different, "there is only one and the same fountain and principle of all the virtues," namely, the Spirit, who pours out all in definitive super-abundance at the Jordan.[27]

Sources in the Old Testament, the early authors think, give a basis for the near equation of Spirit and water, with its eschatological and cosmic connotations. Vigne, to whom I am indebted here, cites the formulation of Tertullian (ca. 160–ca. 225). "[The Spirit] rests on the waters of baptism as if he recognized there his ancient throne, the one who under the form of a dove descended on the Savior [in the Jordan]."[28] The "ancient throne" refers back to Genesis 1:2, where the Spirit hovered over the primeval waters. The Spirit who was at home and at rest on the waters of creation rests on the Lord in the Jordan, associating creation with Jesus' baptism.

The antecedents of *The Gospel of the Hebrews* are clearest in Ezekiel 36:25, 26: "I will sprinkle clean water upon you . . . and a new spirit I will put within you." The pouring out of the 'Spirit-spring of water' marks the beginning of the end-time, with its accompanying cosmological manifestations. New creation takes up the dynamics of first creation. The Spirit which descended on Jesus is the same Spirit which hovered over the primordial waters of Genesis 1:2. Cyril of Jerusalem gives a clear formulation: " 'The Spirit of God was stirring above the waters.' With water the world began; the Jordan saw the beginning of the Gospels."[29] Genesis and gospel both begin with

[26] Ibid.

[27] Ibid.

[28] *On Baptism* 8:3; SC 35:77. For Tertullian the baptism of Jesus is the boundary between the Old and New Testaments. Ibid., 10:5; SC 35:79.

[29] Cyril of Jerusalem, *Catechetical Lectures* 3:5; *Cyrilli Hierosolymarum Archiepiscopi Opera Quae Supersunt Omnia,* 2 vols., W. K. Reischl and

water. Both the heavens and the earth, says Cyril of Jerusalem, are from water. Spirit and water are at the beginning of creation and at the beginning of the gospel. No new creation, no new age is possible without water. Cyril then expands on the cosmological and soteriological role of water.

Jordan Anchored in Cosmic Creation

Clement of Alexandria reminds us that the Son is the principle and head of all creation, and then places the sacrament of baptism in a creation context.[30] Further, he joins the creation of the world through water and the Spirit to recreation through water and the Spirit. In this framework he further refers to the baptism of Jesus: "For this reason the Savior was baptized, though he had no need of it, in order to sanctify all the waters for those who would be regenerated."[31] The baptism of Jesus is thus anchored in first creation, cosmic creation.

Water has a double cosmic relation. Water and Spirit are cosmic because they are the instruments of creation; the water is cosmic because in the baptism of Jesus all the waters of the earth are sanctified. This will become a common theme in the literature of the early Church. To speak only of the Syrians, the sanctification of water is found in Ephrem, Jacob of Serugh, Philoxenus, and Severus of Antioch.[32]

J. Rupp, eds. (Munich: Keck, 1848/1850) 1:70 (hereafter cited as Reischl); Vigne, *Christ au Jourdain*, 171–176.

[30] *A Selection from Prophetic Writings* 4, 5; PG 9:700, 701. The Maurists placed this text among the dubia, but J. Quasten thinks it is genuine, *Patrology*, 4 vols. (Westminster: Newman/Christian Classics, 1953–1986) 2:15. M. Mees seems to accept it as genuine in the *Encyclopedia of the Early Church*, 2 vols. (New York: Oxford University, 1992) 1:180. The work is a collection of excerpts from Gnostic writings, with comments by Clement. The difficulty is in separating the one from the other.

[31] *A Selection from Prophetic Writings* 7; PG 9:701.

[32] B. Varghese, *Les Onctions Baptismales dans la Tradition Syrienne* (Louvain: Peters, 1989) 172. (CSCO 512). G.W.H. Lampe notes that there is no scriptural warrant for the sanctification of water. Early authors often forget that the Holy Spirit descended not on the water but on Jesus. The theme of the sanctification of water is a sign of "the materialistic decadence of much of the post-biblical theology of Baptism." *The Seal of the Spirit*, 2nd ed. (London: SPCK, 1967) 34.

In a seventh-century manuscript, *Treatise on the Feasts of Christmas and Epiphany*, quoting a second-century tradition, we find the stirrings of a cosmic conception of the baptism of Jesus. Ananias of Shirak cites Polycarp, this ancient bishop of Smyrna to whom Ignatius addressed a letter. Irenaeus (ca. 130–ca. 200), who came from Smyrna, claims to have known Polycarp and heard him speak of the contact with John [the apostle or elder?] and with the rest of those who had seen the Lord," and also that Polycarp had been appointed to the see of Smyrna by the apostles.[33] Ananias quotes Polycarp as declaring that the birth of Jesus was on the first day of the week, which was the day of the week on which creation took place,[34] a teaching that will appear in the Syrians later, as already mentioned. Polycarp teaches that the day of Jesus' baptism, thirty years after his birth, fell on the same number of the day in the month, but on the fourth day of the week, that is, Wednesday. "He [Polycarp] declares that the creation of the sun on the fourth day [Wednesday] was for a mystery and foretype."[35] Though Adolph Harnack does not accept the authenticity of this tradition, both F. C. Conybeare and Daniel Vigne do.[36]

The attempt is to link the creation story with the birth of Jesus and then with his baptism. The fourth day of creation was the day when the sun was made, and very early this became a matter of christological, trinitarian reflection. Already Theophilus of Antioch, who became bishop in 169, according to the *Chronicon* of Eusebius, notes that "on the fourth day the great luminaries came into existence."[37] Immediately, Theophilus adds that the creation of the lights on the fourth day "contain a pattern and type of a great mystery," meaning principally the

---

[33] Irenaeus, *Against Heresies* 3, 3, 4; SC 211:38, hereafter cited as *AH*; Eusebius, *Ecclesiastical History* 5, 20, 5; SC 41:62.

[34] Vigne, *Christ au Jourdain*, 69–72.

[35] F. C. Conybeare, "Ananias of Shirak upon Christmas," in *The Expositor*, 5th series, 4 (1896) 337.

[36] Vigne, *Christ au Jourdain*, 72.

[37] *To Autolycus* 15; SC 20:138. Irenaeus also mentions the symbolic nature of the fourth day. *AH* 1, 18, 2; SC 264:277. Vigne, *Christ au Jourdain*, 72, n. 14.

"Trinity," the first recorded use of this term in reference to God.[38]

The move from sun to fire and light is easily made. A tradition exists, going back at least to Justin, that associates the baptism of Jesus with fire. Justin says: "And when Jesus came to the River Jordan, where John was baptizing, he stepped down into the water and a fire ignited the waters of the Jordan."[39] This tradition is also enshrined both in the apocryphal *Gospel of the Ebionites*[40] and *The Preaching of Paul*.[41] The association of fire and light with the baptism of Jesus is, as we shall see, extensive.

This tradition sees the creation of the sun as a mysterious prefiguration of the baptism of Jesus, giving the baptism a cosmic base.

The Father Anoints the Whole Cosmos

Irenaeus comes back to the baptism of Jesus some twenty times, though about ten of those have to do with differing opinions of the sectarians. Most of the others are passing allusions, always touched with polemics. He never stops to comment on the Jordan event for its own sake.[42]

In Irenaeus' short manual of theology, *The Demonstration of the Apostolic Preaching*, the baptism of Jesus in the Jordan is mentioned four times.[43] This work, addressed to a certain Marcianus but destined for the general public, was probably composed in the last decades of the second century, or first decades of the third century, by a bishop who belonged to the third generation of Christian teachers, and was, in the days of his youth, according to Eusebius, an acquaintance of Polycarp in Asia Minor.[44] This places him in contact with the apostolic tradition. Irenaeus

---

[38] Ibid. Though Theophilus is the first to apply "Trinity" *(trias)* to God, it is evident that he uses it as a commonly accepted term, not an unusual one. *To Autolycus* 15; SC 20:138.

[39] *Dialogue with Trypho* 88; PG 6:685.

[40] Schneemelcher, *New Testament Apocrypha*, 1:169. Here, it is a light.

[41] Quoted by Cyprian in *On Rebaptism* 17; CSEL 3/3:90. Here, it is fire.

[42] Bertrand, *Baptême de Jésus*, 109.

[43] 9, 41, 47, 53; SC 62:45, 95, 106–108, 112–114. Reference should also be made to the new edition of Irenaeus' work by Adelin Rousseau in SC 406.

[44] *Ecclesiastical History* 5:5; PG 20:443.

intends to give a short summary of the apostolic teaching "in its integrity and purity,"[45] with considerable emphasis on the continuity between the Old Testament promises and the New Testament fulfillment in Jesus.

The section of the *Demonstration of the Apostolic Preaching* in which the theme of the cosmic anointing occurs has to do with the birth from a virgin of the Christ, "who was with the Father, being the Word of the Father."[46] The Father has the initiative for the incarnation. This is the background for speaking of the two anointings with the Spirit. First, God eternally anoints the Word with the divine Spirit. So by an act before all the ages, the Father anoints the Word, precisely as God. The Word is thus already the "Christ" before the incarnation. Then, through the Word, God anoints and adorns the whole of the created universe with the Spirit. There is a trinitarian dynamic at work here, the Father initiating, working through the Word in the Spirit, though we must not read back more developed trinitarian thought into this early formulation.

When Irenaeus refers to the baptism of Jesus in this passage, the focus is not on images of sun, fire, or light, but on the messianic anointing of Jesus. This anointing has a cosmic referent. From the Father he received the name of "Christ" "because the Father anointed and adorned all things through him."[47] The anointing of the Word of the Father, constituting him Messiah, touches the cosmos. The Father does not anoint the cosmos with the Spirit directly, but only through the intermediary, the Word. This pre-temporal anointing and adorning touches the natural forces of the universe. The cosmic anointing carries echoes of the Christ hymn of Colossians: ". . . all things have been created through him and for him. He himself is before all things and in him all things hold together" (1:16, 17).

But after this eternal anointing of the divine Word, the Father also anointed Jesus as man at his baptism. This means that his anointing at the Jordan is not the only reason why he is called the "Anointed One." At the Jordan "he was anointed by the

---

[45] Ibid., 1; SC 62:28.
[46] 53; SC 62:112, 113.
[47] 53; SC 62:114.

Spirit of God, [the God] who is also his Father."[48] In the
waters of the Jordan, he receives his salvation history anointing.
This is a specifically triadic act. Jesus himself makes this claim
in reference to his baptism: "The Spirit of the Lord is upon
me."[49] Jesus at this moment is anointed Savior because he is
the cause of salvation to those who are freed from all kinds of
ills and from death. He is Savior also to those believers who
come after them, on whom he confers salvation.

Therefore, there is a double anointing: the first, an eternal
anointing as God before creation, and the second as man at the
baptism of Jesus. If the anointing before creation has a cosmic
dimension, would not the anointing at the Jordan also have
cosmic ramifications? In fact, the anointing at the Jordan is a
revelation of the pre-temporal anointing. This is seen in the
way Irenaeus fuses the eternal and the temporal anointing. Indeed, *The Demonstration of the Apostolic Preaching* seems to have
the anointing at the Jordan carry the cosmic freight.

Now the man who descended into the waters of the Jordan
has a double name, the "Messiah/Christ" and the "Jesus/
Savior."[50] Though the two sets of names are related, Irenaeus
treats them separately. First Irenaeus parses "Messiah/Christ."
Though Jesus becomes the salvation history Christ only at the
Jordan—the issue is not simply that of the eternal Word—it is
still through Christ that the Father anointed the whole of the
universe with the Spirit. Here the eternal and the temporal
anointings merge. The cosmic anointing at the Jordan touches
all individuals, all natures, all worlds, and has a soteriological
texture.

Soteriology is the chief concern when Irenaeus parses the
"Jesus/Savior" name. Again at the Jordan the Father anointed
this man with the Spirit, in virtue of which he takes on his saving mission: to preach the good news to the poor, to free from
all manner of ills and from death, and to give eternal salvation
to others who will believe in him. The names of Jesus as the
"Savior/God With Us" and "Wonderful Counselor," to which
Irenaeus addresses himself in the immediate context, are also

[48] Ibid.
[49] Ibid.
[50] See the explanatory note on the sets of names in SC 406:310, 311.

related to soteriology, namely passing from error to truth, from corruptibility to incorruptibility.[51]

The Father's cosmic anointing of the Word with the Spirit is expressed in the Jordan anointing, which has salvation as its burden. Through the two anointings, one eternal, the other at the Jordan, Irenaeus attempts to give a systematic coherence to his doctrine of creation, binding first creation (Genesis) with second creation (redemption) and the Church. The cosmic character of the eternal anointing has echoes in the Jordan anointing.[52]

When Irenaeus fuses the eternal and the temporal anointing, including them in what he claims is "the preaching of the truth in brief," a short exposition that contains only "the main points" of the apostolic doctrine in their "integrity and purity," this has to be significant.[53] Irenaeus would not include secondary material in such a short summary. *The Demonstration of the Apostolic Preaching* is the earliest document we possess professing to give the very basis of the proclamation of the gospel in its apostolic form.

In a quite different context Gregory Nazianzus (329–389) refers in passing to the cosmic meaning of Jesus' baptism. "Jesus comes up out of the water and he makes the cosmos, which he carries, to ascend [out of the water] with him."[54] The cosmic Lord brings the cosmos, which he carries with him in the mysteries of his life, emerging with him from the waters of the Jordan, in which the Spirit was given to him without measure. Can the cosmos be untouched by this mystery?

From Chaos to Cosmos

In an extensive section on the baptism of Jesus, *The Teaching of St. Gregory* (end of the fifth century) places the Jordan event in the context of the Genesis account of the creation of the world. In the beginning the Spirit transformed chaos into cosmos, "moving over the waters, and thence set out the order of the

[51] *Demonstration of the Apostolic Preaching*, 54, 55; SC 62:115–118.
[52] A. Orbe, *La Unción del Verbo* (Rome: Gregorian University, 1961) 521.
[53] Ibid., 1; SC 62:27, 28.
[54] *Oration* 39:16; SC 358:184.

creatures," including the ornamenting of the heavens where the angels dwell.[55] But there is a larger, cosmic role of the Spirit at creation. "He came down to the waters and sanctified the lower waters of the earth."[56]

This theme has a long history in both orthodox and heterodox circles. Already Ignatius of Antioch says: "He was born and has been baptized in order to purify the water by his passion,"[57] a theme taken up by both Clement of Alexandria,[58] and the Gospel of Philip, very likely composed in the second century.[59] Further, the theme is extensive in the literature of the early Church.[60] Jacob of Serugh is explicit in saying that by stepping down into the Jordan Jesus consecrated all waters: "The entire nature of the waters perceived that you had visited them—seas, deeps, rivers, springs and pools all thronged together to receive the blessing from your footsteps."[61]

The baptismal event touches the cosmic waters. This is especially clear in the Teaching of St. Gregory. At creation the Spirit moved over the waters, and from this act "set out the order of the creatures."[62] The Spirit changes disorder to order. Sin "had weakened and enfeebled and deprived [the waters] of the grace of the Spirit," alienated the Spirit from "the old deteriorated earthy matter."[63] In the beginning the Spirit touches created matters, but when Adam sinned, the Spirit left Adam and departed also from the whole of the creation, including the firmament of the heaven. However, Christ stepped down into the Jordan, "and by treading the waters with his own footstep, He sanctified them and made them purifying,"[64] restoring both

[55] 413; Thomson, 89.

[56] Ibid.

[57] Ephesians 18:2; SC 10:74; Schoedel and Koester, Commentary on the Letters of Ignatius of Antioch, 85, n. 9.

[58] Excerpts from Theodotus 81:2; SC 23:206.

[59] 77; The Nag Hammadi Library in English (New York: Harper & Row, 1977) 146.

[60] Brock, "The Epiklesis in the Antiochene Baptismal Ordines," in Symposium Syriacum 1972, 206.

[61] Bedjan, 1:188.

[62] 413; Thomson, 89.

[63] Ibid., 412; Thomson, 89.

[64] Ibid., 414; Thomson, 89.

the lower and the upper waters, a reference to Semitic cosmology.

The renewal of creation through the Spirit is nonetheless a trinitarian act. The Father sends the Son and the Spirit, the two "demonstrating the consubstantial hypostasis of the Trinity, acting together in establishing and united in renewing."[65] As the Son and the Spirit are associated with the Father in creation,[66] they are associated in the restoration of creation, which is itself the context for the transformative elevation of all persons "in the glory of adoption."[67]

By the use of water at creation, God "fattened all plants and reptiles and wild animals and beasts and birds, and by the freshness of the waters they sprung from the earth."[68] The God who nurtured first creation with water likewise nurtures second creation by the baptism of Jesus, where God "made verdant the womb of generation of the waters, purifying by the waters and renewing . . . earthy matter," which sin "deprived [the cosmos] of the grace of the Spirit."[69] In another context the author speaks of "the mortality of creation."[70] If one takes away the Spirit, creation 'dies.'

The sin of Adam stripped creation of the Spirit; the baptism of Jesus restores the Spirit to the whole of the created order. Just as at the beginning "the Spirit of the Deity moved over the waters, and thence set out the order of the creatures," so now at the new creation God sets out the new order at the baptism of Jesus.[71] The author specifically relates cosmic renewal to Jesus' baptism: "He renewed and rejuvenated creation once and for all. He opened the womb of baptism."[72]

---

[65] Ibid., 420; Thomson, 91.
[66] Ibid., 362; Thomson, 73.
[67] Ibid., 414; Thomson, 90.
[68] Ibid., 412; Thomson, 89.
[69] Ibid.
[70] Ibid., 516; Thomson, 120.
[71] Ibid., 413; Thomson, 89.
[72] Ibid., 679; Thomson, 169.

Philoxenus, who belongs to the same broad theological tradition, gives Jesus' baptism a commanding role in cosmic renewal: ". . . the return of all to God, and the gathering up and making new, that everything might become in him and he in all—this was kept for the Son. And its type is baptism [in the Jordan], and its truth in his resurrection."[73] The model of the restoration of all things, the universal gathering up of all history and the whole of creation in the Son, is the Jordan event. At the Jordan, "creation [is] renewed in power."[74] These cosmic mysteries, unsuspected even by John the Baptist, "commenced at [the Son's] baptism."[75] The eschatological return of the universe to the Father begins at the Jordan, though it is revealed only in the resurrection.

This great cosmic vocation of the Son is hidden from every intelligence, but is made known by testimony of the Father and the Spirit. In fact, the revelation of the Trinity here, at the baptism, is the revelation of the Son's role in the cosmic restoration, in which "all things which are seen [are changed] to the other order, which does not fall under the senses."[76] The baptism of Jesus is the inauguration of the new order.

While the emphasis in Paul is clearly on non-human creation, one cannot reduce "creation" to irrational creation. It is not completely impersonal. "Creation," for instance, includes non-Christians.[77] The author of Ephesians repeatedly uses "to create" to describe salvation.[78]

Philoxenus now borrows from Romans 8:18-23. Having terminated his description of the new Christian life, Paul calls on three elements to witness to the reality of that life lived under "the law of the Spirit . . . in Christ Jesus" (Rom 8:2), namely, the groaning of material subhuman creation in labor pains, the

[73] Philoxenus, *Fragments of the Commentary on Matthew and Luke* 11; CSCO 393:9.

[74] Ibid., 12; CSCO 393:16.

[75] Ibid., 11; CSCO 393:9.

[76] Ibid., CSCO 393:10.

[77] A. Vögtle, *Das Neue Testament und die Zukunft des Kosmos* (Düsseldorf: Patmos, 1970) 184.

[78] M. Barth, *Ephesians 1-3* (Garden City: Doubleday, 1974) 104.

hope of Christians for salvation, and for the Spirit itself.[79] Material creation is not a completely passive spectator of the glorious triumph of humanity's liberation and triumph, but shares in the splendor of the victory of God's daughters and sons. By sharing in this expansive gift, creation is delivered from its innate corruption and decay. Paul, speaking in the apocalyptic language of his own tradition, seems to be borrowing categories from Greek philosophers who think of the rebirth of nature in the spring season with images taken from a woman in labor.[80] Within a Christian context, this birthing becomes salvation for all creation. Paul has justification in Jewish literature for speaking of "creation" as meaning irrational creatures and the inanimate. A solidarity exists between humanity and creation. In Paul, when Adam falls, creation is affected. When Adam is restored, creation is not left untouched.[81]

An indissoluble relation exists between humankind and creation. Salvation is a "cosmic totality."[82] In Greek, cosmos and universe are closely associated with "order,"[83] making it susceptible to uses in the plan of salvation. Cosmos is concrete historical reality. The universe is regarded as the setting for human history. Paul does not consider our body as something separate from the rest of creation. Their destinies are bound together. "No creationless redemption" is possible (Rom 8:18-30) and, in the final analysis, "no redemptionless creation" (Eph 1:10; Col 1:20).[84] When the cosmic Lord transforms the universe, it will be a certain participation in the glory of the children of God.[85] Salvation is for the whole of the created order.[86]

The harmony or sympathy between the elements of the universe goes back especially to the Stoic philosopher Posidonius

[79] J. A. Fitzmyer, *Romans* (New York: Doubleday, 1993) 505.

[80] Ibid., 509.

[81] J. G. Gibbs, *Creation and Redemption* (Leiden: Brill, 1971) 40.

[82] Ibid.

[83] L. Lilla, "Cosmos," in *Encyclopedia of the Early Church*, 1:204.

[84] J. G. Gibbs, "The Cosmic Scope of Redemption According to Paul," in *Biblica* 56 (1975) 29.

[85] S. Lyonnet, "Redemptio 'cosmica' secundum Rom 8:19-23," in *Verbum Domini* 44 (1966) 236, 237.

[86] J. Zizioulas, "The Mystery of the Church in the Orthodox Tradition," in *One in Christ* 24 (1988) 296.

(ca. 135 B.C.–51–50 B.C). The harmony he found in humanity he also found in nature. The laws operative in the first were active in the second. God rules the unity of history, symbolized by the "cosmopolis," or city of God. In the harmony of that unitive creation history, the human race has its full share. He believed that everything continues to live as long as it remains in harmony with the whole, the cosmos being permeated by one all-comprehensive life.[87] Though his influence has been overstated, yet "he can be compared to no one but Aristotle."[88] Posidonius influenced Lucretius, Cicero, Manilius, Seneca, and Pliny the Elder.[89] Whether or not dependent on Posidonius, Basil repeats a similar teaching, saying "the ensemble of the cosmos, composed of dissimilar parts, [God] has closely linked in a communion *(koinonia)* and harmony by a law of indissoluble friendship, such that the beings which are the most distant, the one [joined with] the others, appear united by the same sympathy, with due regard to their place they occupy [in the whole]."[90] Philoxenus knew Greek Christian thought and could have drawn on these themes to help him do an exegesis of the Roman passage in relation to the Jordan event.

One needs to be cautious about giving a twentieth-century exegesis of a biblical passage and then read it back into the basis of Philoxenus' text, which comes from the first decade of the sixth century (ca. 505). On the other hand, biblical insight did not begin with the modern scriptural revival and the historical-critical method.

Philoxenus gives more detail on the cosmic dimensions of the Son's baptism. Speaking of the relation of the human body to the visible universe, Philoxenus says that the groans of cosmic labor are changed into cosmic joy. "All created things are groaning and are in travail until today," the 'today' being the

---

[87] *The Cambridge History of Later Greek and Early Medieval Philosophy,* A. H. Armstrong, ed. (Cambridge: Cambridge University, 1967) 128.

[88] "Posidonius," in *The Oxford Classical Dictionary,* 2nd. ed. (Oxford: Clarendon, 1970) 868.

[89] K. Reinhardt, *Kosmos und Sympathie* (Munich: Beck, 1926); "Posidonius," in *The Oxford Classical Dictionary,* 867–868.

[90] *Homilies on the Hexameron* 2:2; SC 26bis:148.

corrupted cosmos in the pain of delivering.[91] The laboring universe cries out for the Jordan event, "that baptism in which Jesus, when he was baptized, fulfilled the will of his Father and created anew all things visible and invisible."[92] The groaning of the enslaved person is within the context of an enslaved universe, wailing and reaching out in hope of a joint liberation, touching visible and invisible creation, rational and irrational creatures.

Humanity stands within the cosmos. The travail of the one is the travail of the other. The cosmic chorus rises from the depths of the world laboring as in childbirth to bring forth that new world where the dominion of the Lord Christ is universal and absolute. "This is the mystery which was fulfilled in the baptism of our Saviour, which [baptism] indeed the Father ratified through his voice and the Spirit by his descent."[93] The triadic involvement is undeniable. The human/cosmic pain reaches out to the baptism of Jesus, where the Father and the Spirit are double witnesses to a trinitarian cosmic event, which is directed to the goal of all history. The first steps to an eschatological consummation begin at the Jordan where, as Philoxenus would say much later, "mystically God [becomes] in all and all in God."[94]

When Philoxenus writes of the cosmic meaning of the baptism, he may also be reflecting an earlier Syrian tradition as expressed in the *Odes of Solomon*, which probably originated in Syria about the mid-second century c.e. *Ode* 24 seems to be about the baptism of Jesus, beginning with the first verse: "The dove fluttered over the head of our Lord Messiah / Because He was her head."[95] (A variant reading has "the dove flew over the head of our Lord, the Savior."[96]) The dove/Spirit comes

[91] Philoxenus, *Fragments of the Commentary on Matthew and Luke* 53; CSCO 393:70.

[92] Ibid.

[93] Ibid.

[94] *Fragments of the Commentary on Matthew and Luke* 12; CSCO 393:16. The formulation is admittedly clumsy.

[95] *The Odes of Solomon: The Syriac Texts*, J. H. Charlesworth, ed. (Missoula: Scholars Press, 1977) 98.

[96] Bertrand, *Le Baptême de Jésus*, 25, n. 2.

over Jesus, designating him as the Messiah, causing a "cosmic upheaval."[97] As *Ode* 42:11 has it: "Sheol saw me and was shattered."[98] Then the author of *Ode* 24 speaks of the "chasms" opening and closing, very likely a reference to the Messiah's triumphant descent into Sheol.[99] Speaking of the just in Sheol, the *Ode* continues: "They were seeking the Lord as those who are about to give birth. . . . For they travailed from the beginning / And the end of their travail was life."[100] Admitting the difficulty of interpreting this highly symbolic language, creation seems in labor pains related to the baptism of Jesus resulting in new life: "For the Lord revealed His way, and spread widely His grace. And those who understood it Knew His Holiness."[101] The resolution of the "chasms'" birth pains is knowing the holiness of God.[102]

Who Sanctifies the Waters?

In Christian baptism the epiklesis of the Holy Spirit consecrates the waters. But at the Jordan, Jacob of Serugh insists, the Holy Spirit does not consecrate the waters. This insistence arises out of the need to safeguard Jesus' sinlessness. He was not in need of baptism. Jacob emphasizes that the Spirit appeared after Jesus' baptism, and the role of the Spirit was simply to testify to Jesus, together with the Father.[103] "The Spirit did not come down to sanctify the water for Christ to be baptized in, for

[97] Ibid., 25.

[98] *Ode* 42; Charlesworth, *Odes of Solomon*, 144.

[99] Bertrand, *Le Baptême de Jésus*, 25; W. R. Newbold, "The Descent of Christ in the Odes of Solomon," in *Journal of Biblical Literature* 31 (1912) 168–209; B. Reiche, *The Disobedient Spirits and Christian Baptism: A Study of 1 Pet.III.19 and Its Context* (Copenhagen: Munksgaard, 1946) 243–245.

[100] Charlesworth, *Odes of Solomon*, 98.

[101] Ibid., 99.

[102] Though not specifically related to the baptism of Jesus, Narsai also has cosmic harmony. "The union between the spiritual and the corporeal must continually function together on every level, so that all creation can know and love God." F. G. McLeod, "Man as the Image of God: Its Meaning and Theological Significance in Narsai," in *Theological Studies* 42 (1981) 467.

[103] Brock, "Baptismal Themes in the Writings of Jacob of Serugh," in *Symposium Syriacum 1976*, 327, n. 12.

sanctification flows from the holy Son. [Only] after Christ had washed and gone up from the water did the Spirit descend in order to indicate [him], and not to sanctify."[104] Using the image of a coal of fire from Isaiah's inaugural vision (6:6), Jacob sees Christ himself as the live coal going down into the Jordan thus inflaming and sanctifying the waters.[105] The move from the live coal in the waters to the Jordan as a furnace is an easy transition.[106]

Christ himself is the sanctifier of the waters as he descends into the Jordan. But once the epiklesis of the Holy Spirit over the water was used for Christian baptism, there was a move, in the name of parallelism, to state that it was the Holy Spirit who sanctified the waters of the Jordan.[107] "The Spirit descended from on high and sanctified the water by her hovering."[108] However, originally it was Christ who consecrates the waters. This is the tradition that Gregory Nazianzus represents: when Jesus is baptized by John, Jesus "sanctifies the Jordan."[109]

[104] Bedjan, 1:159.

[105] Bedjan, 1:183.

[106] Brock, "Baptismal Themes in the Writings of Jacob of Serugh," 326–327.

[107] Brock, "The Epiklesis in the Antiochene Baptismal *Ordines*," in *Symposium Syriacum 1972*, 204, 205.

[108] Ephrem, *Hymns on Epiphany* 6:1; CSCO 187:147. As was said, though the Epiphany hymns are attributed to Ephrem, they may be later. See E. Beck, *Des Heiligen Ephraem des Syrers Hymnen de Nativitate (Epiphania)*, (Louvain: Catholic University, 1959); CSCO 186:vii. See also *The Teaching of St. Gregory* 411; Thomson, 89: "He [the Spirit] Himself came down upon the waters, and made the waters at once purifying and renovating."

[109] *Oration* 39:15; SC 358:183.

Chapter Five

"Come to Me by My Road: Put on Poverty and Freedom"—Asceticism

The baptism of Jesus has strong ascetic overtones. After his baptism Jesus is "led by the Spirit" (Matt 4:1; Luke 4:1), or in Mark's more graphic formulation, "the Spirit immediately drove him out [or "expelled him"] into the wilderness" (Mark 1:12), where he is tempted. The temptations allude to the trials the Israelites suffered in the desert before entering the Promised Land. Coming immediately after the baptism, they symbolize the hostility and rejection he will endure during his public life, factors that are integral to his ministry.[1] But the life in the desert is not a permanent state; on the contrary, it is provisional and transitional, even when it demands great renunciation.

In the later tradition, the desert came to be understood as the place of poverty. "Come to me by my road."[2] But it is also the image of the new freedom, specifically trinitarian in character, pledged by the Father, attested by the Spirit: "Observe the freedom in which Jesus went forth, and do thou thyself also go forth like him,"[3] and "put on freedom."[4] So the Lukan ac-

[1] Fitzmyer, *The Gospel According to Luke I–IX*, 510–512.

[2] *Discourse* 9:272; *The Discourses of Philoxenus*, E.A.W. Budge, ed., 2 vols. (London: Asher, 1894) 2:260. Hereafter cited as Budge.

[3] Ibid., 9:275; Budge, 2:264.

[4] Ibid., 9:268; Budge, 2:257.

count, according to Philoxenus, relates that Jesus "made new his members through his baptism."[5] Philoxenus points out that the genealogy up to Adam, which Luke gives, shows that the newly baptized now belong "to another order, and so [Luke] brought them to the Father."[6] The baptism constitutes a new stage in the unfolding economy,[7] and places history on a movement back to the Father.

Though the relation of the Jordan to the Christian life is a commonplace in the early Church, Philoxenus has a unique way of speaking of it. He wants to say two things: that Jesus' baptism is his, and his baptism is ours. Truly, it is his baptism first, but it is ours "because he was going to give it to us."[8] So he was baptized in the Jordan, and immediately "he gave it to us."[9]

The centrality of Jesus' baptism for understanding of Christian baptism should not diminish the incarnation, which is also of great significance for Philoxenus' doctrine of baptism. The link between the two is soteriology. A double movement from God to humankind and from humankind to God are brought to synthesis in incarnation and baptism.[10] Just as the Word became flesh for our sake, so he was baptized for our sake, leading us back to God.

Earlier, Theodore of Mopsuestia (ca. 350–428), an outstanding representative of Antiochene theology, also wanted to keep the relationship between the Lord's baptism and ours. Still, he wants to remove something of the scandal. Instead of stressing that our baptism is really his baptism, he emphasizes something else. He says the opposite, namely, his baptism is our baptism, or his baptism conforms to our baptism. In other words, Jesus is baptized for the Church. He writes: "Know that you are bap-

---

[5] *Fragments of the Commentary on Matthew and Luke* 12; CSCO 393:16.

[6] Ibid. Contemporary exegetes also call attention to the cosmic dimensions of the baptism of Jesus. Barrett, *The Holy Spirit and the Gospel Tradition*, 23–25; C. B. Caird, *The Gospel of St. Luke* (London: Black, 1963) 77, 78.

[7] A. de Halleux, *Philoxène de Mabbog: Sa Vie, Ses Écrits, Sa Théologie* (Louvain: Imprimerie Orientaliste, 1963) 284.

[8] *Fragments of the Commentary on Matthew and Luke* 13; CSCO 393:16, 17.

[9] Ibid.

[10] De Halleux, *Philoxène de Mabbog*, 419, 454.

tized in the same baptism as that in which Christ our Lord in the flesh was baptized. [The baptism of our Lord] was in fact symbolically drawn to ours."[11] Or more precisely, "He was baptized in our own baptism."[12] The scandal of the Jordan is removed.

The Baptism as Limit

The baptism of Jesus constitutes a boundary, even a fence. But the boundary functions in quite different ways. For Cyril of Alexandria (ca. 375–444) the baptism is taken out of the narrow exegetical framework, out of the dogmatic discussion that sees it as a problem, and makes it a mystery of cosmic dimensions.[13] Cyril sees Adam losing the image of God because he lost the Spirit: "Our father Adam . . . did not preserve the grace of the Spirit, and thus in him the whole nature lost at last [gradually] the God-given goods."[14] If the loss of the image in Adam is tied to the loss of the Spirit, then the restoration of the image can only be linked to the return of the Spirit. The loss of the

[11] *Commentary of Theodore of Mopsuestia on the Lord's Prayer and on the Sacraments of Baptism and the Eucharist*, A. Mingana, ed. (Cambridge: Heffer, 1935) 66. "He was baptized in our own baptism, the symbol of which He depicted in this way." Ibid. Much earlier Clement of Alexandria (ca. 150–ca. 215) has Jesus imaging our baptism. "He did it for us, the Lord being the model; baptized, we are illumined; illumined, we are adopted as sons; adopted as sons, we are made perfect; being made perfect, we receive immortality." *The Teacher* 1:6, 26; SC 70:158. Athanasius has a similar formulation. At the Jordan the Spirit did not descend upon the Word (who has no need of sanctification), but upon us through him." *Oration Against the Arians* 1:47; PG 26:109. Both John Chrysostom and Gregory of Nyssa spell out the relationship of Jesus' baptism to Christian baptism. Chrysostom, *Homilies on Matthew* 12:4; PG 57:206; Gregory of Nyssa, *On the Baptism of Christ*; PG 46:580–600.

[12] *Commentary of Theodore of Mopsuestia*, 66.

[13] Wilken, "The Interpretation of the Baptism of Jesus in the Later Fathers," in *Studia Patristica*, 272. Idem, *Judaism and the Early Christian Mind: A Study of Cyril of Alexandria's Exegesis and Theology* (New Haven: Yale University, 1971) 127–142. I am indebted to Wilken in these paragraphs on Cyril.

[14] *Commentary on John* 5:2; *Sancti Patris Nostri Cyrilli Archiepiscopi Alexandrini in D. Joannis Evangelium*, P. E. Pusey, ed., 2 vols. (Brussels: Culture and Civilization, 1965) 1:691. Hereafter cited as Pusey.

Spirit was universal in Adam; its restoration is universal in the New Adam. Though acknowledging that "at the time of the incarnation he received the Spirit from heaven," the incarnation is not decisive for the permanent, secure return of the Spirit.[15] That is the function of the baptism of Jesus. Working within an Adam christology, the Spirit is returned by the New Adam at the Jordan, thus "restoring human nature to its ancient state, . . . its unshaken state."[16]

For Cyril, as even before him already in the second century, the accent has shifted from Jesus' descent into the waters of the Jordan to the descent of the Spirit on Jesus as he comes up from the waters:[17] "With the descent of the Spirit the time of renewal is at the doors, yea within the doors. . . . The Spirit who fled away from human nature, the one who can gather and form us in the divine image, this one the Savior gives us anew and returns us to our ancient condition and reforms us to his own image."[18] The new age begins. The Spirit that had departed human nature at the sin of Adam has returned, and restores humanity. The image defaced is the image restored and made new.

While granting that the Old Testament prophets had the Spirit, he denies that one can compare the giving of the Spirit in order to prophesy, to the dwelling of the Spirit in Christ beginning at the Jordan so that the whole of humankind can be restored to the ancient image. Through the descent of the Spirit on Jesus, we permanently possess "the full and complete indwelling in men of the Holy spirit."[19] The voice of the Father and the descent of the Spirit lay down the boundary where the old creation ends and the new begins. The dispensation of grace starts here. Cyril's teaching represents one of the most theologically profound reflections on the baptism of Jesus in early Christian literature.[20]

[15] Ibid., 2:1; Pusey, 1:179.
[16] Ibid., 5:2; Pusey, 1:691, 692.
[17] Wilken, "The Baptism of Jesus in the Later Fathers," in *Studia Patristica*, 270.
[18] *Commentary on John* 5:2; Pusey, 1:695, 696.
[19] Ibid.
[20] Wilken, *Judaism and the Early Christian Mind*, 140.

That at the Jordan the Law ends and graces begin was developed by others, John Chrysostom among them.[21] But Philoxenus develops it extensively. So decisive is the baptism of Jesus to Philoxenus' thought that he repeatedly returns to it to divide off the stages in the economy of salvation. There are three stages: from Mary's giving birth to the baptism at the Jordan, from the Jordan to the cross, and, finally, the cross itself.[22] If in this perspective the first beginnings of the economy are at the birth of Jesus, and the end is the cross, then the baptism of Jesus dominates the central stage of the economy.[23] From the moment of his baptism, the way to the cross is prepared by the *kenosis*.[24] During the period extending from the baptism to the cross, Jesus stood "at the limit of spiritual perfection."[25]

For Philoxenus, as for Tertullian, the boundary between the Old and New Testaments is not the incarnation but the baptism of Jesus: "In the Jordan he laid down the boundary of them both; for He ended that path, which was after the law, in which He was journeying because He kept the law, and from it He began the path of perfection, which He shewed in His own person."[26] Before the Jordan experience, Jesus' "rule and conduct of life . . . fell short of perfection."[27] The reason: "Until the Jordan it was bondage, that is to say, He was subject unto the law as a servant, but from the Jordan and henceforth His life and conduct were in freedom."[28] An important aspect of Philoxenus' teaching is the relation of the Jordan to Christian freedom.

[21] *Homilies on Matthew* 12:3; PG 57:206.

[22] Philoxenus, *Fragments of the Commentary on Matthew and Luke* 9; CSCO 393:5; idem, *Commentary on the Johannine Prologue* 2; CSCO 381:3; *Discourse* 8; Budge, 2:244, 245.

[23] De Halleux, *Philoxène de Mabbog*, 402.

[24] Grillmeier, "Die Taufe Christi," in *Fides Sacramenti: Sacramentum Fidei*, 175.

[25] *Discourse* 8; Budge, 2:245.

[26] Ibid., 9; Budge, 2:262, 263.

[27] Ibid., 8; Budge, 2:239.

[28] Ibid., 9; Budge, 2:248.

Before the Jordan Jesus fulfilled the way of life of the law. But "from the Jordan he made the beginning of the way of His own rule of life."[29] Mary, on the other hand, remained on the law side of the Jordan: "For Mary stood in one rule of life, and Jesus stood in another, that is to say, she lived the life of the law, and He lived the life of the Spirit."[30] As evidence that Mary remained behind on the law side of the Jordan, Philoxenus cites the severe rebuke of Jesus at Cana: "What do I have to do with you, woman?"[31]

After the baptism in the Jordan, "the rule of life was more perfect" because Jesus was no longer subject to human authority.[32] At the Jordan the voice of the Father and the descent of the Spirit reveal "that the fence was removed between fleshly (beings) and spiritual (beings)."[33] John of Apamea (mid-fifth century), who belongs to the same theological tradition but slightly earlier, teaches that only after the witness of the Father and the Spirit at the Jordan did Jesus begin to teach. "No knowledge of the divine mysteries are manifested in men before he (Jesus) received baptism."[34] Aphrahat (ca. 270–ca. 345) records that though Jesus was born of the Spirit, after his baptism the Spirit left him so that he could be tempted by Satan; no temptation preceded the baptism.[35] The Jordan is truly a boundary.

What the passage through the Red Sea was for Israel, the passage through the Jordan was for Jesus. He passes from the land of subjection (Egypt) to the "land of freedom,"[36] into "the spiritual country,"[37] "crossing from one world to another."[38]

---

[29] Ibid.

[30] Ibid., 8; Budge, 2:241, 242.

[31] Ibid.

[32] Ibid.; Budge, 2:239, 240.

[33] Philoxenus, *Fragments of the Commentary on Matthew and Luke* 11; CSCO 393:10.

[34] *Dialogues and Treatises* 10:117; SC 311:149. Cyril of Jerusalem has the same teaching: "Jesus Christ was the Son of God, but before his baptism he did not preach the gospel." *Catechetical Lectures* 3:14; Reischl 1:82.

[35] *Demonstration* 7:17; SC 349:405.

[36] Philoxenus, *Discourse* 9; Budge 2:263.

[37] Ibid.; Budge, 2:248.

[38] Ibid.; Budge, 2:263.

For Philoxenus the Jordan is "the beginning of the new order of the Spirit."[39]

"No River Is Good but the Jordan"

The Jordan has a role ascribed to no other river. Because of its role in the history of Israel, and more specifically in the narratives of Joshua, Elijah, and Elisha, the Jordan becomes charged with soteriological significance. The ministry of John and the baptism of Jesus took up and gave new meaning to the river's soteriological past. Early Church authors use the Jordan as a symbol in their exegesis of the narrative of Jesus' baptism.[40] Because in this symbolic framework the Jordan is a tributary of the primordial ocean, it is a soteriological instrument of universalism.

Bertrand records that in the first two centuries there are almost a hundred significant references to the baptism of Jesus in the Jordan, coming from thirty-three different sources; twenty-five of the authors can be determined or are anonymous, and eight are from the sectarians. The scope would suggest that the significance of the Jordan was widely discussed, possibly because of the problems the baptism of Jesus poses.[41]

Already in the earliest years some are speaking of "the Grand Jordan," as Hippolytus records.[42] Origen speaks of "the great mystery of the Jordan,"[43] likening the unique character of the Jordan to the unique Father: "Just as no one is good, except the one only God, the Father, so, among the rivers, no river is good except the Jordan."[44] Gregory of Nyssa (ca. 330–ca. 395) also believes that the "Jordan alone among all rivers had

[39] *Fragments of the Commentary on Matthew and Luke* 11; CSCO 393:9. See F. J. Dölger, "Der Durchzug durch den Jordan als Sinnbild der Christlichen Taufe," in *Antike und Christentum* 2 (1930) 70–79. Ephrem teaches that baptism of Jesus brings John's baptism to an end, and that Jesus baptized again all who had received baptism from John. *Commentary on the Diatessaron* 4:1; SC 121:93.

[40] Bertrand, *Baptême de Jésus*, 127.

[41] Ibid., 134.

[42] *Philosophumena*, 5, 7; PG 163:3139.

[43] *Commentary on John* 6:47; SC 157:312.

[44] Ibid.; SC 157:314.

received the first fruits of sanctification and blessing"; the Jordan itself "spread the grace of baptism throughout the whole world."[45] The cosmic dimension surfaces again. The Jordan as a saving place was foreshadowed by Joshua crossing over into the Promised Land, by Elisha twice passing over the river, and by the cleansing of Naaman.[46]

Not surprisingly, the equation between the Jordan and baptism, with its provenance probably Alexandria, is a commonplace in early Greek, Syriac, and Latin-speaking areas.[47] Ephrem says of Christ that "he took baptism out of the Jordan."[48] In a work uncertainly attributed to the Alexandrian theologian Didymus the Blind (ca. 313–398), the author writes: "The Jordan is immortal baptism."[49] Eusebius relates that Constantine deferred baptism to the end of his life, desiring to be baptized in the Jordan,[50] but the hope was not realized. Jerome made a revision of Eusebius' Onomasticon (ca. 330), which he issued as The Book of Places, remarking that even in his day (usque hodie), many believers come to the Jordan to be baptized.[51] The desire to enter into the mystery of Jesus' baptism by being baptized in the actual Jordan was great enough, even as far away as North Africa, that already Tertullian protests against the practice. Now that Jesus has consecrated all waters by his baptism, "there is no difference between those John [the Baptist] baptized in the Jordan and those Peter baptized in the Tiber."[52] Ambrose, too, looks askance at the elevation of the physical waters of the

---

[45] On the Baptism of Christ; PG 46:593.

[46] Origen, Homilies of Joshua 4:1; 4:4; 5:1; SC 71:146, 148, 156, 158, 160; idem, Commentary on John 6:46; SC 157:308, 310, 314. Dölger, "Der Durchzug durch das Rote Meer als Sinnbild der christlichen Taufe," in Antike und Christentum 2 (1930) 63–69. See also Tertullian, Against Marcion 4:9; Adversus Marcionem, E. Evans, ed., 2 vols. (Oxford: Clarendon 1972) 2:290, 292; Ambrose, On the Sacraments 1:13, 14; SC 25bis:66–68; idem, On the Mysteries 16, 17; SC 25bis:164.

[47] Dölger, "Der Durchzug durch den Jordan als Sinnbild der christlichen Taufe," in Antike und Christenum, 74, 76.

[48] Sermon on Our Lord 56; CSCO 271:53.

[49] On the Trinity 2:14; PG 39:700.

[50] Life of Constantine 4:62; PG 20:1216.

[51] PL 23:931.

[52] On Baptism 4:3; SC 35:70.

Jordan, maintaining that "where Christ is, there also one finds the Jordan."[53] Here Ambrose makes an equation not between the Jordan and baptism but between Jordan and Christ, a view already found in Origen, for whom the Jordan was the Word of God made flesh.[54] Or more expansively, "the Jordan is the figure of the Word who descended with our descent."[55]

The consecration of all waters by Jesus' baptism, and the equation between Jordan and baptism, led to what Augustin Mouhanna calls "the willed confusion of the baptismal font and the river Jordan."[56] Severus (ca. 465–538), patriarch of Antioch, and Sophronius (ca. 560–638), patriarch of Jerusalem, both record that the baptismal font is called "the Jordan."[57] By extension, all baptismal waters are the Jordan. Among the Armenians the blessing of Epiphany water for use in initiation asks God to "endue it with the grace of the Jordan."[58]

---

[53] *Sermon* 38:2; CSEL 6:481. The manuscript text reads: *ubique enim nunc Christus, ubique Iordanis est.* But an editor, wishing to improve the rendering, changed it: *ubi enim nunc Christus est, ibi quoque Iordanis est.* Dölger, "Der Durchzug," in *Antike und Christentum* 75, n. 20. In *The Spiritual Meadow*, John Moschus (ca. 550–619) tells of a Jew who, about to die in a desert, was baptized with sand, and on being rescued, the bishop suggested he be baptized in the Jordan. SC 12:230–232.

[54] *Commentary on John* 6:42; SC 157:296–298.

[55] Ibid., 6:46; SC 157:310.

[56] *Le Rites de l'Initiation dans l'Église Maronite,* 238.

[57] "Come, let us go to the fountain of the Jordan." Severus, *Hymn Sung on the Entry into the Baptistery at Dawn on Sunday* 90; PO 6:131; *Homily* 88; PO 23:95. See also hymn sung at the entry into the baptistery at dawn on Sunday; PO 6:131; Sophronius, *On the Miracles of Saints Cyrus and John,* Miracle 39; *Spicilegium Romanum,* A. Mai, ed., 10 vols. (Rome: Urban College, 1839–1844) 3:436, 437.

[58] "Canon of Blessing the Water on the Day of the Epiphany of Our Lord Jesus Christ," *Rituale Armenorum,* F. C. Conybeare, ed. (Oxford: Clarendon 1905) 176. A tradition exists that understands the Jordan as "the river of death." The symbolism is tied in part to Romans 6:3 ("all of us who have been baptized . . . were baptized into his death") as in Origen's *Homilies on Joshua* 4:2; SC 71:150. P. Lundberg has studied this extensively in *La Typologie Baptismale dans l'Ancienne Église* (Uppsala: Lundequist, 1942). See also Dölger, "Der Durchzug." J. Daniélou brings some correctives to the research of Lundberg in "La Traversée du Jourdain: Figure du Baptême," in *Sacramentum Futuri* (Paris: Beauchesne, 1950) 233–256. The concern here is not with the broader symbolism of the Jordan, but the Jordan in re-

In a long, philologically technical article, Gabriele Winkler has researched the themes of resting and knowing at the Jordan in Syriac and Armenian sources. In spite of its length, I will partly summarize and, in a minor way, supplement this important contribution.[59]

According to a series of Armenian and Syriac witnesses, a tradition that has its origin in Syria, there is a clear relation between Matthew 11:28-29 (rendered not "I am meek and humble" but "I will make you quiet because I am quiet. . . . I will give you rest . . . you will find rest for your souls") and the baptism of Jesus as well as Christian baptism. Besides the Matthaean text, John 1:32 ("I saw the Spirit descending from heaven like a dove, and it remained on him") and Acts 2:3 ("Divided tongues . . . rested on each of them") play a role.[60] The rest promised to believers is based on Jesus' "quiet" and the Spirit resting on him in the Jordan.[61]

The Spirit resting on Jesus, already mentioned by Mark (1:10) and John (1:32) reappears in the *Gospel of the Hebrews.* The text expands on the resting of the Spirit in relation to Christ's baptism: "And it came to pass when the Lord was come up out of the water, the whole fount of the Holy Spirit descended upon him and rested on him and said to him: 'My Son, in all the prophets was I waiting for thee that thou shouldest come and I might rest in thee. For thou are my rest; thou art my firstbegotten Son that reignest for ever.'"[62] History was in expectation,

---

lation to the baptism of Jesus. Vigne has an extensive chapter on the typology of the Jordan, *Christ au Jourdain,* 275-308.

[59] Winkler, "Ein Bedeutsamer Zusammenhang," 267-326.

[60] Ibid., 274-279. Very likely the original Armenian reading of John 1:32 is: "I will make you quiet . . . because I am quiet, . . . and you shall find rest." Unlike the Greek of John 1:32, which reads the Spirit "remained" on Jesus, the Armenian reading is "rested" on Jesus. The Syriac, in contrast to the Armenian, conforms to the Greek. But it is possible that the Armenian, which is generally dependent on the Syriac, represents the original Syriac reading, the Syriac was later changed under Hellenizing influences.

[61] Ibid., 300.

[62] Schneemelcher, *New Testament Apocrypha,* 1:177. This fragment is preserved in Jerome, *Commentary on Isaiah* 4, while commenting on Isaiah 11:2; PL 24:144-145. Winkler, "Ein Bedeutsamer Zusammenhang," 293.

in eager longings, until the full abundance of the Spirit could rest on the Son who then becomes the rest of God. Behind the expression "the whole fount of the Holy Spirit" seems to stand the Johannine "he gives the Spirit without measure" (John 3:34). All of the Armenian and a number of Syriac sources support the view that the Spirit rested on Jesus in fullness.[63]

Justin, too, seems to have had the same idea. He contrasts the Old Testament prophets, each of whom received "one or two powers from God," "one or two gifts,"[64] implying that to Christ was given the fullness. All the many different gifts found in the prophets and kings are gathered together in Christ, who is their goal.[65] In a work ascribed to Tertullian, he also attributes to Christ, at the moment of his baptism, the reception of "all the fullness of the spiritual gifts."[66] Nonetheless, Justin and Tertullian teach that even before his baptism Jesus had received the Spirit.[67]

Ephrem makes it clear that "many were baptized on that day [by John the Baptist], but the Spirit descended and rested only on one."[68] If the Spirit rested on only one of all those baptized, it was for the sake of the Church, or more precisely, Christian baptism. Immediately, Ephrem names the purpose of the descent of the Spirit: "And because the Spirit descended in his baptism, the Spirit is given by his baptism."[69] In the beginning, therefore, the Spirit rested only on Jesus, but afterwards on the disciples at Pentecost, which is also a baptismal event, and on those who receive Christian baptism.[70] As the rest signifies the permanent possession of the Spirit for Jesus, so also the Spirit does likewise, in its way, for his followers. For Ephrem the resting of the Spirit on Jesus "attests that he was the pastor,

[63] Winkler, "Ein Bedeutsamer Zusammenhang," 279–292.
[64] *Dialogue with Trypho* 87; PG 6:684.
[65] Bauer, *Das Leben Jesu*, 131.
[66] *Against the Jews* 8; PL 2:615.
[67] Bauer, *Das Leben Jesu*, 120.
[68] *Commentary on the Diatessaron* 4:3; SC 121:95.
[69] Ibid.
[70] Winkler, "Ein Bedeutsamer Zusammenhang," 300–302. See especially *The Teaching of St. Gregory* 614; Thomson, 151. Winkler (310) conjectures, on the basis of the Syrian and Armenian sources, that "originally Matt 11, 27–29 in a general way stood in a baptismal context."

and that, through the intermediary of John, he received the prophetic and sacerdotal office'' (kingship he received by being born from the house of David).[71] Earlier, Irenaeus had said that the Spirit came down on Jesus so that the Spirit could be accustomed to rest on the human race, to dwell in the work molded by God.[72] Origen was saying that the resting of the Spirit on Jesus means that the Spirit is with Jesus as a permanent possession.[73]

Knowing at the Jordan

The Teaching of St. Gregory relates the mutual knowledge of Father and Son, explained above, to the "rest" of the Spirit and the glorification of Jesus at his baptism.[74] The author of *The Teaching of St. Gregory* cites the Armenian translation of Isaiah 52:13: "Behold, my child will deal prudently, he will be raised up, exalted and glorified exceedingly." This prophecy is fulfilled at the Jordan, for it was there that Jesus "was *first* understood and known as the true Son of God by the voice of his Father and the descent of the Spirit over him."[75] The emphasis on the priority of the Jordan as the place and time where Jesus' sonship was first understood and known—and glorified—has support in another Armenian text, *The Key of Truth*, possibly dating from the seventh to ninth centuries, where this priority is repeatedly insisted upon.[76] As we have seen, it is already

---

[71] *Commentary on the Diatessaron* 4:3; SC 121:94, 95.

[72] *Against Heresies* 3, 17, 1; SC 211:330.

[73] *Homilies on Numbers* 18:4; SC 29:370.

[74] Winkler, "Ein Bedeutsamer Zusammenhang," 302–304.

[75] *The Teaching of St. Gregory* 416; Thomson, 90. Emphasis added.

[76] "First was our Lord Jesus baptized by the command of the heavenly Father, when thirty years old, as St. Luke has declared his years, iii.23: 'And Jesus himself was of years about thirty, beginning with which as he was supposed son of Joseph.' So *then* it was in the season of his maturity that he received baptism; *then* it was that he received authority, received the high-priesthood, received the kingdom and the office of chief shepherd. Moreover, he was *then* chosen, *then* he won lordship, *then* he became resplendent, *then* he was strengthened, *then* he was revered, *then* he was appointed to guard us, *then* he was glorified, *then* he was praised, *then* he was made glad, *then* he shone forth, *then* he was pleased, and *then* he rejoiced. Nay more. It was *then* that he becomes chief of beings

found in Justin. The "rest" of the Spirit on Jesus is decisive in the handing on of the "rest" to believers. Without it there is no divine knowledge in the Christian community, because the Spirit is "the searcher of hearts, knower of secrets, the revealer of all hidden things; for He knows everything. . . ."[77]

These accents in the Syrian and Armenian sources lead Winkler to conclude that an archaic Spirit-christology has its origins in the Jordan event. There the Son is revealed as Spirit-filled and as Only-begotten (First-born) of the Father. She notes the dominance of Spirit-christology, to the complete exclusion of Logos-christology.[78]

---

heavenly and earthly, *then* he became light of the world, *then* he became the way, the truth, and the life. *Then* he became the door of heaven, *then* he became the rock impregnable at the gate of hell; *then* he became the foundation of our faith; *then* he became Savior of us sinners; *then* was he filled with the Godhead; *then* he was sealed, *then* anointed; *then* he was called by the voice, *then* he became the loved one, *then* he came to be guarded by angels, *then* to be the lamb without blemish. . . ." *The Key of Truth*, 74, 75. Emphasis added. This manual is concerned with both doctrine and liturgy. Both Conybeare (viii) and N. G. Garsoïan (*The Paulician Heresy: A Study of the Origin and Development of Paulicianism in Armenia and the Eastern Provinces of the Byzantine Empire* [The Hague: Mouton, 1967] 157, 166, 185) consider this text Adoptionist. P. Lemerle has questioned the position of Conybeare and Garsoïan that the Paulicians were of Adoptionist origins. P. Lemerle, "L'histoire des Pauliciens d'Asie Mineure après les sources grecques," in *Travaux et Mémoires* 5 (1973) 1–144, especially 4. Winkler leaves unmentioned the discussion of Conybeare, Garsoïan, and Lemerle. Even if the text were Adoptionist, now somewhat in doubt, that does not entirely cancel out its worth in the present context.

[77] *The Teaching of St. Gregory* 419; Thomson, 91.

[78] "Ein Bedeutsamer Zusammenhang Zwischen," 325, 327. Winkler's position seems to be supported by the rather obvious avoidance of "the Word was made flesh" by the author of *The Teaching of St. Gregory*. In sections 422–424 (Thomson, 92), the author seems to be taking special pains not to quote John 1:14, though he quotes verses before and after. Of the Prologue to the Fourth Gospel 1–18, *The Teaching of St. Gregory* omits quoting only verses 8, 10, 12, and 14. See also Winkler, "Eine bemerkenswerte Stelle im armenischen Glaubensbekenntnis," 130–162; idem, *Das Armenische Initiationsrituale*, 79, 132, 337. But Logos christology is found in another Syrian writer. Philoxenus quotes John 1:14 in *Fragments of the Commentary on Matthew and Luke* 36, 51 (twice), 54; CSCO 393:32, 66, 67, 71. Winkler also concludes that in the oldest strata of the Syro-Armenian baptismal doc-

The Glorification of Jesus Begins at the Jordan

The Testament of Levi, an apocryphal work begun in the last century before Christ, but edited by Christian hands, already ties the baptism of the Lord to glory: "The heavens will be opened and from the temple of glory sanctification will come upon him, with a fatherly voice. . . . And the glory of the Most High shall burst forth upon him. [variant: "and his glory will elevate him"]. And the spirit of understanding and sanctification shall *rest* upon him [in the water]."[79] The glory, tied to the theology of rest, will be fully manifested in his resurrection, but begins already here. In a similar manner Origen relates the beginnings of Jesus' glorification to the Jordan. In his *Commentary on Joshua,* Origen, as Barnabas and Justin before him, sees Joshua as a type of Christ. In fact, Origen consistently speaks of either Joshua or Jesus, but he means Joshua/Jesus. For instance, he writes: "Where the Jordan is traversed, there it is said to Jesus, 'On this day I will begin to exalt you in the sight of the people.'"[80] The quoted words are the words directed to Joshua as he prepares the people to cross the Jordan (Josh 3:7). Then Origen continues: "Before the mystery of [Jesus'] baptism, Jesus is not exalted, but beginning at this moment, he commences to be exalted, and exalted in the sight of the people."[81] The glorifying of Jesus is specifically that eschatological homage given to God alone, when the universe, that is, those in heaven, on the earth, and under the earth, bend the knee in adoration (Phil 2:9-10). This exaltation, which is proper to the risen Christ after the resurrection, starts at the Jordan.

In the early fourth century, Ephrem also places the first glorification of Jesus at his baptism: "The river in which he [Jesus] was baptized, receives him symbolically anew: the moist

---

trine, the Pauline "death mysticism" of (Rom 6:4), so dear to the West, is absent. "Ein Bedeutsamer Zusammenhang," 327. See also, idem, "The Original Meaning and Implications of the Prebaptismal Anointing," 52, in *Worship* (1978) 39–45.

[79] *Testament of Levi* 18:6, 7; Charlesworth, *The Old Testament Pseudepigrapha,* 795. Emphasis added. Winkler, "Ein Bedeutsamer Zusammenhang," 291.

[80] *Commentary on Joshua* 4:2; SC 71:150.

[81] *Homilies on Joshua* 4:2; SC 71:150.

womb of the water receives him in purity, bore him in splendor, and lets him ascend [out of the water] in glory."[82]

The Teaching of St. Gregory, containing the oldest Armenian baptismal catechesis to come down to us, is most explicit in relating the glorification of Jesus to the Jordan event, which, like the *Testament of Levi*, embraces the rest of the Spirit.[83] In an extended passage on the baptism of Jesus, *The Teaching of St. Gregory* narrates, in relation to the passion, Jesus' request to the Father to "glorify your name." The voice of the Father, speaking as Jesus' "hour" approaches, replies: "I have glorified it, and I will glorify it again" (John 12:28). This hour of glorification is anticipated at the baptism, the Father acknowledging the Son both at the approach of the passion and at the Jordan. "In the same way" as at the passion, so now at his baptism, "the Son, standing in our midst, shows the Father and the Holy Spirit to the world. As the Father cried concerning the Only-begotten: 'This is my only-begotten Son: He is pleasing to myself. I shall set my Spirit over Him [Matt 12:18],' who was revealed at his descending and *resting* on Him; just as He Himself said of the Holy Spirit: 'He glorifies me [John 16:14].'"[84] Through the Spirit's resting on Jesus he is elevated to sonship, but not in the Adoptionistic sense. So the Son proclaims both the Father and the Spirit, while the Father testifies to Jesus' sonship and, finally, the Spirit rests on him. Both Father and Spirit manifest the glory of Jesus at his baptism.[85]

Another Armenian source, *The Key of Truth*, notes that it was "then [first at his baptism] he was glorified, then [first] he was praised . . . then [first] he shone forth."[86] Both the Syrian and

---

[82] *Hymns on the Church* 36:3; CSCO 199:88.

[83] Winkler, "Ein Bedeutsamer Zusammenhang," 302–304.

[84] *The Teaching of St. Gregory* 425; Thomson, 93. Emphasis added.

[85] Winkler, "Ein Bedeutsamer Zusammenhang," 302–304.

[86] *The Key of Truth* 75. For the dating of this source of Winkler, "Ein Bedeutsamer Zusammenhang," 306, n. 156, Lemerle, "L'histoire des Pauliciens d'Asie Mineure d'après les sources grecques," *Travaux et Mémoires*, 4, doubts the early dating, 7th–9th centuries, given by Conybeare, *Rituale Armenorum*, vi, ix, xxx, xxxi and given guarded support by Garsoïan, *The Paulician Heresy*, 96, 108–110, 111, n. 111.

Armenian sources establish a close relationship between the baptism of Jesus, the rest, knowledge, and glory.[87]

The "rest" is manifold. It is the Spirit resting on Jesus, and according to *The Testament of Levi*, "the Spirit of wisdom and knowledge rests on him [in the water.]" In *The Teaching of St. Gregory*, the resting of the Spirit on Jesus is a dimension of the Spirit's glorifying Jesus. Sebastian Brock has pointed out that it was very likely Origen who first gave baptismal connotations to the phrase "he leads me by restful waters" of Psalm 22 (23):2. The theme was afterwards taken up by Eusebius, Athanasius, Hesychius of Jerusalem (d. after 451), and Theodoret (ca. 393–ca. 466). In the Antiochene epiclesis of the baptismal rite, the theme becomes "the water of rest."[88] Precisely because the divine rest has descended on Jesus in its fullness, and is there first actualized, the Son can both promise and impart the rest to the Christian community.[89] The baptism of Jesus is the substance of Christian baptism; the Spirit resting on him is the Spirit resting on the Church; his rest is our rest.

[87] Winkler, "Ein Bedeutsamer Zusammenhang," 304–318.
[88] Brock, "The Epiklesis in the Antiochene Baptismal Ordines," in *Symposium Syriacum 1972*, 187, 206, 207.
[89] Winkler, "Ein Bedeutsamer Zusammenhang," 314.

Chapter Six

The Lukan Variant and the Jordan as Birth Event

In the narrative of Jesus' baptism at Luke 3:22, the best Greek manuscripts read "You are my beloved son; in you I have taken delight." Most commentators follow this tradition. But in manuscript D (= Codex Bezae Cantabrigiensis, located in Cambridge) and in seven Old Latin texts (a, b, c, d, ff², 1, r¹), as well as in some patristic writers, the last phrase reads "today I have begotten you," a quotation from Psalm 2:7. On the basis of the hermeneutical principle that the more difficult reading (*lectio difficilior*) is given priority, this last reading is preferred by a number of commentators (Grundmann, Harnack, Klosertmann, Huck, Lietzmann, Leaney, W. Manson, Moffat, Streeter, Zahn, Cullmann).[1] D. Plosij notes that the Lukan variant "is always the text with the earliest attestation," though he does not consider it the original.[2] The more difficult reading makes the Jordan experience the birth of the Son. This is not necessarily an Adoptionistic view.

Vigne has reviewed the evidence and has come to the conclusion that the phrase "today I have begotten you" is not a vari-

---

[1] Fitzmyer, *The Gospel According to Luke I–IX*, 485.

[2] "The Baptism of Jesus," *Amicitiae Corolla*, Festschrift for J. Rendel Harris, H. G. Wood, eds. (London: University of London, 1933) 246.

ant reading but, in fact, the original authentic reading of Luke
3:22. The phrase "in you I have taken delight," he contends,
was introduced into the Greek text in the fourth century and
into the Latin text in the fifth century.[3]

In favor of Vigne's position is the theological competence of
the scribe. "The additions, omissions, and alterations of the text
(especially in Luke and Acts) betray the touch of a significant
theologian."[4] Besides, the quality of the scribe is the quality of
the text with which he was working. The manuscript he transcribed and adapted "was an outstanding example of the early
text."[5] The basic form of this early text is much older than the
manuscript D, dating from the second century, when there was
a considerable variety in texts. The scribe was copying the older
text to make D about 400, the place of D's composition being
debated, but a good case can be made for Berytus (Beirut). It
appears that the scribe made D for liturgical use in church, indicating a conservative attitude.[6]

Making one less sure of the Lukan variant in D's text of Luke
3:22 are the thousands of places where the reading of D is
unique. Also, thousands of examples of harmonization are
found in the Gospels.[7]

What has been recognized as the variant reading is widely attested in the early authors.[8] Some of the authors of antiquity

---

[3] *Christ au Jourdain*, 106–132, especially 107.

[4] K. Aland and B. Aland, *The Text of the New Testament* (Grand Rapids:
Eerdmans, 1989) 109.

[5] Ibid.

[6] D. C. Parker, "Codex, Codex Bezae Cantabrigiensis," in *The Anchor
Bible Dictionary*, 6 vols. (Doubleday: New York, 1992) 1:1070.

[7] Ibid.

[8] In early Greek literature it is found in *The Letter to Diognetus*; Justin in
The Dialogue with Trypho; Clement of Alexandria in *The Teacher*; Celsus, as
quoted by Origen in *Against Celsus*; Origen in the *Commentary on John* and
the *Homilies on Ezekiel*; Methodius of Olympus in *The Banquet*; and in *The
Gospel of the Ebionites, The Passion of the Apostles Peter and Paul, The Acts of
Peter and Paul, The Apocryphal Acts of the Apostles, The Apostolic Constitutions*.
In early Latin texts it appears in the Latin *Didascalia*; Lactantius in *The Divine Institutions*, Juvencus in *The Books of the Gospels*; Hilary in *On Matthew,
Commentary on the Psalms*, and *On the Trinity*; Augustine in *The Consensus of
the Four Books of the Gospels* and in the *Enchiridion to Lawrence*; Ambrosiaster
in *Questions on the Old and New Testament*; Tyconius the Donatist in *Book on*

quoting the variant of Luke 3:22 pre-date the great editions.[9] When the authors are writing *before* the great editions were made, and they are citing Scripture, their formulations may be preferable to the manuscript tradition.[10] If they depart from the manuscript tradition, it is not necessarily because they are quoting from memory. It can be that they have before them a different text.[11] Obviously this also holds for those writing after the date of the great editions. The weight of these early authors in determining the authentic text should be given full consideration.

It is possible that the variant was actually the original text and was suppressed for dogmatic reasons, namely, the early rise of Adoptionism. The first to suggest a form of Adoptionism was a learned Byzantine leather merchant, Theodotus, who brought it to Rome about 190. Until his baptism, Theodotus teaches, Jesus lived as an ordinary but supremely virtuous man. At the Jordan the Spirit descended on him and he became the Christ; from that time on he began to work miracles, without, however, becoming divine. Some of his followers said Jesus became divine at the resurrection.[12] Theodotus was influential enough to be

---

the Seven Rules; Maximinus the Arian in *Against Ambrose*; Faustus the Manichaean in Augustine's *Against Faustus*. It is also found in the Syriac version of the *Didascalia*. The precise bibliographical references are given in Bauer, *Das Leben Jesu*, 110–141, and in H. Usener, "Christliche Epiphanie: Das Alte Tauf- und Geburtfest," in *Religionsgeschichtliche Untersuchungen* (New York: Olms, 1972) 40–52. The text also appears in the other Syriac sources. See G. Winkler, "Zur frühchristlichen Tauftradition in Syrien und Armenien unter Einbezug der Taufe Jesu," in *Ostkirchliche Studien* 27 (1978) 283, 293.

[9] Légault, "Le baptême de Jésus," 148. Vigne, *Christ au Jourdain*, 23.

[10] The authors or texts in which the Lukan variant is found dating before the great editions are Tatian *(Diatessaron)*, Clement of Alexandria, Justin, Origen, Ephrem, Methodius of Olympus, Lactantius, Juvencus, Cyprian, Didascalia Apostolorum, *(The Apostolic Constitutions)*, and in the apocryphal *Passion of the Apostles Peter and Paul, Acts of Peter and Paul*. Perhaps one can add Maximinus. Ibid., 107–132.

[11] M. E. Boismard, "Critique textuelle et citations patristiques," *Revue Biblique* 57 (1950) 388.

[12] Hippolytus, *Philosophumena* 7:35; Hippolytus, *Refutatio Omnium Haeresium*, M. Marcovich, ed. (Berlin: de Gruyter, 1986) 318, 319; Epiphanius of Salamis, *The Panarion* 34 but 54 of the series; *The Panarion of Epiphanius of Salamis*, 2 vols., F. Williams, ed. (Leiden: Brill, 1987–1994) 2:72-77 (hereafter cited as Williams).

condemned by Pope Victor (186–198), but his ideas were immediately taken up and modified by another man of the same name, a banker, who lived in Rome about 250.[13] Adoptionism in a much more sophisticated form lived on in Paul of Samosata (3rd c.), bishop of Antioch, who was condemned by two, possibly three, synods and deposed in 268. Though they are not strictly Adoptionists, the Ebionites belong to the broad Adoptionist tradition.

The Gospel of the Ebionites

Vigne contends that it was in reaction against *The Gospel of the Ebionites* that provoked the change in the manuscript tradition at Luke 3:22, that is, the suppression of "today I have begotten you."[14] The great biblical codices were produced mostly in the fourth and fifth centuries.[15] If Epiphanius (ca. 315–403) is to be followed,[16] and H. J. Schoeps thinks he is trustworthy here,[17] the Ebionites, who were carriers of some form of the Adoptionist tradition, very likely began as a distinct group at the fall of Jerusalem in 70 B.C.E. The last traces of them disappeared in the fifth century in eastern Syria.[18] Augustine already speaks of them as a people in the past.[19] They were, therefore, a force to contend with for a period of about 250 years.[20] So the threat of the Ebionites could have influenced the great editions of the Scriptures.

---

[13] Hippolytus, *Philosophoumena* 7:36; Hippolytus, *Refutatio Omnium Haeresium* (Marcovich) 319, 320; Eusebius, *Ecclesiastical History* 5:28; PG 20:512–517.

[14] *Christ au Jourdain*, 120.

[15] Codex Alexandrinus, fifth century; Codex Bezae Cantabrigiensis, shortly before 400; Codex Claromontaus, fifth or more probably sixth century; Codex Ephraimi Rescriptus, fifth or sixth century; Codex Sinaiticus, fourth century; Codex Vaticanus, fourth century; Codex Washingtonianus, fourth or fifth century.

[16] *Panarion* 2, 311; Williams, 1:121.

[17] *Jewish Christianity* (Philadelphia: Fortress, 1969) 18.

[18] Ibid., 136.

[19] A.F.J. Klijn and G. J. Reinink, *Patristic Evidence for Jewish-Christian Sects* (Leiden: Brill, 1973) 71.

[20] Schoeps, *Jewish Christianity*, 120.

More specifically, who are they? The Ebionites are an undetermined number of Judeo-Christian sects with common characteristics. *The Gospel of the Ebionites* seems to issue from the beginning of or in the first half of the second century.[21] One needs to move with caution in making theological judgments, because the surviving texts are so meager.[22] According to Tertullian, they taught that Jesus was "a mere man."[23] The Ebionite witness is significant for the issue at hand because *The Gospel of the Ebionites* omits the infancy account and starts with the Jordan event, the account of which includes the Lukan variant, "Today I have begotten you."[24] Martin Dibelius believes that the infancy account is omitted not because they did not know it but "because they [did] not want it."[25] As remarked, though classed with Adoptionists, the term may not be properly applied to them. The sonship may not come through adoption but simply by union of the Spirit with Jesus at the baptism.[26] All reference to the Fourth Gospel is avoided, possibly because of its support for the pre-existence of Jesus. Ebionites seem to deny the virgin birth. His sonship rests solely on his baptism. For them the Jordan event is "the absolute beginning."[27] Though not Adoptionists in the strict sense, they are their herald.[28] Having been judged heretical, they were held up as a warning to later generations even after they had ceased to exist.[29]

Though the proponents of the early form of Adoptionism came from Byzantium, proposed by the two men named Theodotus, it was mostly a Roman affair, where it seems to have affected the Gentile-Christian population. In this form it

[21] P. Vielhauer, *Geschichte der urchristlichen Literatur* (Berlin: de Gruyter, 1975) 656.

[22] Also, there was a general tendency in early orthodox circles to judge that everything Jewish-Christian was Ebionite. Klijn and Reinink, *Patristic Evidence for Jewish-Christian Sects*, 43.

[23] *On the Flesh of Christ* 14:5; SC 216:270, 272.

[24] Schneemelcher, *New Testament Apocrypha*, 1:169.

[25] Vielhauer, *Geschichte der urchristlichen Literatur*, 56.

[26] Ibid., 655.

[27] Vigne, *Christ au Jourdain*, 129.

[28] Ibid., 130.

[29] Klijn and Reinink, *Patristic Evidence for Jewish-Christian Sects*, 43.

was "an isolated and unrepresentative movement."[30] From the number of early Christian writers cited by Klijn and Reinink, the Ebionites had a much broader impact, geographically and theologically. It was a force in the period just before the composition of the codices, which might account for the omitting of the offending "today I have begotten you." On the other hand, it is easier to believe that one codex (Bezae Cantabrigiensis) inserted a phrase than to believe that six others (Alexandrinus, Claromontanus, Ephraimi Rescriptus, Sinaiticus, Vaticanus, Washingtonianus) omitted it. As Augustine observed, about 400: "The oldest Greek manuscripts do not contain this variant."[31] Still, if doctrinal stances were reflected in the text of the codices, it is possible, but not demonstrated, that "today I have begotten you" was deleted from most codices.

Jordan Event: The Day of Jesus' Birth

In any case, the conviction that the baptism of Jesus was the day of his birth "was extremely strong in Armenia."[32] The liturgical expression of this can be found in the Syrian celebration of the nativity and the baptism of Jesus on the same day, January 6, as is the case to this day among the Armenians.[33] On this basis Winkler suggests that the understanding of the baptism as a birth event "probably" has its origin among the Syrians (who influenced the Armenians).[34]

To be remembered: "Today I have begotten you" is not necessarily Adoptionist. The birth proclaimed at the Jordan does not cancel out the infancy narratives. At the Jordan the "birth" is in a broader sense of the bold beginning of Jesus' public

[30] Kelly, Early Christian Doctrines, 117.

[31] The Consensus of the Four Books of the Gospels 2, 14, 31; PL 34:1093.

[32] Garsoïan, The Paulician Heresy, 229.

[33] Brock, "Clothing Metaphors," in Studies in Syriac Christianity, XI:26, n. 64.

[34] Winkler, "Zur frühchristlichen Tauftradition," in Studies in Syriac Christianity, 299. One should note the presence of the Lukan variant in two apocryphal writings: The Passion of the Apostles Peter and Paul 8, and The Acts of Peter and Paul 29. Acta Apostolorum Apocrypha, R. A. Lipsius, ed., 2 vols. (Hildesheim: Olms, 1959) 1:127, 192.

ministry, in Mark's words, "the beginning of the Gospel" (Mark 1:1). Whether the reformulation of the problem of the Lukan variant made by Vigne, together with his recommendation that the variant "should now be accepted as authentic,"[35] remains to be tested by the community of textual critics.

Where the Lukan variant appears in the tradition, it carries a profound insight into the mystery of Jesus. To this I now turn.

The Jordan: "The Economic Perfection"

If the Lukan variant is found in some early texts, what is the theological import? What is its theological weight?

The original Greek source of the Ethiopic *Didascalia Apostolorum* goes back to a Greek text that may be as early as the beginning second century, though the text we have dates from the fourth century.[36] The Alexandrian version views the baptism of Christ as a birth event not unlike our own regeneration at baptism, when we become children of God. By his baptism in the Jordan, Jesus attains his "economic perfection," that is, the reception of the Spirit and the manifestation of himself as the Son of God, empowered with all that is necessary for the fulfillment of his redemptive mission.[37]

In the Syriac version the baptized person is exhorted to honor the bishop from whom baptism is received. In the rite of baptism believers become children of light when the bishop lays his hands on them and says in the voice of God, the Father, "You are my Son, today I have begotten you."[38] In Christian baptism the begetting at the Jordan event is in some way actualized again in the believer, the bishop representing the Father. In the Ethiopic version this is clearer; the verse from Psalm 2:7 has been modified. During the rite of baptism the bishop lays his hands on the candidates and says "You are my sons, today I

---

[35] Vigne, *Christ au Jourdain*, 107.

[36] P. Nautin, "Didascalia Apostolorum," in *Encyclopedia of the Early Church*, 1:235.

[37] J. Dupont, "Filius Meus es Tu," in *Recherches des Science Religieuse* 35 (1948) 526, n. 5.

[38] *Didascalia Apostolorum*, R. H. Connolly, ed. (Oxford: Clarendon, 1929) 93.

have begotten you."[39] By direct address the bishop speaks to the baptized the words spoken by God to Christ. The variant also appears in *The Apostolic Constitutions*,[40] which in taking over much material also transcribed the variant from the *Didascalia Apostolorum*. Though Clement of Alexandria does not cite the Lukan variant, he has a strong view on the Jordan as a birth event, and the supposition is that the variant stands behind his position.[41] In fact, the Jordan forces adversaries to recognize that the Word, "the Perfect One born of the Perfect One," is begotten again for the sake of the economy.[42] The taunt of the adversaries is: If Christ has this degree of perfection, why does he come to be baptized? Could it be that the Lord becomes perfect at the Jordan. Surprisingly, Clement answers, "on the basis of all the evidence, yes."[43] But the perfection is of an economic order, that is, he is perfected in his role within the economy of salvation. The Lord receives from the Father "a perfect regeneration in order to give a prefiguration of the God's economy."[44] What the perfect One models in the Jordan is the regeneration that determines the whole economy. The baptism of Christ is programmatic for the life of the Church, especially its trinitarian life.

Justin, who is older than Clement by fifty years, cites the Lukan variant at the end of his section on the baptism of Christ. The begetting that interests Justin here is not concerned with the origin of the Son of God but with the manifestation of Christ to humankind. Up to the moment when John "sat by the river Jordan and preached the baptism of repentance" Christ was "considered the son of Joseph the carpenter," himself a carpenter.[45] But when the Spirit descends and the voice of the Father declares his identity, he becomes for us what he was before his manifestation, the Son of God. When he is

[39] *Didascalia Apostolorum* 9; *The Ethiopic Didascalia*, J. M. Harden, ed. (London: SPCK, 1920) 53.
[40] 2:32; SC 320:252.
[41] Usener, *Religionsgeschichtliche Untersuchungen*, 41.
[42] *The Teacher* 6:25.3; SC 70:158.
[43] Ibid.
[44] Ibid.
[45] *Dialogue with Trypho* 88; PG 6:687.

recognized by us as the Son of God, at that moment he, in some mysterious fashion, is born Son of God for us, for the Church.[46] To be known is to be born.

Ephrem has a relation to Justin's tradition. Tatian was a student of Justin's in Rome. Tatian composed the *Diatessaron*, an edition of the four Gospels in continuous narrative. Inspired principally by the order in Matthew, destined for liturgical use, it circulated widely in Syriac-speaking churches and was the standard text for the Gospels in Syria down to the fifth century, when it was replaced by the Peshitta, the official text of the Scriptures for Syriac-speaking Christians. The influence of the *Diatessaron* was enormous, both in Syria and beyond.[47] Of Tatian's *Diatessaron* we have only fragments, the closest to the original text being the *Commentary on the Diatessaron*, the text of which is Ephrem's, though the form in which we have it may not be entirely his.[48]

Ephrem speaks of the Jordan event as "a second birth,"[49] giving rise to the speculation that behind this formulation is the Lukan variant "today I have begotten you." If the nativity account is the account of the first birth, the baptism of Jesus must be the second birth.[50] The suggestion is that Justin, Tatian, and Ephrem share the same manuscript tradition, with Justin handing on the Lukan text to Tatian, who in turn passed it on to Ephrem in the *Diatessaron*.[51]

---

[46] Dupont, "Filius Meus es Tu," 526, n. 5.

[47] Leloir, *Doctrines et Méthodes de S.- Éphrem d'après son commentaire de l'Évangile Concordant* 6.

[48] E. Beck, *Oriens Christianus* 73 (1989) 1–37.

[49] *Commentary on the Diatessaron* 4:3; SC 121:94.

[50] The question of the relation of the anointing to a second birth of Jesus was widely discussed even late. Why would the Christ who was anointed at birth need an anointing at his baptism? Getatchew Haile discusses the seventeenth-century debate on the issue in Ethiopia and provides texts and translation: *The Faith of the Unctionists* (Louvain: Peeters, 1990) CSCO 518.

[51] M. J. Lagrange suggests that the variant was mediated to the early authors less through Codex D than by the authority of Justin. *Critique Textuelle II La Critique Rationnelle* (Paris: Gabalda, 1935) 172; Vigne, *Christ au Jourdain*, 121.

Origen, who preceded Ephrem by 120 years, too, speaks of the
baptism of Jesus as "a second birth," that is, he began his real
life and his real work after his baptism.[52] One might accuse
Origen of indecision. He employs both the Lukan variant and
the standard reading. What is striking is that in texts where he
is treating of Jesus' baptism, in his *Against Celsus* and the *Homilies on Numbers,* and even when he is preaching on the very text
of Luke where the variant usually occurs in his *Homilies on Luke,*
he uses the standard text: "You are my beloved son, in you I
am well pleased," without mention of the variant.[53] On the
other hand, in his *Commentary on John* and his *Homilies on Ezekiel,*
when he is speaking in a more general context, therefore, not
specifically of Jesus' baptism, he uses the Lukan variant, which
in Luke is concerned with the Jordan event.[54] Why this shyness
in linking "today I have begotten you" to the Jordan event,
even though he uses it in other contexts? It is not clear. Whatever the answer, when Origen does use the Lukan variant, he
points out that the "today" is a "today that lasts for ever."[55]

Here we have a major contribution to trinitarian doctrine.
Origen was the first to state explicitly the eternal generation of
the Son from the Father.

However, when he speaks of Jesus' baptism in his *Homilies on
Luke,* he relates it to Jesus' resurrection. The Spirit which came
upon Jesus in the Jordan is the very Spirit which Jesus imparts
when, as the risen Lord, he says "Receive the Holy Spirit"
(John 20:22).[56] If there is no reception of the Spirit at Jesus' baptism, there is no imparting of the Spirit at his resurrection. The
baptism is more than introduction into public life. The Jordan
establishes order.

Lactantius (ca. 240–ca. 320) also cites the Lukan variant when
he is mustering witnesses in support of the divinity of Jesus as

[52] *Homilies on Luke* 28:4; SC 87:356.

[53] Origen, *Against Celsus* 2:72; SC 132:456; *Homilies on Numbers* 18:4; SC
29:370; *Homilies on Luke* 27:5; SC 87:348.

[54] *Commentary on John* 1:29; SC 120:160; *Homilies on Ezekiel* 6:3; SC 352:218,
220.

[55] *Commentary on John* 1:29; SC 120:160.

[56] *Homilies on Luke* 27:5; SC 87:348.

the source of his miracles, against the view that from the day of his baptism on, Jesus "began to perform the greatest wonders" by magic.[57] Very likely Lactantius took the Lukan variant from a collection of what is technically called "Testimonia," that is, a collection of extracts or biblical texts gathered, for instance, around an apologetic theme. The Testimonia are the proof texts.

We know that Lactantius and other ancient authors were greatly influenced by Cyprian's *Testimonies to Quirinus*.[58] Especially in the matter at hand, establishing the biblical text, it is significant because it quotes the oldest of the Latin versions of the Bible. It was also a handy reference for those looking for the biblical sources around a given topic. The second book of Cyprian's *Testimonies* is christological in intent, having as its purpose to gather the scriptural proofs for the coming of the Messiah, demonstrating the correspondence between the life of Jesus and the prophecies of the Old Testament. In this section of the *Testimonies*, the issue is the textual evidence for the position that though Jesus was the Son of God from all eternity (*a principio*), he did have to be begotten again in the flesh if he wanted to redeem humankind. He not only quotes Psalm 2:7, "You are my son; today I have begotten you," but goes on to quote the following verse, "Ask of me, and I will make the nations your heritage."[59] Possibly Lactantius saw in Cyprian's text a way of linking the baptism of Jesus and the miracles following it ("so many that one book would not be enough to include the accounts of all of them") with the miracles "long announced by the prophets."[60] After his baptism Jesus works wonders not by magic but "by a word and a command" of him who is the divine Word of God.[61]

[57] The Divine Institutes 4:15; CSEL 19:330.

[58] While it is possible that Lactantius took the Lukan variant from a biblical text, the bulk of the evidence indicates that he borrowed it directly from Cyprian's *Testimonies*. P. Prigent, *Justin et l'Ancien Testament* (Paris: Gabalda, 1964) 178; J. Quasten, *Patrology*, 4 vols. (Westminster: Newman, 1951–1986) 2:362–363. J. Doignon thinks Lactantius may derive the Lukan variant from Justin. "La scène évangélique du baptême de Jésus," in *Epektasis*, 66.

[59] *Testimonies* 2:8; CSEL 3:73.

[60] Ibid., 4:15; CSEL 19:330.

[61] Ibid., CSEL 19:331.

Slightly earlier than Ephrem, Methodius of Olympus (d. ca. 311) composed a work between 260 and 290 in imitation of Plato's *Banquet,* and carrying the same name. It is a manual of doctrine, and instrument of catechetical instruction, in which he returns more than once to the physiology of giving birth. Instead of explaining Christian baptism by the baptism of Christ, he does the opposite. Christian baptism tells us what the baptism of Christ is because there is congruence between the two.

Having explained that the Church is a pregnant mother bringing her children to baptism, thus effecting a "transfiguring illumination in the Word" by the communion in the Holy Spirit, he calls baptism "the second birth."[62] Between Christian baptism and the baptism of Jesus, there is "a concordance and harmony."[63] So at the Jordan one hears the voice of the Father saying "You are my son; today I have begotten you." The Father declares this paternity "without any chronological precision,"[64] that is, without specifying whether the Father is speaking in God's eternity or humankind's history or, more likely, both simultaneously. The second birth at the Jordan is real, but it has a trans-temporal character, embracing the eternal and the temporal. Today is forever.

In other words, says Methodius, the Father did not say "You will become my son."[65] The sonship declared at the Jordan is not a recent acquisition. Although already brought to birth as a son, still the Father says "Today I have begotten you." Methodius has the Father explain: "You (the Son) who were pre-existing in the heavens before the origin of the ages, I have wished to bring to birth in the world [Jordan], which is to say, to make known you of whom they were previously ignorant."[66] In other words, the Father "begets according to knowledge and intelligence."[67] Here, as in Justin, the argument is: To be made known is to come to birth. About the same time as Methodius,

---

[62] Methodius of Olympus, *The Banquet* 8:9; SC 95:221.
[63] Ibid., SC 95:222.
[64] Ibid.
[65] Ibid.
[66] Ibid.
[67] Ibid.

that is, the early fourth century, Juvencus, a Spanish presbyter of noble birth, composed *Four Books of the Gospels*, a narrative harmony of the Gospels in hexameter verse as a tool of evangelization. Juvencus wishes to combine Matthew and the Lukan variant. When Christ is entirely suffused by the breath of the Spirit, the voice of God declares: "I am well pleased with you, my first-born, whom I beget this day."[68] Here, too, the one who is the first-born of the Father is the one the Father begets in the Jordan. The prior begetting does not cancel out the propriety, even necessity, of the Jordan as a birth event.[69] In a slightly different context Augustine, like Juvencus, confronts the two versions. He does not want to chose between the Matthaean "in you I am well pleased" and the Lukan variant "today I have begotten you." Both, Augustine says, are declarations of divine sonship.[70]

Birth of the Perfect Son: True Man, True God

Hilary of Poitiers, whom I have already mentioned, refers three times to the Jordan as a birth event. In his early years as a bishop, therefore before 356, in a written rather than oral commentary, *On Matthew*, destined very likely to his presbyterium,[71] he emphasizes that "when he [Christ] is baptized, the gates of heaven open, the Spirit is sent under the appearance of a dove, and he bathes (is baptized?) in this sort of unction of the Father's love."[72] The image is one of luxuriant abundance. This reference to bathing in the anointing of the Father is immedi-

[68] *Four Books of the Gospels* 1:362, 363, CSEL 24:21.
[69] Though the interpretation is Arian, this point is made clearer by Maximinus, who writes: "The Father says to the Son he has already begotten, 'Today I have begotten you.'" *Dissertation Against Ambrose*; PL Supplement 1:717. Faustus, a Manichee and one-time teacher of Augustine during his Manichaean period, notes that the phrase "Today I have begotten you" was not spoken at the nativity but at the purification at the Jordan. So Jesus became a son of God only at his baptism. The reconstruction of Faustus' position can be made from Augustine's text *Against Faustus the Manichaean* 23:2; PL 42:467. Vigne, *Christ au Jourdain*, 123.
[70] *The Consensus of the Four Gospels* 2, 14, 31, PL 34:1093.
[71] J. Doignon, Introduction, Hilaire de Poitiers, *Sur Matthieu*; SC 254:19, 20.
[72] *On Matthew* 3:6; SC 254:110.

ately followed by "The voice from heaven said: 'You are my Son; today I have begotten you.' "[73] The Jordan event is the day of Jesus' birth in that his sonship is proclaimed. This will be determinative of Christian baptism as giving birth to children of God.

Twice in *On the Trinity* he returns to the Lukan variant. "After the birth that took place in baptism," that is, after Jesus Christ is anointed with the Spirit, the Father declares "Today I have begotten you."[74] The purpose of this manifestation is that "through the mystery of the perfect and true birth" the true humanity and true divinity might be confirmed.[75] The authenticity of the two natures is declared at the Jordan.

In his last years, between 356–359, Hilary returns to the theme in his *Tract on the Psalms*, where he twice cites the Lukan variant. Although Jesus existed before his baptism, that event is truly a birthing of "the perfect Son" because "the Son of man and the Son of God are joined together in baptism," without detriment to the fullness of either his humanity or divinity, a clear defense of the Jordan experience against accusations of Adoptionism.[76] Hilary was not deterred by the threat of Adoptionism from seeing the baptism as a birth event.

"Today Is Forever"

Augustine returns to the same point in *Enchiridion to Lawrence*, writing toward the end of his life, 423–424. This is a manual giving a brief, clear synthesis of Augustine's theology. The Christ who is generated, says Augustine, does not need regeneration. So when the voice of the Father sounds at the Jordan "Today I have begotten you," he speaks not of the one single temporal day on which he was baptized but of an immutable eternity. The day referred to is not begun when the day before is terminated, nor ended when the day after begins. "Today is forever" (*semper hodiernus est*).[77] The "today" of the Jordan is

---

[73] Ibid.

[74] *On the Trinity* 8:25; PL 10:254.

[75] Ibid. See also *On the Trinity* 11:18; PL 10:412.

[76] *Tract on the Psalms* 2:29, 30; CSEL 22:59. See J. Dupont, "Filius Meus es Tu," 522–543; E. Lövestam, *Son and Savior* (Lund: Gleerup, 1961).

[77] *Enchiridion to Lawrence* 1:49; PL 40:255.

taken up into the ageless "today." The begetting at the Jordan is integral to the eternal begetting.

Proceeding with caution, Vigne concludes that the "today" of the Lukan variant "cannot be taken in an exclusive or literal sense."[78] If this means that the "today" of the Jordan cannot mean the only birth of Christ, excluding at least the nativity accounts and possibly the whole pre-existence dimension, he is, of course, correct. If the Jordan is isolated from the total mystery—yes, one cannot understand it in an exclusive or literal way. But the formulation is misleading. The strictly exegetical question is very complicated. However, at least in the tradition, the "today" of the Jordan is taken up into the eternal begetting. It partakes of the exclusive and literal quality of that begetting before all the ages.

The Feminine Spirit Gives Birth at the Jordan

Though there is considerable evidence of the Spirit as mother in Syrian and Armenian sources, at the Genesis creation account and at Christian baptism, the Mother-Spirit at the Jordan is found only in the *Gospel of the Hebrews* and Aphrahat.[79] As was mentioned, in the *Gospel of the Hebrews*, the full wellspring of the Spirit rests on Jesus: "It happened that when the Lord had come up from the water, the whole source of the Spirit descended on him, and rested on him, and said to him: 'My Son, I was waiting for you in all the prophets, I was waiting for you, so that I might rest myself on you. For you are my rest, you are my first-born Son who reigns forever.' "[80] In this case it seems that the Holy Spirit is the one who says "My

---

[78] *Christ au Jourdain*, 129. Vigne notes that the birth character of the Jordan event does not imply the rejection of the nativity account. The "today" of the Jordan does not pronounce on the origins of Jesus. Rather it ignores them. Ibid., 108, 109.

[79] Winkler, "Ein Bedeutsamer Zusammenhang," 324. For the Holy Spirit as mother at Christian baptism, see Winkler, "Die Tauf-Hymnen der Armenier: Ihre Affinität mit syrischem Gedankengut," *Liturgie und Dichtung*, H. Becker and R. Kaczynski, eds., 2 vols. (Munich: St. Ottilian, 1983) 1:381–420; idem, *Das armenische Initiationsrituale* 456, 457. Vigne treats the "Mother-Spirit" extensively: *Christ au Jourdain*, 205–232.

[80] Schneemelcher, *New Testament Apocrypha* 1:177.

Son." In another fragment this same Spirit is again identified as the Mother-Spirit: "Even so did my mother, the Holy Spirit, take me by one of my hairs and carry me away on to the great mountain Tabor."[81] Aphrahat refers to the baptism of Jesus as one in which he was "born of the Spirit."[82] Elsewhere in the *Demonstrations* Aphrahat identifies the Spirit as mother when speaking of celibacy: "If a man has not yet taken a woman [in marriage], he loves and honors his Father and the Holy Spirit, his mother, and he has no other love."[83] Aphrahat is only one witness to the prevalence of the Mother Spirit in the early Churches formed in the Semitic tradition.[84] According to Aphrahat, the feminine Spirit gives birth to Jesus at the Jordan.[85]

[81] Ibid. Schneemelcher notes that Origen refers twice to the text (*Commentary on John* 22:12; SC 120:262; *Commentary on Jeremiah* 15:4; SC 238:122) and Jerome three times (*On Isaiah* 40:9; CCh 73.459; *On Micah* 7:6; CCh 76:513; *On Ezekiel* 16:13; CCh 75:178). In his *Commentary on John*, Origen goes out of his way to point out the feminine nature of the Spirit.

[82] *Demonstrations* 6:17; SC 349:405.

[83] 18:10; SC 359:761.

[84] W. Cramer, *Der Geist Gottes und des Menschen in frühsyrischer Theologie* (Münster: Aschendorff, 1979) 29.

[85] For the feminine Spirit in the Syrian tradition, see Cramer, *Der Geist Gottes und des Menschen in frühsyrischer Theologie* 27, 36–38, 68, 84. Aphrahat's teaching on the feminine Spirit at the Jordan is in keeping with the considerable role the Mother-Spirit plays in early, but not later, Syrian literature. See Brock, *The Luminous Eye: The Spiritual World Vision of St. Ephrem* (Rome: Centre for Indian and Inter-Religious Studies, 1985) 140–144; idem, *Holy Spirit in the Syrian Baptismal Tradition* 4, 5. Brock notes that *Logos*, "Word," was also feminine in Syriac, and that from the late fourth century on, Spirit was construed as masculine. In a conversation with Brock, June 17, 1981, he noted that when the Syriac tradition began to speak of the Spirit in the masculine, possibly under the influence of developing trinitarian doctrine, no protests are recorded within the Syrian tradition.

Chapter Seven

The Jordan as Womb
and the Great Fire/Light

The baptism of Jesus as a birth event is linked to the Jordan as a womb, both in relation to Christ and to Christians. This relationship has a highly diverse history,[1] but it is especially characteristic of Syriac writers and the related Armenian tradition.[2] Aphrahat writes: "A number of prophets came who were not able to reveal baptism—until the great prophet would come

[1] W. M. Bedard, "The Font as Womb or Mother," in *The Symbolism of the Baptismal Font in Early Christian Thought* (Washington, D.C.: Catholic University, 1951) 17–36; Brock, "Baptismal Themes in the Writings of Jacob of Serugh," in *Symposium Syriacum 1976*, 325–329; idem, "The Baptism of Christ and Christian Baptism," in *The Luminous Eye*, 70–76; idem, *Spirituality in the Syriac Tradition*, 60–66; Lundberg, *La Typologie Baptismale dans l'Ancienne Église*; Benoit, *Le Baptême Chrétien au Second Siècle*; Winkler, "Zur frühchristlichen Tauftradition." There is a related theme, namely, the Church as mother. See J. C. Plumpe, *Mater Ecclesia: An Inquiry into the Concept of the Church as Mother in Early Christianity* (Washington, D.C.: The Catholic University of America, 1943); J. Daniélou, *Bible and Liturgy* (Notre Dame: Notre Dame University, 1956) 47–49.

[2] S. Brock, "A New Syriac Baptismal *Ordo* Attributed to Timothy of Alexandria," *Muséon* 83 (1970) 418, 419; idem, "St. Ephrem on Christ as Light in Mary and in the Jordan: *Hymni de Ecclesia 36*," in *Eastern Churches Review* 7 (1975) 142.

who alone opened it [baptism] up, and was baptized."[3] Ephrem
ties the act of opening to the Jordan: "Our Lord opened baptism in the blessed Jordan river."[4] Narsai (399-503—*sic*) hands
on the tradition, saying, "Our Lord opened up for us the sweet
spring of baptism."[5] In *The Teaching of St. Gregory*, it is the
Spirit who opens up baptism: "The invisible Spirit opened
again the womb by visible water, preparing the newly born
fledglings for the regeneration of the font."[6] Jacob of Serugh
wants to link Jordan to Calvary: "Christ came and opened up
baptism on his cross so that it should be 'mother of living
things,' in place of Eve."[7] Philoxenus points out the relationship of opening baptism to the theme of womb and birth: "I
have been baptized and have prepared baptism that it may become the spiritual womb which gives birth to men anew."[8]

The Teaching of St. Gregory places the womb image in the context of cosmic creation. Just as God made "the first earth
emerge from the waters" of creation, and by the freshness of

---

[3] *Demonstrations* 4:6; SC 349:300. Aphrahat can also say that John the
Baptist opens up baptism, ibid., 6:13; SC 349:398.

[4] *Hymns on Epiphany* 11:2; CSCO 187:170. Though the authorship of the
Epiphany hymns are in some doubt, the expression is also found in his
undoubted *Hymns on Virginity* 15:3; CSCO 224:50, 51: "Happy are you little
river Jordan. . . . For the Holy One condescends and washes himself in
you; through his baptism he opened [the door of] baptism. . . ."

[5] *Homily* 21; *On the Mysteries of the Church and on Baptism: The Liturgical
Homilies of Narsai*, R. H. Connolly, ed. (Cambridge: Cambridge University,
1909) 46. Hereafter cited as Connolly.

[6] 412; Thomson, 89.

[7] Bedjan 1:162. My major source for Jacob of Serugh is Brock, "Baptismal
Themes in the Writings of Jacob of Serugh."

[8] *Fragments of the Commentary on Matthew and Luke* 50; CSCO 393:59. See
also 57; CSCO 393:80: ". . . when he was baptized in it [Jordan] he made
the new womb which gives birth to sons of God." Philoxenus, however,
more typically attaches Christian initiation to the mystery of the incarnation. See de Halleux, *Philoxène de Mabbog*, 455. See Ephrem's formulation:
"Baptism has become a mother," *Hymns on Epiphany* 13:1; CSCO 187:175.
Or *The Teaching of St. Gregory* 679; Thomson, 169: "He renewed and rejuvenated creation once for all. He opened the womb of baptism. . . ." In
The History of the Armenians, those who receive the sacrament of baptism
are reborn "from water and the womb of the Spirit," in Agathangelos, *The
History of the Armenians*, R. W. Thomson, ed. (Albany: State University of
New York, 1976) 365.

water all plants, reptiles, and wild animals were fattened, so "by treading the waters with his own footsteps" at the Jordan, he made green "the womb of regeneration" so that the second earth "might be renewed through the Spirit by the waters."[9] In the beginning the Spirit moved over the waters, thus setting out "the order of creation," so at the baptism of Christ the Spirit, who now "dwells in the water," sets out the order of the new creation for those who are born children of God.[10] "The invisible Spirit opened again the womb by visible water," bringing children to rebirth, to "the glory of adoption."[11]

In Philoxenus, the baptism of Jesus, turning the Jordan into "the new wombs" is the beginning of the larger mystery in which "the Trinity was revealed, the creation renewed in power, the church united to Christ, the rebellious powers condemned and sin and evil destroyed."[12] The baptism manifests the basic mystery of faith, the Father revealing the Son, the Son receiving the Spirit. By the descent of the Spirit, the new creation is begun, and in the unity found in the Spirit and baptism, the Church finds its unity. Through the powers there imparted (demonstrated in the temptation that immediately follows) evil spirits and sin are overcome. Jesus' baptism not only opens up our baptism, our rebirth as children of God, but opens up the whole economy of salvation.

Ephrem—The Three Wombs

Ephrem uses the womb image to link the mysteries of incarnation, Christ's baptism, and the universal proclamation of salvation symbolized by the descent into Sheol, which, we will see, represents misty, generic life for both good and evil.

Ephrem postulates three wombs: Mary's womb, the womb of the Jordan, and the womb of Sheol.[13] Because Ephrem is thinking in sacred (or liturgical) time rather than historical time, he can move backward and forward, without the restrictions of

---

[9] *The Teaching of St. Gregory* 412, 414; Thomson, 89.
[10] Ibid., 413, 414; Thomson, 89
[11] Ibid., 412, 414; Thomson, 89, 90.
[12] *Fragments of the Commentary on Matthew and Luke* 12; CSCO 393:16.
[13] Brock, *The Luminous Eye*, 71, 72.

linear time. The baptism of Jesus can be the source of Christian baptism even though in a temporal sequence the death and resurrection do not occur until later.[14] Brock recalls that Ephrem, and early Syriac poets, see the incarnation effective at any single "staging post" in the economy, of which the Jordan experience is one.[15] As Brock points out, events that are situated at different posts, such as nativity, baptism, crucifixion, descent into Sheol, and resurrection, all participate in the same saving content. The baptism is located on a redemptive spectrum along with the other major mysteries of Jesus' life.

The womb image is also used without explicit reference to Sheol. In a hymn concerning the Jordan event, Ephrem has Christ's baptism in the womb of the Jordan looking back in time to his conception in the womb of Mary. From both wombs issue Christ the Light. Because Christ dwelt in both the womb of the Jordan and the womb of Mary, both the Jordan and Mary are themselves clothed with light from within. The womb of Mary becomes the source of her own baptism, and the womb of the Jordan becomes the source of Christian baptism. Because of its importance, I quote extensively:

"The river in which Christ was baptized
conceived Him again symbolically;
the moist womb of the water conceived Him in purity,
bore Him in chastity,
made Him go up in glory.

"In the pure womb of the river
you should recognize Mary, the daughter of man,
who conceived, having known no man,
who gave birth, without intercourse,
who brought up, through a gift,
the Lord of that gift.

"As the Daystar in the river,
the Bright one in the tomb,

---

[14] Ibid., 16.

[15] Ibid.; Brock, *Holy Spirit in the Syrian Baptismal Tradition*, 8, 9; idem, "Clothing Metaphors," in *Studies in Syriac Christianity*, XI:12.

He shone forth on the mountain top
and gave brightness too in the womb;
He dazzled as He went up from the river,
gave illumination at His ascent.

"The brightness which Moses put on
was wrapped on him from without,
whereas the river in which Christ was baptized
was clothed in light from within;
so too did Mary's body, in which He resided,
gleam from within."[16]

In one stanza Ephrem starts with the baptism of Jesus, which
he then links with the tomb, Tabor (or ascension), womb, again
baptism, and finally ascension, therefore the mysteries of his
baptism, death, transfiguration (or ascension), incarnation, and
ascension.[17] He associates baptism with the chief mysteries of
Christ's life.

In a much quoted stanza, Ephrem carries the linkage further.
He connects the womb of Mary (incarnation), Christ's baptism
in the Jordan, our baptism, and the Eucharist:

"Fire and Spirit are in the womb of her who bore you (Christ),
Fire and Spirit are in the river in which you were baptized,
Fire and Spirit are in our baptism,
and in the Bread and Cup is Fire and Holy Spirit."[18]

In all four mysteries, Fire and Spirit are the constants.

John of Apamea (writing between 430–450) wants those who
have problems finding significance in many mysteries of the
faith to concentrate on Christ's birth, baptism, and resurrection,
as each of these gives entrance into the whole dispensation

---

[16] *Hymns on the Church* 36:3–6; CSCO 199:88. Translation from Brock, "St.
Ephrem on Christ as Light in Mary and in the Jordan: *Hymni De Ecclesia*
36," 138. I have borrowed extensively from Brock's translations.

[17] Ibid., 138, 142, 143. Brock thinks that the reference to the mountain is
not to the transfiguration, which plays a minor role in Ephrem's theological thought, but rather there are two references to the ascension, as there
are two to his baptism.

[18] *Hymns on Faith* 10:17, CSCO 155:35, 37.

manifest in Christ Jesus.[19] This ranging of the baptism among the major mysteries of the faith (incarnation, baptism, death, resurrection) is seen earlier in a great semi-credal doxology by Ignatius of Antioch.[20]

That the baptism is placed in the company of the other major mysteries is seen in the practice of swearing by the baptism of Jesus.[21] Swearing or taking an oath is a way of establishing credibility. The dignity and weight of the baptism of Jesus is called upon to establish trust in the veracity of the word of the person taking the oath. One would not swear by a minor mystery.

The Jordan Is Ablaze with Fire

Fire/light associate themselves with Jesus' baptism. Here there is a rich symbolic development having its origin in the earliest tradition. Justin writes: "As Jesus went down into the water, the Jordan was set ablaze."[22] He seems to have taken this conception from either *The Gospel of the Ebionites* ("Thou art my beloved Son, in thee I am well pleased." And again: "I have this day begotten thee. And immediately a great light shone around about the place")[23] or from the apocryphal *The Preaching of Paul* ("When he was baptized, fire appeared upon the water").[24] Quite possibly the original conception was inspired by the eschatological words of John the Baptist that Jesus "will baptize you with the Holy Spirit and fire" (Matt 3:11). Fire in this context carries the threat of God's own judgment.

---

[19] "Second Treatise on the Mystery of Christ," in *Dialogues and Treatises* 10; SC 311:153.

[20] *Smyrnaeans* 1:1-2, SC 10:132. See also *Ephesians* 18:2; SC 10:74. See Schoedel and Koester, *A Commentary on the Letters of Ignatius of Antioch*, 220-222.

[21] "I abjure thee by him who was baptized in the river Jordan . . ." See Brock, "A New Syriac Baptismal *Ordo* Attributed to Timothy of Alexandria," 378.

[22] *Dialogue with Trypho* 88; PG 6:685.

[23] Schneemelcher, *New Testament Apocrypha*, 1:169.

[24] Quoted in what appears to be a third-century text, Pseudo-Cyprian, *On Rebaptism* 17; CSEL 3/3:90.

Two Old Latin codices, Vercellensis and Sangermanensis, have expanded the text at Matthew 3:15 ("then he [Jesus] consented [to be baptized]"), the first codex adding "and when he was baptized, a flaming light shone round the water."[25] The second codex goes further, remarking on the purpose of the light, namely "so that all who come might fear,"[26] very likely a reference to the divine judgment. The themes of fire kindling the Jordan and baptism of fire were not received in the Church at large, possibly because of excessive attention given to them in certain Judeo-Christian and Gnostic circles.[27]

While Justin is also concerned with fire as judgment, his focus is rather on power (dunamis). "As soon as he was born he possessed powers," but in his condescension he exercised only those powers appropriate to the stage of his own growth.[28] He was baptized because men "had become subject to death."[29] Jesus' baptism marks a stage in his growth; here the appropriate exercise of power is in weakness, namely, being baptized by John. Justin sees this as proof of the gifts Christ received. A parallel exists between Jesus' descent into the Jordan to struggle there with the powers of evil and death (a Sheol reference) and the passing through the fire of judgment.[30] In mediating the tradition on the fire at the Jordan, it was especially Tatian who had such a great influence through his Diatessaron.[31]

But there is another perspective on fire: the sanctification of the waters. Though this theme lacks an exegetical foundation,[32] it is a persistent thread in early Christian writings. It is, however, an authentic theological development.

Jacob of Serugh uses the coal of fire of Isaiah 6:6: "[Christ], the coal of fire went down to wash in the stream, and the

[25] Bauer, Das Leben Jesu, 134.

[26] Ibid.

[27] Vigne, Christ au Jourdain, 270.

[28] Dialogue with Trypho 88: PG 6:685.

[29] Ibid.

[30] Daniélou, The Theology of Jewish Christianity, 228.

[31] C. M. Edsman, Le Baptême de Feu (Uppsala: Almquist & Winksell, 1940) 183.

[32] S. Légasse, Naissance du Baptême (Paris: Cerf, 1993) 69. I thank Justin Taylor for this reference.

flames of its sanctifying power poured forth."[33] The coal of fire sanctifies the waters. Or in a different mode: "The Holy Spirit proceeds from him and he rests upon the waters; the heat of his power warms the waters; and his fire sets the waves on fire before [Christ] descends."[34] In Jacob, the Jordan becomes, indeed, "a furnace" where Christian baptism recasts the original image marred by sin.[35] According to Philoxenus, by going down into the Jordan, Jesus "set fire and Spirit within baptism."[36] The fire can have a purgative function, but it also signifies sanctification and transformation.[37]

The Splendor of Light on the Jordan

Sometimes the emphasis is not on fire as heat, but as light. This is the more common theme. Ephrem writes of the dazzling light: "The splendor of a light appeared on the water."[38] As we

[33] Bedjan, 1:184 (Grillmeier, 164). Though usually it is Christ who heats the water of the Jordan, in one passage it is the Holy Spirit. Brock, "Baptismal Themes in the Writings of Jacob of Serugh," in *Symposium Syriacum 1976,* 334; idem, "A New Syriac Baptismal *Ordo* Attributed to Timothy of Alexandria," 409, n. 64. Influenced by the theology of Christian baptism, where it is the Spirit who comes down upon the water, the role of heating the water in the Jordan event is attributed to the Holy Spirit. I am indebted to the research of S. Brock.

[34] Bedjan, 1:174.

[35] Bedjan, 1:181. Narsai (d. ca. 503) has a similar formulation where the Spirit heats the water. "The furnace of the waters His purpose prepared mystically, and instead of fire He has heated it with the Spirit of the power of His will." *Homily* 22; Connolly, *On Baptism, The Liturgical Homilies of Narsai,* 41.

[36] *Fragments of the Commentary on Matthew and Luke* 12; CSCO 393:12.

[37] The theme of fire at the Jordan is found especially in Syriac iconography, but it is also present in Armenian and Ethiopic baptismal art. Edsman, *Le Baptême de Feu,* 183.

[38] *Commentary on the Diatessaron* 4:5; SC 121:95. See also Ephrem, *Commentary on the Diatessaron,* Armenian Version; CSCO 145:36. On qualifications of the attribution to Tatian, see Black, *An Aramaic Approach to the Gospel and Acts* 267, 268. For other early witnesses, see G. Quispel, *Tatian and the Gospel of Thomas: Studies in the History of the Western Diatessaron* (Leiden: Brill, 1975) 164.

A much later Jacobite witness is Dionysius Bar Salibi (d. 1171), who writes that at Jesus' baptism "a mighty light flashed upon the Jordan," in

have seen, for Ephrem there are two light bearers, Mary and the Jordan. In both cases the radiance comes from Christ dwelling in their wombs. The light of Christ also dwelt in Moses in an exterior and temporary way, while it is interior and permanent in Mary and the Jordan.[39] The light of Christ illumines the chief personages in both the Israelite and the Christian narrative, making them one in a history of light. Gregory Nazianzus, in celebrating the feast of Jesus' baptism, seems to recall the tradition of fire/light at the Jordan. He exhorts the faithful: "Christ is illumined: let us burn bright."[40] Gregory has John the Baptist, "the lamp," addressing Christ, "the Sun."[41] "The Great Light," Christ, is assisted by "perfect lights," that is, the baptized, who should become "as stars in the world."[42]

The Feast of Epiphany, as the Feast of Light (*photismos*, illumination), made this transition from the light on the Jordan to Christ the Great Light and from there to Christians being stars. Already Justin calls Christian baptism "enlightenment" (*photisma*),[43] and, similarly, Clement of Alexandria.[44] Before the tradition is hardly launched, Clement sums up the development still to come, saying that what happens to Jesus at the Jordan happens to us: "Baptized, we are illumined; illumined, we are adopted as sons; adopted, we become perfect; perfect, we receive immortality."[45]

Commentary on the Gospels, purporting to be citing Tatian's *Diatessaron*. *Evangelion da-Mepharresche: The Curetonian Version of the Four Gospels*, F. C. Burkitt, ed., 2 vols. (Cambridge: Cambridge University, 1904) 1:115. See Leloir, *Le Témoignage d'Éphrem sur le Diatessaron*; CSCO 227:106.

[39] *Hymns on the Church* 36:1–7; CSCO 198:87, 88. Brock, "St. Ephrem on Christ as Light in Mary and the Jordan: *Hymni de Ecclesia* 36," 143. In Jacob of Serugh, it is the Spirit that is the light "shining between the waves." Leloir, *Le Témoignage d'Éphrem sur le Diatessaron*; CSCO 227:1061

[40] *Discourse* 39:14; SC 358:180.

[41] Ibid., 39:15; SC 358:182.

[42] Ibid., 39:20; SC 358:194, 196.

[43] *First Apology* 61; PG 6 421.

[44] *The Teacher* 6, 26, 1; SC 70:158. P. T. Camelot, "La triple Épiphanie de la gloire du fils de Dieu," in *La Vie Spirituelle* 92 (1955) 5–15; idem, "Le baptême du Christ et le baptême du chrétien," in *Spiritualité du Baptême* (Paris: du Cerf, 1960) 257–281.

[45] *The Teacher* 1, 6, 26; SC 70:158.

In Proclus (b. before 390), the patriarch of Constantinople, the result of Jesus' baptism is that "fire is baptized by water."[46] Here it is not the fire sanctifying the water, but the water making the fire holy.

The theological perspective in these texts is not restricted to inner spiritual experience but is cosmic in range.[47] The tradition sees fire and light and water as part of the witness of the created universe to the baptism of Jesus.

---

[46] *On the Holy Epiphany* 2; PG 65:760. Wilken, "The Interpretation of the Baptism of Jesus in the Later Fathers," 275.

[47] Daniélou, *The Theology of Jewish Christianity,* 213.

Chapter Eight

The Messianic Anointing of Jesus with the Spirit

When Christians confess that Jesus is the Christ, they confess their belief that he is the Messiah, the Anointed One whom the prophets foretold. This cannot be considered a secondary title. Rather it defines who he is by becoming part of his personal name, Jesus Christ. Jesus is anointed with the Spirit at his baptism, thus becoming the Christ. Anointing and the baptism of Jesus are inextricably linked. And in the Gospels, the baptism is linked to the title of Christ.

Justin—Committed but Uneasy

As we have seen earlier, Justin is an important witness to the role of the baptism of Jesus in the early Church. But he proceeds with the caution of one who is wary. In no way was Jesus in need of the Spirit, which he possessed from the day of his birth.[1] He believes that the Spirit came over Jesus to signify that the Spirit will no longer be poured out on the Jews but will be restricted to Jesus and to those to whom Jesus imparts the Spirit, his disciples. His concern is also, as was said, with power. The baptism in the Jordan is a sign, a proof, that he,

---

[1] *Dialogue* with Trypho 87; PG 6:681, 684.

Jesus, is endowed with power and is the Christ. The birth of Jesus is at the Jordan where persons first recognized who he is, the Son and the Messiah.[2] The Jordan is, therefore, a birth event with messianic content.

Most important is the linking of the descent of the Spirit to the design (oikonomia) of the plan of salvation. It was for the sake of humankind that the Spirit descended on Jesus. Justin is careful not to give the baptism of Jesus an Adoptionist interpretation. In fact, he seems in a quandary as to what to make of the event.[3] "The baptism of Jesus has become a problem" for Justin.[4] He gives the impression of being hesitant to fully exploit the pouring out of the Spirit on Jesus at the Jordan lest it place the divinity of the pre-existent Logos in peril.[5] As we have seen, he was also concerned lest he give a handle to the Jews whom he criticized for their attachment to external rites. Could Justin also have been put on guard by the presence of Valentinus and his followers? Justin and Valentinus were in Rome at the same time. The latter came to Rome about 140 and returned there after a trip to the East, dying about 160. Justin was martyred about five years later. The Valentinians had a developed view of Jesus' baptism in the Jordan.[6] This would prompt Justin to write looking over his shoulder for persons whom he thought might exploit the baptism in an unacceptable way.

According to Justin the anointing of the Word takes place first in pre-existence, and then at the baptism in the Jordan.[7] Here Justin is in agreement with the Valentinians and other Gnostics.[8] For Justin the anointing is another name for divinity. When he writes of the anointing of Christ, he wants to speak two truths: the unimpeachable divinity of Christ and his undoubted claim to be the Messiah.[9] But here, he does not even use the more

[2] Ibid., 88; PG 6:685, 688.

[3] Benoit, Le Baptême Chrétien au Second Siècle, 179.

[4] R. Seeberg, Dogmengeschichte, 4 vols. (Darmstadt: Wissenschaftliche Buchgesellschaft, 1965) 1:347.

[5] Houssiau, La Christologie de Saint Irénée, 184.

[6] Orbe, La Uncion del Verbo, 390–394.

[7] Second Apology 6; PG 6:4S3; Dialogue with Trypho 88; PG 6:685, 688.

[8] Orbe, La Uncion del Verbo, 96–113, 642–647.

[9] Dialogue with Trypho 38, 56, 63; PG 6:557, 601, 621.

precise religious sense of anointing found in the Jewish tradition, but uses a Greek meaning, that is, the anointing which is the final touch on a work of art.[10] Jesus does not need the anointing of the Spirit to establish or empower his person. This he received already at the incarnation. The anointing at the Jordan is as an example for others. Jesus is anointed so he can be seen to be the Messiah.

In spite of his positive stance on the baptism of Jesus, his position is compromised by two misreadings: he confuses the Word with the Spirit in Jesus and confuses the divine dignity with Jesus' messianic character.[11] Justin's hesitation regarding the baptism of Jesus is a herald of future trouble when the baptism will be set aside as a defining moment in establishing Jesus' identity. Even before the rise of Adoptionism in Rome, about 190, a person of Justin's stature is uneasy about the uses to which the Jordan event could be put.

Theophilus—No Reference to the Mysteries

Justin is not the only one who failed to fully exploit Jesus' baptism. Theophilus of Antioch, who became bishop about 169, answers the ridicule heaped on the name "Christian" by stressing the utility of the name. A boat is caulked before it is put into the water. A house or tower is whitewashed to enhance its beauty. A newborn babe is anointed as well as the athlete before the games. He concludes: "What is anointed is sweet and useful. . . . Do you not want to be anointed with the oil of God? We are actually called Christians just because we are anointed with the oil of God."[12] Remarkable is the complete absence of any reference not only to the messianic Christ but to his baptism. Appropriate would have been an argument saying, "We are anointed because Christ was anointed at the Jordan."

However, the lack of any allusion to the Jordan event should not be taken for a want of appreciation of its importance. Rather it stems from the apologetic intent. The absence of any reference to the work of Christ is part of the general reluctance

[10] Houssiau, *La Christologie de Saint Irénée*, 170.
[11] Ibid., 184.
[12] *To Autolycus* 1:12; SC 20:84.

of Theophilus, and the other apologists, to speak openly of Jesus Christ. Not only does Theophilus not refer to Jesus' baptism; he makes no reference at all to his birth, miracles, death, resurrection, or ascension. He is the most radically monotheistic of the Greek Christian apologists. Occasionally, Theophilus speaks of the Logos and the Son of God, but never of the Logos made flesh in Jesus Christ.[13] He is only alluded to. When quoting Jesus, Theophilus does not attribute the saying to Jesus but to the Gospel.[14] Theophilus has a Jewish mind-set and very large Jewish sympathies. The Jews are the legitimate heirs of the patriarchs, and Theophilus' defense of Jewish Christianity is also in part a defense of Hellenistic Judaism. So the failure to mention the baptism of Jesus in relation to the anointing belongs to this larger apologetic context.

Tertullian—From Literary Meaning to the Jordan

Tertullian, writing his *Apology* about 197 (which may be his most important work), therefore after the death of Valentinus and the rise of non-Valentinian Adoptionism, takes refuge in etymology as Theophilus had done. He says that anointing refers to "sweetness and kindness," adding "Christian is derived from anointing."[15] Tertullian derives the name "Christian" (those anointed) not from Christ but from "to anoint." They are called Christians because they have been anointed with the oil of God. In his *On Baptism*, written about the same time as his *Apology*, the relation of the anointing of Jesus at the Jordan to the anointing of the neophyte at Christian baptism is more explicit. First he derives "Christian" from those anointed (*christi dicti a chrismate*) whose content is determined from the anointing of Aaron, and then that of Christ.[16] But he further specifies that the Christian is anointed at baptism because Christ was anointed by the Father.[17] Ostensibly, this means the Jordan

---

[13] J. Lortz, *Tertullian als Apologet*, 2 vols. (Münster: Aschendorff, 1928) 2:5; R. Grant, "Introduction," *Theophilus of Antioch: Ad Autolycum* (Oxford: Clarendon, 1970) xv, xviii.

[14] *To Autolycus* 3:13, 14; SC 20:230, 232.

[15] *Apology* 3:5; CSEL 69:10.

[16] *On Baptism* 7:1; SC 35:76.

[17] Ibid., 7; SC 35:76.

event. Here there is an evident development in Tertullian's thought.

In his very influential defense of trinitarian doctrine, *Against Praxeas*, written in his Montanist period, about 213, Tertullian has his most extensive treatment of the anointing. In this treatise Tertullian is not preoccupied with the meaning of the name "Christian" but with the trinitarian implications of Jesus' anointing by the Father and with the meaning of the name "Christ." Here, he again clearly ties the name "Christ" to the Jordan event: "He is called Christ from the sacrament *(sacramentum)* of anointing."[18]

Sacramentum is found with frequency in Tertullian, where it is rich and various in its meanings. Already by the second century the word *sacramentum* has a liturgical and sacramental (though somewhat abstract) sense, and is still associated with the more concrete biblical Greek *mysterion*, which carries connotations of the sacred, the mysterious, and of initiation.[19] The sacrament of anointing in Tertullian's text would then refer to the mystery of the Jordan as Jesus' initiation, already looking upon that anointing and the whole Jordan experience in somewhat sacramental terms. In support of his understanding of Jesus' baptism, Tertullian calls upon Luke's oblique reference to the action of the Father at the Jordan in Acts 4:27 (". . . your holy servant Jesus, whom you anointed . . ."). For Tertullian, that anointing of Jesus at the Jordan had meaning for what is essential to the Christian life. Those who believe in the anointing of Jesus "have fellowship with the Father and with his Son, Jesus Christ."[20] Trinitarian *koinonia/communio* has its roots in the baptism of Jesus.

There is, therefore, a development in Tertullian from a more literary understanding of the anointing of Christians ("sweetness and kindness") to viewing anointing in relation to Christ's anointing at the Jordan.

[18] *Against Praxeas* 28; CCh 2:1200.
[19] Mohrmann, "Sacramentum dans des plus anciens textes chrétiens," *Études sur le Latin des Chrétiens* 1:236, 241, 243, 244. *Sacramentum* tended to take over meaning from the biblical *mysterion*, and to supplant it, but never fully succeeded.
[20] *Against Praxeas* 28; CCh 2:1201.

Like Theophilus and the earlier Tertullian, Clement of Alexandria also fails to make a connection between the anointing of Christians in baptism and the baptism of Jesus. *The Exhortation to the Greeks,* addressed to unbelievers, calls them to conversion to the true religion, promising a life that will fulfill the deepest human longings because this life is salvation and immortality. Speaking of Christian initiation, he writes: "I will anoint you with the unguent of faith."[21] This is nearer one biblical tradition where the name of Christian is not related to anointing but to faith in Jesus and the following of his teachings (Acts 11:26; 26:28). But 1 Peter 4:16 ties "Christian" to bearing Christ's name.

While in *The Exhortation to the Greeks* Clement is addressing pagans, in *The Teacher* he is speaking to those who have already been baptized, presenting to them the Christ/Logos as the master and model. Those who are baptized are "regenerated by water" and "made to grow in the Spirit" so that "they practice on earth the heavenly life which divinizes us, receiving the anointing of a joy that is always young, considering the mode of life of the Lord as a brilliant example of incorruptibility and following the footsteps of God."[22] Given his Greek philosophical background, *mimesis* (imitation) appears to be inner participation in the life of Jesus rather than just an exterior moral following. The reference to joy seems to refer to the experience of anointing during initiation, and to the following of the Lord that flows from baptism. There is no attempt in either work to relate the anointing received in Christian initiation to Jesus' anointing at the Jordan.

Irenaeus—Eternity, the Jordan, and the Cosmos

Irenaeus, the first theologian to develop themes systematically (who nevertheless fell into obscurity until rediscovered by Erasmus[23]), has one of the most extensive teachings on anointing.

[21] *The Exhortation to the Greeks* 12:5; SC 2:191.
[22] *The Teacher* 1, 12, 3; SC 70:284, 286.
[23] *Epistola nuncupatoria*; PG 7:1321.

How different Irenaeus' approach in comparison to the tentative Justin and Theophilus! He has no hesitations about exploiting the Jordan expansively. Unlike Justin he is not shy of the baptism for fear that it imperils the divinity of Christ, nor is he shy of the external rite. On the contrary, Irenaeus "pushes the doctrine (of the outpouring of the Spirit on Christ at the Jordan) to its ultimate."[24] Two reasons can be given for this attention to the Jordan. First his biblicism. He never wanders far from the text of Scripture. Again and again he returns to the biblical source. Secondly, he is prompted by the very great attention the Gnostics, especially the Valentinians, give to the baptism of Jesus. Indeed, it is one of their principal preoccupations. Therefore the need to give the baptism of Jesus an orthodox interpretation. Irenaeus peels back the layers of meaning and expands on them in confrontation with his theological opponents, the Gnostics.[25]

As we have seen above in relation to the cosmos, Irenaeus names two anointings. The first anointing: the Word in the bosom of the Father from all eternity; the second: the Lord in time at the Jordan.[26] The anointing at the Jordan has large messianic content related immediately to mission. The anointing comes out of the prophetic tradition which promises that the Spirit of God will descend on the Expected One. Accompanying the anointing is the imparting of the seven gifts of the Spirit (Isa 11:1-4) that empower the Lord to carry the good news to the poor, to deliver the captives, to free from sins. Though conceived in the power of the Spirit, and possessing the Spirit from the moment of conception, only at the baptism does the

[24] Houssiau, *La Christologie de Saint Irénée*, 184.

[25] Hans-Jochen Jaschke, *Der Heilige Geist im Bekenntnis der Kirche* (Münster: Aschendorff, 1976) 209, 210.

[26] Enrique Fabbri ("El bautismo de Jesus y la unción del Espiritu en la teología de Ireneo" *Ciencia y Fe* 12 [1956] 37) cites *Demonstration of the Apostolic Preaching* 53; SC 62:114 as referring to the anointing at the incarnation. This appears, however, to be a reference to the anointing at the baptism. This seems to be confirmed by other references where the Spirit plays a role in the incarnation, but in these instances Irenaeus does not use the vocabulary of anointing. See *AH* 3, 16, 2; SC 211:292; *AH* 3, 21, 4; SC 211:410; *AH* 4, 23, 1; SC 100:692; *AH* 5, 1, 3; SC 153:24; *Demonstration of the Apostolic Preaching* 40, 71; SC 62:95, 138.

Lord receive the Spirit in order to communicate it to others. In Irenaeus' words: "It is, indeed, the Spirit which descends for the sake of the economy."[27]

The descent of the Spirit at the Jordan is the anointing, and it has to do only with the humanity of the incarnated Son, not with his divinity.[28] To emphasize this point Irenaeus uses a crude expression. He says that John the Baptist declares that this particular person is the Christ "on whom the Spirit of God, mixing himself with the flesh, rests."[29] In this way Irenaeus takes the baptism out of the Gnostic context that related the anointing to the divinity of Christ. Still he wants to keep the divinity related to the event. So he insists that only a human person can receive the anointing, and that this human person is the Son of God.[30] The Jordan event, therefore, is not a revelation of the union of the human Jesus with the divine Christ but rather the manifestation of the descent of the Spirit on the flesh assumed by the Word.[31] From the point of view of the Spirit, the action of the Spirit is a resting on the Lord; from the point of view of the Lord, it is an anointing.[32] From the moment the Spirit descends and anoints the Lord at the Jordan, this Jesus is called "the Christ."[33] Before the baptism Jesus is not the Christ. The baptism of Jesus is a clear messianic boundary.

The Triune Anointing

The anointing of Jesus at the Jordan is set in the revelation of the trinitarian God and in the broad range of the mysteries of Christ. The Spirit descends on Jesus, this event declaring that

[27] *AH* 3, 17, 4; SC 211:336, 338.

[28] This is the position of Houssiau, *La Christologie de Saint Irénée*, 166–186, and of A. Rousseau and L. Doutreleau, SC 210:248–262, in opposition to the position of A. Orbe, "La unción de Cristo en la Teología de S. Ireneo," *La Unción del Verbo*, 501–520.

[29] *Demonstration of the Apostolic Preaching* 41; SC 62:95.

[30] *AH* 3, 18, 3; SC 211:347–352. Houssiau, *La Christologie de Saint Irénée*, 180, 181.

[31] *AH* 3, 9, 3; SC 211:106–112.

[32] Vigne, *Christ au Jourdain*, 80.

[33] *AH* 3, 9, 3; SC 211:108.

he is the Christ who will suffer, die, and rise. The Spirit character of the baptism is constitutive of the paschal mysteries. The descending and resting on Jesus is itself the anointing declaring him the Christ.

But under the name "Christ," "anointed," is the understanding "of the One who has anointed, the One who is anointed, and of the Unction with which one is anointed."[34] Irenaeus specifies the meaning: "The one who has anointed is the Father; the one who has been anointed, this is the Son; and the Unction is being in the Spirit."[35] The whole triune life is manifested here at the very beginning of the public economy. Irenaeus uses the anointing to demonstrate the unity of the one God but also the unity of Jesus Christ (unlike the Gnostics who believe that Christ and Jesus are two).[36]

But the perspective is even larger. The baptism reveals and communicates to humanity the eternal anointing that the Son received from the Father. The earthly anointing at the Jordan has to do with the Son insofar as he is human; the eternal anointing has to do with the Son in so far as he is divine. As we have seen earlier, he fuses the two anointings. Only Irenaeus gives such messianic breadth to the baptism.[37]

At the Jordan the Spirit Becomes
Accustomed to the Human Race

The participation of believers in the anointing of Jesus at the Jordan is central to Irenaeus' teaching on the baptism of Jesus. He applies a much loved category, namely, "becoming accustomed to." The Spirit descends on Jesus so that the Spirit "might get accustomed to dwell in the human race, to repose on men, to reside within the work God has modeled, working the Father's will in them and renewing them from oldness to newness in Christ."[38] All this is the work of the Spirit descending on Jesus at the Jordan. Elsewhere he names the Hands of

[34] *AH* 3, 18, 3; SC 211:350. See also *AH* 3, 6, 1; 3, 9, 3; SC 211:66, 110, 112.
[35] *AH* 3, 18, 3; SC 211:350.
[36] Houssiau, *La Christologie de Saint Irénée*, 174.
[37] Vigne, *Christ au Jourdain*, 81.
[38] *AH* 3, 17, 1; SC 211:330.

God that formed and molded the work of the Father, namely the Son and the Spirit.[39] The Spirit descends and rests on us as the Spirit descended and rested on Jesus, anointing him at his baptism. This anointing is an expression of the fullness of the gifts of the Spirit imparted to Jesus, a sign of what the gifts of the Spirit mean in the Christian life. In this way the Spirit is becoming accustomed to dwell among us, renewing us from within. "We ourselves receive from the superabundance of this anointing, and thus we are saved."[40] In a word, if we participate in the anointing of Jesus at his baptism, we are saved. Strong words!

From Church to the Whole Earth

Irenaeus sees the Church as "the paradise in this world."[41] The bishop of Lyons is careful not to isolate the Jordan event from the Church, this anointing of Jesus, in which we share. Rather the Spirit anointing Jesus at his baptism is the very Spirit, with all of the rich variety of charisms, given to the Church.[42] The anointing at the Jordan has to do with the fullness and perfection of salvation offered to humankind in the Church, which, as Origen notes, is "the cosmos of the cosmos."[43]

Irenaeus further specifies the ecclesiological significance of the Jordan event. The Spirit resting in such abundance on Jesus in the Jordan "is the same Spirit which the Lord in his turn has given to the Church, in sending the Paraclete from heaven onto the whole earth."[44] The Church is not a prison for the Spirit; the Spirit given to the Church is destined for the whole of creation. The Jordan event opens universalist perspectives.

[39] *AH* 5, 6, 1; SC 153:72. See J. Mambrino, "Les deux mains de Dieu dans l'oeuvre de saint Irénée," *Nouvelle Revue Théologique* 79 (1957) 216.

[40] *AH* 3, 9, 3; SC 211:112.

[41] *AH* 5, 20, 2; SC 153:258.

[42] *AH* 3, 17, 3; SC 211:336.

[43] *On John* 6:59; SC 157:360. See Irenaeus, *AH* 3, 6, 1; SC 211:66, and *Demonstration of the Apostolic Preaching* 47; SC 62:106–108. This view is also found in Clement of Alexandria, who places cosmos alongside of salvation and the Church. So there is a certain similitude between cosmos and Church. *The Teacher* 1, 27, 2; SC 70:160. Orbe, *La Unción del Verbo*, 521, 522.

[44] *AH* 3, 17, 3; SC 211:336.

The Spirit coming down on Jesus is the same Spirit coming down on the disciples on the day of Pentecost, opening the Church to universal vistas in the multiplicity of nations speaking one language of praise.[45] To this end the Father sends "Water from Heaven," or "Rain from Above," that is, the Spirit.[46] Without this divine moisture, Irenaeus continues, the dry flour cannot become bread; without moisture dry wood will not bring forth fruit. Further, Christian baptism inherits the spiritual gifts from Jesus' baptism. As at the Jordan, the Spirit is united to the body of Christ. Thus our bodies, through the bath of baptism, have been joined to the Incorruptible One (Christ), while our souls have received the Spirit.[47]

While it is true that "there where the Church is, there also is the Spirit, and where the Spirit of God is, there the Church and all grace is to be found"—this again is not a narrow ecclesiasticism.[48] The "economy" has to do with that spacious plan of God for the whole of humanity, as the Pentecost event demands. The Spirit is poured out on all flesh. The Spirit comes "with power over all the nations in order to introduce them into the life and to open to them the New Testament. Therefore the disciples celebrate the praises of God in all of the tongues, (all) animated with the same sentiment, while the Spirit leads to unity the separated tribes, offering to the Father the first fruits of all the nations. This is the reason why the Lord has promised to send us the Paraclete, which makes us apt for God."[49] The unity of humanity demonstrated in the unity of all tongues praising God is a first work of the Spirit. From the anointing at the baptism to the pouring out of the Spirit at Pentecost on the separated nations, leading them into a universal unity, the Spirit makes the whole of humanity "apt for God" (qui nos aptaret Deo). This is why "the Spirit is sent over all the earth."[50] The first work of Pentecost is the unity of humanity. The unity of humanity signs the unity of the

---

[45] AH 3, 17, 2; SC 211:330.

[46] Ibid.; SC 211:333.

[47] AH 3, 17, 1; SC 211:330.

[48] AH 3, 24, 1; SC 211:473, 475.

[49] AH 3, 17, 2; SC 211:330, 332.

[50] Ibid.; SC 211:335.

Church. The unity of the Church is not conceived apart from the unity of the nations. Irenaeus is innocent of a cramping, foreshortened churchiness.

The Cosmic Anointing

The horizon expands. In Irenaeus' view the anointing at the Jordan is cosmic, which I have already treated above. The anointing of the Son at the Jordan is a reflection of the eternal anointing. In this eternal/temporal anointing, the Father anoints the whole of creation through him. To this, one can add Irenaeus' forceful but crude concern that God not be wasted. The Word, the creator of the universe, already existed as the one who saves. Out of fear that this Savior might lose reason for existing, it was necessary for the Savior to have something to save: "Since the One who would save already existed, it was necessary that whoever would be saved, come into existence, so that this Savior would not be without reason for existing."[51]

A certain impulsion toward creation is rooted in the saving nature of the Word, lest the saving character of the Word be squandered. But this Word/Son whom the Father has anointed with the oil of gladness, that is, the Spirit, is also the only access to the Father. Likewise, the Father anoints others, the prophets, the just, and disciples, with the Spirit, giving them also access to the Father through the Word and only through the Word.[52] The Spirit with which the Father anoints the Word, who in turn will anoint the universe, is the same Spirit with which the God anoints the just. Though there are differences in effects, the distinction in Irenaeus between the anointing of the just and the anointing of the world must not be pressed.[53] Irenaeus' teaching on the anointing describes a cosmic universalism embracing persons and the whole of the created universe.

What is significant historically is Irenaeus' realization of the "autonomous" character of the Holy Spirit in the baptism of Jesus. The Spirit is not to be viewed as merely a constituent

[51] "Since the One who would save already existed, it was necessary that which would be saved come into existence," *AH* 3, 22, 3; SC 211:439.
[52] *Demonstration of the Apostolic Preaching* 47; SC 62:106–108.
[53] Orbe, *La Unción del Verbo*, 522.

part of the person of the Redeemer, as some might want to interpret the descent of the Spirit at the annunciation. The "autonomy" of the Spirit in the Jordan event makes an orthodox christology possible.[54] Also, it places trinitarian theology on a sure road.

If Enrique Fabbri is correct, the whole theological structure of Irenaeus' thought is built upon the Spirit resting on Jesus and his anointing with the Spirit at the Jordan.[55] Hans-Jochen Jaschke likewise contends that for Irenaeus "the whole of the human development finds its center in the anointing of Christ with the Spirit," which takes place at the Jordan.[56]

Irenaeus is more aggressive in his treatment of the baptism of Jesus than Justin, with whom he is usually compared. That the bishop of Lyons is more successful is partly due to the clarity with which he distinguishes between the Word and the Spirit, unlike Justin. Further, he does not confuse the anointing of Christ with his divinity, again unlike Justin. While stressing the descent and resting of the Spirit on Jesus, which is the anointing, he still maintains the divinity of Jesus born of Mary, that is, he is divine from birth, not just from the baptism. Yet he gives the humanity of Jesus the fullest, most generous role in mediating the anointing to us. The salvation of humanity begins in the humanity of Jesus.[57] An impressive achievement.

Cyril—"The Exact Image of Christ's Anointing"

The anointing of Christ at the Jordan becomes the basis of anointings in Christian baptism. What happened to Christ at the Jordan through the anointing with the Spirit happens to Christians in baptism. Christian baptism is a *mimesis* of the baptism of Jesus. One example will suffice. Cyril of Jerusalem announces the principle: "Baptized in Christ, and having put on Christ, you have become conformed to the Son of God. . . . Henceforth, as participants in Christ, you are justly called

---

[54] Jaschke, *Der Heilige Geist im Bekenntnis der Kirche*, 212.

[55] "El bautismo de Jesús y la unción del Espíritu en la teología de Ireneo," 22.

[56] *Der Heilige Geist im Bekenntnis der Kirche*, 215.

[57] Houssiau, *La Christologie de Saint Irénée*, 184.

'christs.' . . . You have become christs in receiving the imprint of the Holy Spirit, and all is accomplished in you as in an image, because you are the images of Christ."[58] The justification of this is the verse of Isaiah that Jesus quotes in reference to his own baptism: "The Spirit of the Lord is upon me because he has anointed me." When Jesus bathed in the Jordan, the Holy Spirit visited him "in essential presence, *like* resting on *like*."[59] So also, when the neophyte ascends from the waters of baptism, the newly baptized is anointed with chrism, "the exact image of that with which Christ was anointed' at the Jordan.[60]

The Anointing Succession

We need to turn from the Greek and Latin tradition to the Syrian and Armenian witness. In the theology of Ephrem, the word "ointment" is a synonym for the word "baptism." "By baptism, the Lord has put on the justice of the Old Testament, in order to receive the perfection of the anointing."[61] The Armenian witness of *The Teaching of St. Gregory* at first speaks extensively of the baptism of Jesus in the Jordan; then, as if to expand on the theme, again speaks at length of an anointing succession to which the baptism of Jesus is heir through John the Baptist.

The author introduces the theme of the baptism of Jesus with a reference to Moses. Speaking of the baptism that John the Baptist administers, the author says that John, "a descendant of Moses," mandates a cleansing, just as Moses did (Exod 19:10).[62] As in the age of Moses, so when God sent John, "the greatest of the prophets," a washing is prescribed "so that they might become worthy of the revelation of the divine glory."[63] This linkage between Moses and John the Baptist is essential for understanding the ministry of John, the baptism of Jesus, and the revelation of the glory at the Jordan.

[58] *Mystagogical Catecheses* 3:1; SC 126:120.
[59] Ibid.; SC 126:122. Italics mine.
[60] Ibid.
[61] *Commentary on the Diatessaron* 4:2; SC 121:94.
[62] *The Teaching of St. Gregory* 429; Thomson, 94.
[63] Ibid., 408; Thomson, 88.

When "the vision of the glory of the Lord was burning like fire (burning bush)," God gave Moses "a type of the anointing of Christ, that first he might present examples, and then the truth might come."[64] The anointing that Moses institutes is the type; the anointing of Christ is "the truth." God commands Moses to make a horn of anointing, "from which were anointed the priests, prophets, and kings."[65] So the history of anointing, according to the text, begins with Moses, and from him "proceeded in orderly fashion the unction in succession."[66] All those who were anointed in the Old Testament were anointed with "the anointing of Christ."[67] The mystery of the anointing is preserved in the succession of priests, prophets, and kings, until it comes to John, "priest, prophet, and baptist."[68] John, "worthy of anointing,"[69] "evangelist of Jerusalem,"[70] and "keeper of the tradition, . . . gave the priesthood, the anointing, the prophecy, and the kingship to our Lord Jesus Christ."[71] Or again: "Thus in succession the traditions were

[64] Ibid., 431; Thomson, 95.
[65] Ibid., 433; Thomson, 96.
[66] Ibid. Translation modified.
[67] Ibid., 432; Thomson, 95.
[68] Ibid., 433; Thomson, 96. Ephrem also appeals to the tradition starting with Moses to safeguard the imposition of hands in which "the order [of succession]" is transmitted through Aaron to John the Baptist and handed on to the Lord, and passed on by the Lord to the apostles, which accounts for its presence in the Church. The issue is the ordination of heretics who either reject the ordination of the Church or have the temerity to ordain their own priests. Ephrem appeals to the line of succession embedded in the imposition of hands, contending that Christ honored the tradition of succession, saying to John the Baptist: "Justice demands that I be baptized by you lest the order [of succession] be lost. Our Lord transmitted it to the apostles, and this is the reason for the tradition in our Church." *Hymns Against Heresies* 22:18, 19; CSCO 170:81, 82. According to Ephrem, John the Baptist imposed hands on Jesus at the Jordan, or rather, Jesus took John's hand and placed it on his own head, saying "Allow us now to fulfill all justice." *Commentary on the Diatessaron* 4:2; SC 121:94.
[69] Ibid., 429; Thomson, 94.
[70] Ibid.
[71] Ibid., 433; Thomson, 96. Ephrem in his *Commentary on the Diatessaron* 4:3; SC 121:94, 95, has Jesus receive priesthood and prophecy from John, but kingship from his birth from the house of David. See also 3:9; SC 121:86, 87.

handed down to John, and John gave the tradition of his trust to his Lord (Jesus Christ)."[72]

The handing on of the succession of anointings takes place at the Jordan when the Spirit descends on Jesus. So both Old and New Testaments are "a revelation of the anointing of Christ and his name."[73] Christ, in fact, "surpassed the types and established the truth" by the anointing with the Spirit at his baptism.[74] John, "the keeper of the tradition of the inheritance, . . . gave the priesthood and the power and the prophecy and the kingship to our Savior Christ: and Christ gave them to the apostles, and the apostles to the children of the church."[75] The anointing succession has a continuing history in the life of the Church. When Jesus comes to be baptized by John he does so in order "to give life to all by the illuminating and life-giving baptism."[76]

The Jordan as Imitation

The author presents the baptism of Jesus as the object of imitation. The baptism of Jesus is the image, icon, primary paradigm, source, and fountain that Christian baptism imitates and reproduces. This imitation is a participation in the interior reality and dynamics of the Jordan event. Using the rhetoric of universalism, the author writes: "(Christ) ordered all men born from the earth, all humans, to imitate the divine image of salvation."[77] The baptism of Jesus is the icon of salvation because the Spirit imparted in the past, to priests, prophets, and kings—part of the Old Testament charismatic succession—and imparted to Jesus in his baptism, is now, in the new order, imparted to all the faithful. Priests, prophets, kings were bearers of the Spirit and therefore bearers of the memory of Israel. As

[72] Ibid., 435; Thomson, 96. In a broader and more exhaustive context, G. Winkler has treated this subject in *Das Armenische Initiationsrituale*. See also her important article "The Original Meaning of the Prebaptismal Anointing and Its Implications," 24–45.

[73] Ibid., 441; Thomson, 98.

[74] Ibid., 423; Thomson, 92.

[75] Ibid., 468; Thomson, 106.

[76] Ibid., 410; Thomson, 88.

[77] Ibid.

Gerhard von Rad says, they represent charism, "an absolutely constitutive factor in Jahwism."[78] Through John the Baptist, the baptism of Jesus is the heir to this tradition, a major theme of *The Teaching of St. Gregory.*[79] The author saw in the baptism of Jesus the revelation "of salvation to all" through a new kind of water, the water of baptism in which the Spirit dwells, which clothes "all with robes of light."[80] The Spirit manifested at the baptism of Jesus is poured out at Pentecost when the apostles "drank of the fire of the Spirit of joy, and became cupbearers throughout the world."[81]

So the succession of anointing beginning with the anointing that Moses instituted, handed down in the tradition of priests, prophets, and kings, is mediated through John to Jesus by means of his baptism in the Jordan, and Jesus, in turn, hands the succession on to the apostles, who assures the succession to the Church. The anointing succession is constitutive of Yahwism, constitutive of the economic Christ, and constitutive of the Church. The anointing at the Jordan has a central role in salvation history. Jesus Christ himself orders all to imitate his baptism, sharing in the interior substance of his baptism, a way of sharing in the divine life. The anointing lives on.

The anointing of Jesus at the Jordan, therefore, is an instrument of theological cohesion spanning the Old and New Testaments. Christ's anointing is proleptically given to the anointed personages of the Old Testament. In the New Testament, the Father anoints the Christ with the Spirit, and the Father in that Spirit-anointing binds from within Word, Church, world, universe. The finger of the Father reaching out to anoint the Christ with the Spirit also extends beyond the triune self to touch the world and the cosmos. The trinitarian dynamic is cosmic.

---

[78] G. von Rad, *Old Testament Theology*, 2 vols. (New York: Harper & Row, 1962) 1:102. The author of *The Teaching of St. Gregory* would make a simple identification of the spirit in the Old Testament with the Holy Spirit in the New.

[79] 430, 431, 433, 435, 468; Thomson, 94, 96, 95 n. 1, 106.

[80] Ibid., 420, 414, 412; Thomson, 91, 89.

[81] Ibid., 508; Thomson, 118.

Chapter Nine

Taking the Robe of Glory from the Jordan—Divinization

The idea of divinization is not peculiar to Christianity, but has a long history in pre-Christian poetry, philosophy, and the mystery religions. Within Christianity it is broadly represented in both the Greek and Latin traditions.[1]

Irenaeus seems to have been the first to give it explicit formulation in the Greek tradition, saying that "the Word of God, Jesus Christ our Lord, who, because of his superabundant love, made himself what we are in order to make of us what he is."[2] But the formulation having the greatest influence is that of

[1] "Divinisation," *Dictionnaire de Spiritualité* (Paris: Beauchesne, 1957) 3:1370–1459; P. Nellas, *Deification in Christ: The Nature of the Human Person* (Crestwood: St. Vladimir's Seminary, 1987); V. Lossky, "Redemption and Deification," in *The Image and Likeness of God* (Crestwood: St. Vladimir's Seminary, 1985) 97–110.

[2] *AH* Preface, 5, 1, 1; SC 153:14. Irenaeus gives similar formulations: ". . . having promised to render his 'Salvation' visible for all flesh in such a manner that the Son of God would become the Son of man so that in his turn man might become the son of God." *AH* 3, 10, 2; SC 211:118. The same formulation appears in 3, 16, 3 and 3, 19, 1; SC 211:298, 374. Theophilus of Antioch (probably became bishop about 169) makes tentative approaches of a similar nature. *To Autolycus* 2:27; SC 20:164, 166. Later, Origen picks up the theme in *On First Principles* 1, 6, 2; SC 252:196–200; idem, *Against Celsus* 3:28; SC 136:69.

Athanasius: "God became man so that we might become god."[3] The same theme is taken up by Gregory Nazianzus: "God is made Man; man is rendered god."[4] And likewise in Gregory of Nyssa: "Because our nature is mixed with the divine nature, our nature is made divine."[5] Gregory of Nyssa uses clothing images specifically in relation to the baptism of Jesus as a way of effecting divinization. Old Testament types, he recalls, instruct us that the baptismal experience entails stripping ourselves of our "ill-favored raiment" to put on "clean and fair apparel."[6] More specifically, "in the baptism of Jesus all of us, putting off our sins like some poor and patched garment, are clothed in the holy and most fair garment of regeneration."[7] In the baptism of Jesus we are clothed in the garments of rebirth, and are divinized.

Harnack and the Secularization of the Gospel

Though this same theme under various titles is found in Latin sources, the Greek view of this "real redemption," as A. Harnack calls it, became its most typical formulation.[8] And Gregory Nazianzus, that mighty champion of the divinity of the Spirit—he chafed under the reticences of Basil in this regard and wanted to shout out the divinity of the Spirit from the highest mountain[9]—gave expression to the theme of divinization in the

---

[3] On the Incarnation of the Word 54:3; SC 199:458.

[4] Dogmatic Poem 10:5; PG 37:465. Also: "If the Spirit has no right to my adoration, how can the Spirit divinize me by baptism?" Oration 37:28; SC 250:332.

[5] Catechetical Oration 25; PG 45:65, 68.

[6] On the Baptism of Christ; PG 46:593.

[7] Ibid.

[8] History of Dogma, 7 vols. (New York: Dover, 1961) 2:240.

[9] "We will go up a high mountain and shout, if we are not heard here below; we will exalt the Spirit; we will not be afraid. Or if we are afraid, it shall be [fear] of keeping silence, not of proclaiming [the divinity of the Spirit]," Oration 31:3; SC 250:280. Basil, mostly for religious/political reasons in a highly charged theological atmosphere, makes a distinction between dogma and kerygma. The divinity of the Spirit belongs to dogma, but at this moment in history, not to kerygma. Not once in the whole of his treatise On the Holy Spirit, written to defend the divinity of the Spirit, does he explicitly say the Spirit is God. Basil argues for the divinity of the Spirit

celebration of the baptism of Jesus. Referring to the divinity of the Spirit and the divinity of Jesus, Gregory writes: "The Spirit testifies to the divinity, because the Spirit hastens toward the One [Jesus at the Jordan] to whom the Spirit is like."[10] The divine Spirit hastens to the divine Jesus. Like rushes to like. It is this divine Spirit that divinizes those who follow Jesus down into the waters of baptism: "How could He (the Spirit) not be God, the one through whom you become god."[11]

But Harnack would have none of it. For him, divinization is part of that process of "the gradual hellenising of Christianity," which he viewed as a secularization of the good news, a point that Brock notes.[12] From a historical point of view Harnack was part of the nineteenth-century anti-metaphysical stream, looking for a simpler form of Christianity, uncomplicated by theological and philosophical formulas.[13] Divinization tangles the gospel.

---

more by indirection. This was called Basil's "economy." His purpose was to lead those of good will to acknowledge the divinity, who would balk at a straightforward open declaration. This position stupefied Basil's friends, Gregory Nazianzus among them, but in the end, even the Council of Constantinople (381) adopted his position. Basil prevailed at the council even though Gregory Nazianzus, the champion of a loud proclamation of the divinity of the Spirit, was present, while Basil was not, dead then for about two years. J. Gribomont, "Intransigence and Irenicism in St. Basil's 'De Spiritu Sancto,' " in *Word and Spirit* 1 (1979) 113, 11; A. Laminski, *Der Heilige Geist als Geist Christi und Geist der Gläubigen: Der Beitrag des Athanasios von Alexandrien zur Formulierung des trinitarischen Dogmas im Vierten Jahrhundert* (Leipzig: St. Benno, 1969) 140, 141. For clarification of Basil's concept of economy, see H. Dorries, *De Spiritu Sancto: Der Beitrag des Basilius zum Abschluss des trinitarischen Dogmas* (Göttingen: Vandenhoeck & Ruprecht, 1956) 23–28, 125–128.

[10] *Oration* 39:16; SC 358:184.

[11] Ibid., 39:17; SC 358:186. In another formulation, Gregory argues back from divinization of believers to the divinity of the Spirit. "If he is in the same rank with myself, how can he make me God, or join me with the godhead?" *Oration* 31:4; SC 250:282.

[12] Harnack, *History of Dogma* 2:247, 251, 297, 328; 3:295, 296, 287. H. Rondet, *The Grace of Christ: A Brief History of the Theology of Grace* (Westminster: Newman, 1967) 66; Brock, *The Luminous Eye*, 123.

[13] G. W. Glick, *The Reality of Christianity* (New York: Harper & Row, 1967) 152, 153.

If Divinization Is Greek, What About the Syrians?

But, Brock suggests, if divinization is essentially a Greek philosophical category and a Greek preoccupation, then it would be difficult to explain the presence of the same idea in Syrian sources, Ephrem for instance.[14] We know from Theodoret that Ephrem "had not tasted Greek culture."[15] He had some awareness of Greek civilization, had picked up some individual Greek words, but knew no Greek as a usable language. Though Ephrem was not militantly anti-Greek, he could deliver himself of an anti-Greek jibe: "Happy the man who has not tasted of the venom of the Greeks."[16] What Ephrem seems to have had in mind is the application of logic to matters of theology.[17] Ephrem represents a Syrian Christianity in all its purity, at least in his Nisibis period. He, together with Aphrahat, represents a truly Semitic form of Christianity, a Christianity that is "un-hellenized," "uneuropeanized."[18] So when the Syrian Ephrem says of the Son "He gave us divinity, we gave him human-ity,"[19] or "Our body was Your clothing, Your Spirit was our robe,"[20] he is echoing neither Irenaeus, nor Athanasius, nor any of the Greeks. He is being authentically Syrian. Though the content of divinization is close to the Greek, its mode is Semitic.[21] Ephrem is borrowing neither from philosophy nor Greek ecclesiastical sources, but from the symbolic world of the Scriptures.[22]

---

[14] S. Brock, *St. Ephrem the Syrian: Hymns on Paradise* (Crestwood: St. Vladimirs Seminary, 1990) 73.

[15] *Ecclesiastical History* 4:26; PG 82:1190. S. Brock, "From Antagonism to Assimilation: Syriac Attitudes to Greek Learning," in *Syriac Perspectives on Late Antiquity* V:19.

[16] *Hymns on Faith* 2:24; CSCO 155:7.

[17] Brock, "From Antagonism to Assimilation: Syriac Attitudes to Greek Learning," V:18, 19.

[18] Brock, *The Luminous Eye*, 2, 3; idem, "Early Syrian Asceticism," in *Syriac Perspectives on Late Antiquity*, 1, 11.

[19] *Hymns on Faith* 5:17; CSCO 155:17.

[20] *Hymns on the Nativity* 22:39; CSCO 187:105.

[21] Brock, *St. Ephrem the Syrian: Hymns on Paradise* 74.

[22] Robert Murray, "Der Dichter als Exeget: Der Hl.Ephraem und die Heutige Exegese," in *Zeitschrift für Katholische Theologie* 100 (1978) 485, 486.

In both the Greek and the Syrian tradition, the divinization of believers is a major preoccupation.[23] In the Semitic languages the word *bar* may mean "sharing in the attributes" or "belonging to the category of"[24] or related to "son of" (as in "Simon bar Jonah," Matt 16:17; John 1:42). Divinization is, of course, a poetic exaggeration, referring to the wondrous sharing of the life of the Spirit, abundant divine life, proper to God, by which believers are made adopted daughters and sons of God. The poetic expression of divinization is a mark of the great seriousness with which the tradition takes the central insight about sharing in God-life. This is not poetry.

Divinization is not a scandalous compromise between Hellenism and the gospel, not a post-biblical Hellenistic import into the Scriptures, as Harnack thought. Though a hyperbole, it is a biblical hyperbole: "Our God and Savior . . . called us by his own glory and goodness . . . [so that we] may become participants of the divine nature" (2 Pet 1:1-4). The bold expression "divine nature" is found only here in the Scriptures. This biblical text attracted much attention from the early Christian and medieval authors, playing a large role in the development of the doctrine of grace.[25] It seems to mean the membership in God's covenant that brings with it all that is necessary for life and holiness, implying a call to a new and special world, God's own realm of glory.[26]

The author of 2 Peter himself borrows from popular Greek philosophy, especially Stoicism, to emphasize how the pagan convert is freed from that world opposed to God through baptism, where the convert is clothed in Christ, becoming a new person (Eph 4:22-24). Similar ideas using other vocabularies are found elsewhere in Scripture (1 John 1:3; 3:2, 9; John 15:4; 17:22, 23; Rom 6:5; 8:14-17). The divinization the Greeks pursued

---

[23] The book of Nellas, *Deification in Christ: The Nature of the Human Person*, lays out the Greek teaching on divinization or theosis, but does not relate it to the baptism of Jesus.

[24] Brock, *The Luminous Eye*, 128.

[25] H. Rondet, *The Grace of Christ*, 65–88, especially 70; Z. Alszeghy, *Nova creatura* (Rome: Gregorian University, 1956) 129–157.

[26] J. H. Neyrey, "The Second Epistle of Peter," in *The New Jerome Biblical Commentary*, 1018.

through philosophy, *gnosis,* and the mystery religions, the Christians attain by communion with the being and life of Father, Son, and Holy Spirit, by putting on Christ.[27] In the secular Greek philosophical tradition, divinization is totally dependent on human effort. "No divine help, no grace."[28] A person has only to know the self. In the Scriptures it is wholly dependent on divine promise and free gift, eliciting a free human response. According to the biblical teaching, what is effected by the communion with God is not a distant image but assimilation in some real sense to the divine life so that believers are truly adopted daughters and sons of the Father. As this biblical tradition is appropriated by the Syrians, it does not stand alone but belongs to the nature of creation as manifested in revelation. The Syrian teaching is rooted in the exegesis of the creation/paradise accounts of Genesis, and in the incarnation, baptism, and resurrection.[29]

When treating of divinization, the *Dictionnaire de Spiritualité* devotes extensive sections to the Greek and Latin witness, but there is no section given to the Syrian tradition,[30] a not untypical assumption that when one has looked at the Greeks and the Latins, one has adequately covered the ancient sources, forgetting that there is a whole religious culture of great antiquity expressed in Syriac, a dialect of the language Jesus very likely spoke.

The Trinitarian Cosmology

Cosmology in a trinitarian mode constitutes the prolegomena for Ephrem's view of divinization and Jesus' baptism. The Sun corresponds to the Father, the light to the Son, and the heat to the Spirit: "Behold the image! Son and Father, light and sun,

---

[27] A. J. Festugière, *L'Idéal religieux des Grecs et l'Évangile* (Paris: Gabalda, 1981) 47–53; C. Spicq, *Les Épîtres de Saint Pierre* (Paris: Gabalda, 1966) 212; Bo Reicke, *The Epistles of James, Peter, and Jude* (Garden City: Doubleday, 1964) 153.

[28] Ibid., 52.

[29] Ibid., 128; S. J. Beggiani, *Early Syriac Theology: With Special Reference to the Maronite Tradition* (New York: University Press of America, 1983) 73.

[30] 3:1370–1459.

the Holy Spirit, heat.''[31] Within this trinitarian view he expands
on the relation of the Spirit to creation. The heat of the Spirit
informs the whole of God and the whole of creation: ''The
power of the Spirit's heat resides in everything (the whole of
the created universe), with everything [the Spirit] is whole, yet
entirely [whole] with the One (God), and is not cut off from the
Radiance (Son), being mixed with it, [nor is the Spirit divided]
from the Sun (Father), being mingled with it.''[32] The Spirit in
the Father and the Son. The Spirit, whole and undivided in
God, the Spirit whole and undivided in creation, all warmed by
the same heat. Here is the broad trinitarian and cosmological
background for divinization.

Divinization and the Jordan are the source of Christian baptism. Ephrem sets up the argument in reference to the eternal
begetting of the Son, the incarnation, and ''our Lord's'' baptism in the Jordan—in this treatise he uses this denomination
instead of Jesus or Christ:

"It is He who was begotten of Divinity,
according to His nature,
and of humanity,
which was not according to his nature,
and of his baptism
which was not His habit.''[33]

Here Ephrem uses the abstract ''divinity'' for the Father.[34] The
Son took on humanity, though it was a foreign nature, and
likewise he went down in the Jordan, though this, too, was
alien. Then Ephrem tells of the purpose of this divine largesse:

"So that we might be begotten of humanity,
according to our nature,
and of divinity,
which is not according to our nature,

---

[31] *Hymns on Faith* 73:1; CSCO 155:192.

[32] Ibid., 74:3–4; CSCO 155:194.

[33] *Sermon on Our Lord* 2; CSCO 271:2.

[34] *St. Ephrem the Syrian*, K. McVey, ed. (Washington, D.C.: The Catholic
University of America, 1994) 276, n. 14.

and of the Spirit,
which is not according to our habit.''[35]

The believers' divine birth from the Father, a birth alien to who
they are, a birth of the Spirit given at sacramental baptism, also
alien to human identity, is caught up in the trinitarian dynamics,
as the Father reaches out beyond the divine self to impart
God's life.[36]

Re-clothing Adam with "the Best Garments"

The Syrian teaching relates themes of divinization to the Jordan
experience in a way not true of the Greek and Latin theologies,
with great attention to clothing images. The use of "robe"
imagery is not peculiar to the Syrians but is already found in
Melito of Sardis and widely in other Greek and Latin Christian
authors.[37] Cyril of Jerusalem uses it in a baptismal context.[38] In
the Syrian tradition, it is found already in Aphrahat. He speaks
of clothing oneself in Christ as putting on one's "best garments."[39] Aphrahat can shift the image. He speaks of putting
on the Spirit of Christ. At the baptismal rite the priests call on
the Spirit, and the Spirit "opens the heavens, descends, hovers
over the waters, and those who are being baptized clothe themselves [in the Spirit of Christ]."[40]

But to special effect, Ephrem and Jacob of Serugh use the
image of the robe to bind together the various mysteries of
Christ and the history of salvation, starting with the incarna-

---

[35] *Sermon on Our Lord* 2; CSCO 271:2.

[36] Similar ideas can be found in Ephrem's *Hymns on Virginity 46*; CSCO
224:132–134, and in his *Hymns on Faith* 10 and 18; CSCO 155:33–36; 53–55.
McVey, *St. Ephrem the Syrian*, 276 n. 15. See below.

[37] *On Pascha* 18, 19, 20, 100; Melito of Sardis, *On Pascha*, S. G. Hall, ed.
(Oxford: Clarendon, 1979) 20, 57. Fragment 14; ibid., 81; New Fragment 2:17;
ibid., 92; Brock, *St. Ephrem the Syrian: Hymns on Paradise* 66.

[38] *Mystagogical Catecheses* 3:1; SC 126:118.

[39] *Demonstrations* 9:4; *Patrologia Syriaca* 1:414. M. J. Pierre, in Sources
Chrétiennes, translates the phrase "good garments." 359:476. See E. J.
Duncan, *Baptism in the Demonstrations of Aphraates the Persian Sage*
(Washington, D.C.; The Catholic University of America, 1945) 43–49.

[40] *Demonstrations* 6:14; SC 349:400.

tion.[41] These authors are less well known in the West and they are the focus of these pages, in which I am largely summarizing Brock.[42]

The controlling idea is the image of clothing, either putting on Christ or putting on the Spirit. The New Testament roots are in Galatians 3:27: "As many of you as were baptized into Christ have clothed yourselves with Christ." And in Romans 13:14: "Put on the Lord Jesus Christ." Using this biblical image Ephrem ranges over the history of salvation. He has been speaking of the various moments in Jesus' life when he put on clothing: the swaddling bands in the manger, garments as a young man, in the Jordan when "he put on water," in the grave when he was wrapped in linen bands. Note the central place of the clothing of the Son with humanity at the incarnation. Ephrem continues:

"All these changes did the Merciful One make,
stripping off glory and putting on a body;
for He had devised a way to reclothe Adam
in that glory which he had stripped off.
He was wrapped in swaddling clothes,
corresponding to Adam's leaves;
He put on clothes
in place of Adam's skins;
He was baptized for Adam's sin;
He was embalmed for Adam's death;
He rose and raised Adam up in His glory;
Blessed is He who descended;
put Adam on and ascended."[43]

The lines are determined by the images of Adam and of stripping off and putting on. The Son strips off the divine glory that is properly his, and he puts on a body so that he can clothe the naked Adam who was stripped of divine glory after the Fall. Having put on a body, Christ is wrapped in swaddling clothes. He puts on water in the Jordan for Adam's sin, and in the

[41] Ibid.
[42] "Clothing Metaphors."
[43] *Hymns on the Nativity* 23:13; CSCO 187:109.

tomb was wrapped in linen for Adam's death; he rose from the dead and raised Adam in his glory. In a word, Christ went down and put on Adam's nature as a garment so Adam could put on glory. With Adam in hand the Son then gloriously ascended.

Obviously, the clothing image works both ways. If the Christians put on Christ in baptism, it is because Christ first put on humanity in the incarnation. Ephrem writes with awe of creation, but with even greater awe of God taking on human nature: "What took place later on [at the incarnation] surpassed what happened at Creation: He did not just create man, He actually put man on."[44] Before the majesty of this mystery Ephrem bows down in wonder and praise.

When treating of Jesus' baptism, Ephrem moves from the Jordan event to Christian baptism: "Because the Spirit descended in his baptism [in the Jordan], the Spirit has been given [to believers] through his baptism."[45] Jesus comes to John to be baptized, but, be it noted, Jesus already has the Spirit and brings the Spirit with him when he approaches John for baptism. This he does so "he might mix the Spirit, who cannot be seen, with the visible water, so that those whose bodies perceive the wetness of the water might perceive in their minds the gift of the Spirit."[46]

When the Spirit "Mingles" the Spirit Divinizes

The Syriacs use the words *mazzeg* or *hlat*, having no apparent biblical origin, meaning "mingling." Also Syriac writers use them to express the mingling of the Spirit with the eucharistic bread and the wine, and the baptized themselves.[47] The play in the strophe just cited is on invisible Spirit with visible water, and the mingling of the two. In Ephrem, Jesus mixes the Spirit

---

[44] *Hymns of Nisibis* 69:11; CSCO 103:99.

[45] *Commentary on the Diatessaron* 4:3; SC 121:95.

[46] *Sermon on Our Lord* 50; CSCO 270:52. *The Teaching of St. Gregory* has a similar formulation: "Then the invisible Spirit opened again the womb by visible water, preparing the newly born fledglings for the regeneration of the font [Titus 3:5], to clothe all with robes of light who would be born once more." Thomson, 89.

[47] Brock, *Holy Spirit in the Syrian Baptismal Tradition* 7, 8.

with the water, leaving the Spirit in the water so Christians can
go down into the water there to put on "the robe of the
Spirit,"[48] the mingling between the Spirit and the believer.
These are images on interior transformation.

When the Son brings the Spirit to the waters of the Jordan,
the Son brings light, warmth, and fire, all of which are shared
in the process of divinization: "When the light (Son) withdrew
towards its Source (Father), it left its warmth here below: so
our Lord left the Holy Spirit with his disciples."[49] The engage-
ment here is specifically trinitarian.

In a different context we noted the role of Fire and Spirit. It
needs to be recalled here in the context of divinization. In a
hymn addressed to Christ, Fire and Spirit effected the incarnation: "See! Fire and Spirit and in the womb of her who bore
you."[50] The same Fire/Spirit is present in Jesus' baptism: "Fire
and Spirit are in the river in which you were baptized."[51]
Because of the relation of Christ's baptism to ours, "Fire and
Spirit are in our baptism."[52] Then Ephrem extends the same
theme to the Eucharist: "In the Bread and the Cup is Fire and
the Holy Spirit."[53] Or more expansively: "In your Bread there
is hidden the Spirit who is not consumed, in your Wine there
dwells the Fire that is not drunk: the Spirit is in your Bread,
the Fire in your Wine, a majestic wonder, which our lips have
received."[54] Here Ephrem links incarnation to the Jordan, Christian baptism, and the Eucharist, in a pneumatology of some

[48] Ibid.
[49] Hymns on Faith 73:18, 19; CSCO 155:193, 194.
[50] Ibid., 10:17; CSCO 155:35, 36.
[51] Ibid.
[52] Ibid.
[53] Ibid.
[54] Ibid., 73:8; CSCO 155:34. Not in the context of Jesus' baptism, but in relation to Pentecost, The Teaching of St. Gregory uses the fire image to speak
of the Spirit, fire, and joy. The Spirit fills the elect "with the cups of joy
of the Spirit" so that they might be "illuminated by the power of the fiery
Spirit . . . becoming the cupbearers of the whole world," 507; Thomson,
117, 118. Referring to the apostles on the day of Pentecost, the same text
says: "[The apostles] drank of the fire of the Spirit of joy, and became
cupbearers throughout the world. They hastened and served delightful
drink in the cups of joyful sweetness to the worthy at the wedding banquet of the kingdom," 508; Thomson, 118.

force.[55] Fire and Spirit are consistently the instruments of divine indwelling and of divine change, interior transformation.

The Adamic History

The broader patterns of the Syriac teaching on divinization are defined by an Adam/Christ typology, both an identification and a non-identification between the Adam of Genesis (First Adam) and Christ (Second Adam).[56] Brock identifies four main scenes in the Syriac Adamic view of history.[57]

Scene One: Building on the Jewish speculation concerning "garments of skin" in Genesis 3:21, Adam and Eve in paradise before the Fall are presented as clothed in "robes of glory," or "robes of light."

Scene Two: After the Fall, Adam and Eve are stripped of their "robes of glory/light." Unlike the Greeks, who loved to speculate on the nature of the clothes with which God clothed Adam and Eve in paradise, the Syrians were little interested in theoretical considerations and were, at this level, more concerned with what they took off.

Scene Three: To rectify this lamentable state of nakedness of Adam/humankind brought about by the Fall, Divinity itself "puts on Adam" when God "puts on a body." The specific purpose of the incarnation is to reclothe humankind in "the robe of glory." The incarnation is an act of glory. Further, the

---

[55] P. G. Saber, *La Théologie Baptismale de Saint Éphrem* (Kaslik [Lebanon]: University of Kaslik, 1974) 104, remarks with surprise "that Christ does not fill a very efficacious role in the baptismal mystery [of Christian baptism]; one would want to admit that he institutes baptism by his baptism, that is to say, he gives the Spirit, but apart from that, he seems to disappear to leave the Spirit in charge of realizing and applying the baptismal work. The Christian who receives baptism has part in the Spirit, but what is there of Christ in this? . . . The difficulty is rendered even more grave. In speaking of the Eucharist, Ephrem has the air of understanding this less as the body of Christ than as a habitation of the Spirit."

[56] But in Aphrahat, Christ is the First Adam and the Adam of Genesis the Second Adam. See Cramer, *Der Geist Gottes und des Menschen in frühsyrischer Theologie*, 73, 74.

[57] "Clothing Metaphors," XI, 12.

incarnation itself is an ongoing mystery, having three main staging posts: nativity, baptism in the Jordan, and descent into Sheol/resurrection, linked to three successive wombs: the womb of Mary, the womb of the Jordan, and the womb of Sheol, a topic we have already touched on.[58]

Scene Four: Of central importance to this Adamic view of history is the baptism of Jesus, or the descent into the womb of the Jordan. Jesus, as the definitive Adam, goes down into the water precisely to deposit there "the robe of glory/light" thus making it possible for the naked Adam/humankind to descend into the waters to put it on. In this way the "robe of glory" lost in paradise by Adam is reclaimed and put on by the Christian in the baptismal font. Adam is both the individual of the Genesis account and a corporate personality for the whole of humanity. This individual/corporate Adam finds in the Jordan the glory that had been his among the trees of paradise; he took the glory from the water of the Jordan which Jesus had deposited there, put it on, clothed himself in it, and ascended gloriously out of the water.[59]

Adam Steals Divinity

Ephrem's presupposition is that had Adam and Eve not sinned they would have had all their desires fulfilled: they would have eaten of the Tree of Life and of the Tree of Knowledge; they would have possessed infallible knowledge, and they would have "acquired divinity in humanity," that is, they would have been divinized in their proper humanity.[60] With this background in mind, Ephrem states the thesis: "The Exalted One knew that Adam had desired to become a god, so he sent his Son, who put on Adam in order to give him his desire."[61]

The divinization Adam tried to steal comes about by the incarnation, when the Son clothed himself with a full humanity. "Divinity flew down and descended to raise and draw up humanity. The Son has made beautiful the servant's deformity,

---

[58] Brock, "Baptismal Themes in the Writings of Jacob of Serugh," 326.
[59] *Hymns on Epiphany* 12:1; CSCO 187:173.
[60] *Commentary on Genesis* 2:24; CSCO 153:29.
[61] *Hymns of Nisibis* 69:12; CSCO 240:100.

and he has become a god, *just as he desired.*"[62] What Adam
tried to steal in first paradise is now given his thieving heart.
Though by no means peculiar to the Syrian tradition, references
to clothing are especially abundant in Syriac sources. Through a
series of clothing images, including "robe(s) of light," "robe of
glory," "garment of regeneration," Aphrahat, Ephrem, and
Jacob of Serugh point to the divine life communicated through
the baptism of Jesus at the Jordan.

"The robe of glory" and other clothing images form a con-
tinuum, touching incarnation, the Jordan event, descent into
Sheol, the ascension (possibly the transfiguration), resurrection,
and informing Christian baptism, the Eucharist, binding anthropology, christology, Christian life, ecclesiology, and eschatology.[63] Clothing images are pervasive.

Putting on Light from Within

The authors describe the robe in a variety of ways. Ephrem sees
the baptism of Jesus as God "mingling in," divinity taking on
human experience from within.[64] Jesus himself is the Light,
"the Brilliance," "the Daystar in the river," who dazzles a
series of what might be called "economic places," namely, the
river Jordan, the tomb, and the locus of the ascension.[65] In
Ephrem, "the river in which Christ was baptized put on Light
from within, and so did [Mary's] body, in which he resided,
gleam from within."[66] Ephrem returns to the image of brilliance
or splendor in relation to the robe: "Swiftly Adam lost the robe
of brilliance; swiftly you [candidates for baptism] have put on
the robe of splendor."[67]

The Teaching of St. Gregory says that because the Jordan contains the splendor of Christ's light, "the invisible Spirit . . .
clothes all [candidates for baptism] with robes of light" at the

---

[62] *Hymns on Virginity* 48:17, 18. Brock, *St. Ephrem the Syrian,* 72, 73. Emphasis added.

[63] Ibid.

[64] *Hymns on Epiphany* 4:1; CSCO 187:142.

[65] *Hymns on the Church* 36:5; CSCO 199:88.

[66] Ibid.

[67] *Hymns on Epiphany* 6:9; CSCO 187:148.

bath of new birth.[68] For Jacob of Serugh, all who come to baptism receive "a garment, wholly of light . . . woven with fire and Spirit,"[69] "a garment of living fire."[70] In a delightful formulation, Jacob has the making of the robe for the baptismal candidates the result of the combined efforts of the Trinity: "The Father prepared the robe, the Son wove it, the Spirit cut it [from the loom], and you went down [into the waters] and put it on in divine fashion."[71] The industry of the divine weavers and garment makers results in believers putting on the robe, wholly made of light and glory, in no ordinary way. This robe divinizes its bearer.

Christ Deposits the Robe of Glory in the Jordan

Through sin, Adam himself became lost and forfeited the robe of glory. To find Adam and restore the robe, divinity itself "puts on Adam" by putting on a body at the incarnation.

By the descent of Jesus into the womb of Mary, the Son becomes the Second Adam, the Ultimate Adam, the Definitive Adam. At the descent of Jesus into the Jordan, as the Second Adam, he places the robe of glory in the water so the Adam (individual and corporate) could go down and recover it: "Christ came to baptism, he went down and placed in the baptismal water the robe of glory, to be there for Adam, who had lost it."[72]

As we shall see, a dimension of Christ's descent into the Jordan is his descent into Sheol to look for the lost Adam to

---

[68] 412; Thomson, 89. Gregory Nazianzus also has catechumens putting on "robes of light" at baptism. *Oration* 40:25; SC 358:254.

[69] Bedjan, 1:208.

[70] Ibid., 1:196.

[71] Ibid., 1:211.

[72] Ibid., 3:593. Other formulations by Jacob of the same thought: "[Christ] placed in the womb of baptism the robe of glory." Ibid., 1:168; "Christ wove garments of life for Adam in the baptismal water." Ibid., 5:681; "Baptism gives back to Adam the robe of glory which the serpent had stolen from him among the trees," Ibid., 1:197. Earlier, Ephrem had developed the same thought: "[Christ] came to find Adam who had got lost, and to return him in the garment of light to Eden." *Hymns on Virginity* 16:9; CSCO 224:55.

give him the robe of glory. Jacob has Christ explain to John the Baptist why he seeks baptism at his hands: "I am trying to find the lost Adam; let me go down and look for Adam, the fair image."[73] Jacob runs together the descent into the Jordan and the descent into Sheol, where Adam is sometimes identified as a lost pearl that has to be recovered.[74]

As we shall see, the going down into Sheol takes place not in historical time but in sacred time, not in geographical space but in sacred space. Fusing the descent into the Jordan with going down into Sheol is a way of declaring that the process of incarnation affects all historical time, all geographical space, wherever Adam is lost.

At Christian baptism the candidate goes down into the waters to take up the robe of glory which Adam had lost, and which Christ had recovered and deposited in the Jordan. In an Epiphany hymn (therefore used at the celebration of the Jordan event), Adam is both an individual and a corporate personality, including the catechumens: "In baptism Adam finds that glory which had been his among the trees of Paradise; he went down and took it from the water, put it on, and went up and was held in honor in it."[75] Ephrem directly addresses the catechumens: "Go down, my brothers, and put on the Holy Spirit from baptism."[76] Aphrahat, Ephrem's older compatriot—even less affected by Greek culture—also has the baptismal candidates take the robe of the Spirit from the water and re-vest themselves as Adam was before the Fall: "By baptism, in fact, we have received the Spirit of the Messiah; at the hour when the priests invoke the Spirit, [the Spirit] opens the heavens, descends, and hovers over the water, and those who are being baptized, re-clothe themselves with the Spirit."[77]

Yet the Jordan event also has a more pronounced ecclesiological dimension. The baptism of Jesus is seen as the betrothal of

[73] Bedjan, 1:177.
[74] Ibid., 2:599.
[75] Ephrem, *Hymns on Epiphany* 12:1; CSCO 187:173. Brock, *The Luminous Eye*, 73. "At his baptism He vivifies all baptized by having Himself received baptism." *The Teaching of St. Gregory* 414; Thomson, 90.
[76] *Hymns on Epiphany* 5:1; CSCO 187:145.
[77] *Demonstrations* 6:14; SC 349:400.

the Church and Christ, with the Church as "the bride of light" and John the Baptist as the best man.[78] Jacob sees the Church at the incarnation and the Jordan in terms of clothing: "Christ put on the Church in the virgin's womb, and she [Church] put him on in the waters of baptism."[79] A mutuality of putting on typifies the relationship between Christ and the Church. A text from the Syrian Orthodox Fenquitho (breviary) has the Church speaking: "He put us on and we put him on."[80] This is what the later tradition will call "the admirable exchange" (O admirabile commercium). Because the robe Christ recovered is the garment Adam had in paradise, the putting on of that robe at baptism, according to the Maronite rite, is an entry "into paradise, that is, the believing Church."[81]

---

[78] Brock, "Baptismal Themes in the Writings of Jacob of Serugh" in *Symposium Syriacum 1976*, 328.

[79] Bedjan, 3:288.

[80] Quoted in Brock, "Clothing Metaphors," XI:18.

[81] *Codex Liturgicus Ecclesiae Universae, 2 De Baptismo,* J. A. Assemani, ed., 13 vols. (Rome: Apud Angelum Rotilium, 1749–1766) 2:331.

Chapter Ten

The Cosmic Jordan and
the Robe of Glory—
Divinization and Eschatology

Baptism and death/resurrection are usually linked through the use of Romans 6:4, 5:

"We have been buried with him by baptism into death, so that, just as Christ was raised from the dead by the glory of the Father, so we too might walk in newness of life. For if we have been united with him in a death like his, we will certainly be united with him in a resurrection like his."

But this view, joining Christ's death to the believer in baptism, "seems to have faded" from the memory of the early Church.[1] It was not Jesus' death but his baptism that was the primary model for Christian initiation. Very likely the demise of the baptism of Jesus as the primary model was in process by the time of Cyril of Jerusalem, about the last quarter of the fourth century.[2] In Antioch the Romans text, with the element of death,

---

[1] J.N.D. Kelly, *Early Christian Doctrines*, 5th ed. (New York: Harper & Row, 1976) 194.

[2] G. Kretschmar, "Recent Research on Christian Initiation," in *Studia Liturgica* 12 (1977) 92. However, B. Varghese remarks that there is only one

caught the religious imagination only toward the end of that period.[3] But from the beginning, the baptismal paradigm at Antioch was the Jordan event—a birth, not a death event. There is little hint of the Pauline teaching of baptism as participation in death and resurrection of Jesus.[4]

So it is not surprising that Ephrem, belonging to an earlier age, is more influenced by John 3:5 ("No one can enter the kingdom of God without being born of water and Spirit"), and therefore conceives baptism as a birth event, relating "the robe of glory" to the resurrection without reference to the Romans text. When Christians go down into the waters to pick up the "robe of glory" deposited there by Christ, they are proleptically being clothed with the resurrection "robe of glory."[5]

The Jordan as Stress-Point Between Two Edens

Though the putting on of the robe is real, it is incomplete; its full glory is revealed only at the end of time, at the general resurrection. So the Christian baptism places one in eschatologi-

---

reference to the Romans text in the *Catechetical Lectures* of Cyril (3:12), while he has many references to the baptism of Jesus in the Jordan. *Les Onctions Baptismales dans la Tradition Syrienne*, 69.

[3] E. C. Ratcliff, "The Old Syrian Baptismal Tradition and Its Resettlement Under the Influence of Jerusalem in the Fourth Century," *Liturgical Studies* (London: SPCK, 1976) 142; G. Winkler, "The History of the Syriac Pre-baptismal Anointing in the Light of the Earliest Armenian Sources," in *Symposium Syriacum 1976* (Rome: Oriental Institute, 1978) 317-324; idem, "The Original Meaning of the Pre-Baptismal Anointing and its Implications," 24-45; idem, "Zur frühchristlichen Tauftradition in Syrien und Armenien unter Einbezug der Taufe Jesu," 281-306.

[4] Brock, *Holy Spirit in the Syrian Baptismal Tradition*, 38. Some historians find the Pauline view of Romans 6:4 in the Epistle of Barnabas. While Barnabas (11) insists that the remission of sins obtained in baptism has its source in the sacrifice accomplished by the death on the cross, the idea expressed in Romans 6:4 is quite different. There is nothing about dying and rising with Christ in Barnabas' text. "This idea is totally foreign to the conception of Barnabas." Benoit, *Le Baptême Chrétien au Second Siècle*, 38.

[5] Ephrem, *Letter to Publius* 12; Brock, "Ephrem's Letter to Publius," *Muséon* 89 (1976) 284. The same link between baptism and resurrection without reference to Romans is at least twice embedded in East Syrian rites. See Brock, "The Epiklesis in the Antiochene Baptismal Ordines," in *Symposium Syriacum 1972*, 207, 208.

cal tension, the stress-point between what is given now, and its full flowering in paradise. While the paradise lost and paradise regained stand in intimate relationship, what is regained is more glorious than what was lost. In paradise regained, God will give, with greater liberality, the divinity, which Adam and Eve tried to steal from the Tree of Life.[6]

In an Epiphany hymn attributed to Ephrem, the poet is moving back and forth in the freedom of sacred rather than chronological time, stating this eschatological tension without excessive concern for sequence:

"In baptism Adam found [again] that former glory of the garden. Christ ascended [out of the water of the Jordan], and took him [Adam] out of the water, clothed himself [Christ] in him [Adam, a reference to the incarnation] and [Christ], ascended on high and with him [Adam], is glorified. . . . Instead of leaves from the trees, he [Christ] clothed them [Adam and Eve] with glory from the water."[7]

The glory the baptized takes from the Jordan when one descends into the water is the glory of the Garden of Eden, and is the glory one ascends with into the eschatological paradise. The baptized stands poised between "two" paradises that are in fact one.

Speaking directly to Eve, who after the Fall had her robe of glory stripped from her, Ephrem says "in Eden [paradise future] women shall be clothed in light, resembling you [Eve in Eden of paradise past]."[8] The robe of glory belongs to the Genesis paradise of Adam and Eve at the beginning of time, but also to the restored paradise of Adam and Eve at the end of time, the eschatological fulfillment. This two-directional orientation, to paradise past and to paradise future, is succinctly expressed by Ephrem: "Among the saints their nakedness is clothed with glory, none is clad with leaves or stands ashamed, for they have found, through our Lord, the robe that belongs to

---

[6] Brock, "Clothing Metaphors," XI:12, 13.
[7] *Hymns on Epiphany* 12:1; CSCO 187:173.
[8] *Hymns on Faith* 83:2; CSCO 155:216.

Adam and Eve."[9] The robe of glory received in paradise future is the same as the robe of glory of paradise past, only, as noted, far more glorious. When the Christian goes down into the Jordan, that is, into Christ's baptism, to take up the robe of glory Christ deposited there, the Christian takes on the tension of a realized eschatology, already and not yet. Baptism is the wedding feast of Christ and the Church, with the catechumens as the guests, who have been given a wedding garment, which, not surprisingly, is the robe of glory.[10] The wedding robe is to be kept spotless until one enters fully into the eschatological paradise.

In a quite different context, Philoxenus interprets the baptism of Jesus as the beginning of all that the Father intended when the Son took flesh, including the final consumption: "The return of all to God, that gathering up and the making new, that everything might become in him and he in all: these mysteries commenced at [Jesus'] baptism."[11] Eschatology begins at the Jordan.

The Cosmic Jordan Flows from Paradise into Paradise

The theology of the robe as an instrument of divinization becomes linked with the Jordan as the cosmic river having its origins in the paradise of Genesis and emptying into the eschatological paradise. The tradition belongs to the mystagogic exegesis of the Jordan.

In the *Life of Adam and Eve*, probably written in Hebrew by a Jewish author between 100 B.C. and 200 B.C.E., Adam and Eve discuss the penitence they should impose upon themselves. Adam decides that Eve should stand in the Tigris River up to her neck for thirty-seven days, while he will do the same in the Jordan River for forty days. The Jordan is asked to summon all living creatures, to witness to Adam's penance and to weep with him: "I tell, you water of the Jordan, mourn with me and gather to me all swimming creatures which are in you and let

[9] *Hymns on Paradise* 6:9; CSCO 175:20.
[10] Ephrem, *Hymns of Nisibis* 43:21; Brock, "Clothing Metaphors," XI:19, 20.
[11] *Commentary on Matthew and Luke* 11; CSCO 393:9.

them surround me, and so lament together with me."[12] In a play on the Joshua narrative (3:13-17), the Jordan stands still: "At once all the living beings came and surrounded him (Adam) and the water of the Jordan stood, its current not moving, from that hour."[13] So the Jordan, universal and cosmic in character, is placed within the paradise of Genesis where it is the cosmic witness, indeed participant, in Adam's repentance.[14]

Hippolytus (ca. 170–ca. 236) records the Gnostic tradition of a cosmic ocean—borrowed from Homer[15]—that is identified with the Jordan. This cosmic ocean/Jordan flows out of the middle of paradise and surrounds the whole domain of Eden. The ocean/Jordan "flows forth" from paradise and "flows back" into paradise.[16] The river has a negative aspect as boundary: it inhibits the children of Israel from leaving Egypt. In addition it has a positive aspect: the instrument of communication with paradise, indeed, bearing believers into the Promised Land. In the Gnostic tradition Hippolytus records, "the great Jordan" is placed in relation to Jesus' words that "what is born of the flesh is flesh, and what is born of the Spirit is spirit" (John 3:6), a baptismal text.[17] The cosmic Jordan is the river of baptism.

Odes of Solomon—"My Crown Is Living"

In the Odes of Solomon the theme of the cosmic Jordan is joined to the robe of glory. No scholarly agreement exists on the original language of the Odes. Some think it was Hebrew;[18] many others incline toward the Syriac,[19] while C. Kannengiesser

[12] Life of Adam and Eve 6 and 7; Charlesworth, The Old Testament Pseudepigrapha, 2:258–260.

[13] Ibid.

[14] Lundberg in La Typologie Baptismale, 146, interprets The Epistle of Barnabas 6:8, 13 ("Enter into the land flowing with milk and honey, and rule over it") as referring to the Jordan. Though the author treats of baptism (11:1-8), the reference is too generic to be convincing.

[15] Odyssey 24:9f.

[16] Hippolytus, Philosophoumena 5:7; PG 16/3:3137-3140. The text is found among Origen's works because it was formerly attributed to him.

[17] Ibid.; PG 16/3:3140.

[18] J. Carmignac, "Recherches sur la langue originelle des Odes de Salomon," in Revue de Qumrân 4 (1963) 429-432.

[19] A. Vööbus, "Neues Licht zur Frage der Originalsprache der Oden Salomos," Muséon 75 (1962) 275-290, especially 290; Brock, Holy Spirit in the

seems certain the language of composition was Greek, but coming from a Judeo-Christian community in Syria sometime in the second half of the second century.[20] They are mystical poetic compositions with sacramental interests. Whether J. H. Bernard goes too far when he contends that "they are baptismal hymns intended for public worship, either for catechumens or for those recently baptized."[21] At least they are much preoccupied with baptism and the Eucharist. Unlike many other compositions of this genre, they are not taken up with disasters, but are filled with newfound joy. They rejoice in the experience of the Messiah, in the triumph of the risen Christ, in their acknowledgment of him as living Lord and Savior.[22]

"They who trusted in me sought me, because I am the living.
Then I arose and am with them,
And will speak by their mouths."[23]

The *Odes* exult in the sense of God's presence:

"Abundantly helpful to me was the thought of the Lord,
And His everlasting fellowship.
I was lifted up in the light,
And I passed before Him.
And I was constantly near Him,
While praising and confessing Him."[24]

Paradise begins now, here on earth, and is not a promise of a distant future. The images are of some kind of immediate experience and transformation.

"And He (the Lord) caused His immortal life to dwell in One,

Syrian Baptismal Tradition 27; Charlesworth, *The Old Testament Pseudepigrapha,* 2:726.

[20] "Odes of Solomon," in *Encyclopedia of the Early Church,* 2 vols. (New York: Oxford University, 1992) 2:609.

[21] J. H. Bernard, *The Odes of Solomon* (Cambridge: Cambridge University, 1912) 42.

[22] Charlesworth, *The Old Testament Pseudepigrapha,* 2:728.

[23] *Ode* 42:5, 6; J. H. Charlesworth, *The Odes of Solomon* (Chico: Scholars, 1977) 145.

[24] *Ode* 21:5–7; Charlesworth, *Odes,* 88.

And permitted one to proclaim the fruit of His peace.[25]

"Then I was crowned by my God,
And my crown is living."[26]

As we shall see below in the chapter on Sheol, *Ode* 24 makes
specific reference to Jesus' baptism in the Jordan, linking it to
the risen Christ's descent into hell. This makes it likely that in a
baptismal context the reference in *Ode* 11 to "the river of gladness" issuing out of and flowing back into paradise refers to
the Jordan flowing out of the Genesis paradise and into the
eschatological paradise.[27]

"For the Most High circumcised me by His Holy Spirit,
Then He uncovered my inward being towards Him,
And filled me with His love. . . .
And speaking waters touched my lips
From the fountain of the Lord generously,
And so I drank and became intoxicated,
From the living water that does not die."[28]

Then paradise is described in luxuriant images:

"And He took me to His Paradise,
Wherein is the wealth of the Lord's pleasure,
((I behold blooming and fruit-bearing trees,
And self-grown was their crown.
Their branches were sprouting
And their fruits were shining.
From an immortal land (were) their roots.
And the river of gladness was irrigating them,
And round about them in the land of eternal life.))
Then I worshipped the Lord because of His magnificence.
And I said, Blessed, O Lord, are they
Who are planted in Thy land,
And who have a place in Thy Paradise;

[25] *Ode* 10:2; Charlesworth, *Odes* 48.

[26] *Ode* 17:1; Charlesworth, *Odes* 74.

[27] T. M. Finn, *Early Christian Baptism: Italy, North Africa and Egypt* (Collegeville: The Liturgical Press, 1992) 26. Bernard, *Odes of Solomon*, thinks that
Ode 11 is baptismal. *The Odes of Solomon*, 72–74.

[28] *Ode* 11:2, 6, 7; Charlesworth, *Odes* 52.

And who grow in the growth of Thy trees,
And have passed from darkness into light. . . .''[29]

In the final strophes the text returns to the waters of the river
and the glory of paradise:

''((Blessed are the workers of Thy waters,)) . . .
Indeed, there is much room in Thy Paradise.
And there is nothing in it which is barren
But everything is filled with fruit.
Glory be to Thee, O God, the delight of Paradise forever.''[30]

It is in this framework that *Ode* 11 picks up the image of clothing as a way of speaking of stripping off the garments of fool-
ishness and putting on the garment of light, that is,
divinization:

''And I turned towards the Most High, my God,
And was enriched by His favours.
And I rejected the folly cast upon the earth,
And stripped it off and cast it from me.
And the Lord renewed me with His garment,
And possessed me by His light.
And from above He gave me immortal rest.''[31]

This is not an isolated use of the garment as an instrument of
divinization.

''I put on incorruption through His name,
And took off corruption by His grace.''[32]

''I put off darkness,
And put on light.''[33]

''I was covered with the covering of Thy Spirit,
And I removed from me my garments of skin.''[34]

[29] *Ode* 11:16-19; Charlesworth, *Odes* 52, 53.
[30] *Ode* 11:22-24; Charlesworth, *Odes* 53.
[31] *Ode* 11:9-12; Charlesworth, *Odes* 52.
[32] *Ode* 15:8; Charlesworth, *Odes* 68.
[33] *Ode* 21:3; Charlesworth, *Odes* 88.
[34] *Ode* 25:8; Charlesworth, *Odes* 102.

"Joy is for the holy ones.
And who shall put it on but they alone?"[35]

The vigor and intensity of these images is a way of asserting that "immortality is geographically here and chronologically now."[36] In a word:

"Give me yourself,
So that I may also give you myself . . .
For in the will of the Lord is your life,
And His purpose is eternal life,
And your perfection is incorruptible."[37]

"Indeed he who is joined to Him who is immortal
Truly shall be immortal."[38]

Some of the *Odes of Solomon* seem to stand in the tradition of the cosmic Jordan in which Jesus was baptized. Here the robe of glory, more specifically the robe of incorruption, is not promised to the faithful in the future but already clothes them from within with divine life, girds them with joy and immortality this side of death. The heightened Johannine vocabulary (light, life, truth) conveys the immediacy of the experience.

*The Jordan Flows Out of Paradise Past
and Into Paradise Future*

The relation of the cosmic Jordan to the baptism of Jesus, to paradise and to the clothing as an image of divinization, is more explicit in a short passage from Gregory of Nyssa's *Against Those Who Baptize in a Different Manner.*[39] Gregory has been warning against treating matters of grace as one does business affairs and recreation. "For you have given much time to pleasure, take leisure also for philosophy."[40] In this context

[35] *Ode* 23:1; Charlesworth, *Odes* 94.
[36] Charlesworth, *The Old Testament Pseudepigrapha*, 2:731.
[37] *Ode* 9:2, 4; Charlesworth, *Odes* 45, 46.
[38] *Ode* 3:8; Charlesworth, *Odes* 19. "His possession is immortal life, And those who receive it are incorruptible." *Ode* 40:6; Charlesworth, *Odes* 138.
[39] PG 46:415–432.
[40] Ibid.; PG 46:419.

philosophy is contemplation. He then introduces the clothing metaphor: "Put off the old man, like a filthy garment, shameful, full of defilement from a multitude of sins. . . . Receive the clothing of immortality which Christ has laid out and extends to you. Do not refuse the gift so that you may not insult the one who has given it."[41] Then he introduces the Jordan: "Hasten, O man, to my Jordan. John is not calling, but Christ. For the river of grace is running everywhere."[42] Christ is the one who invites catechumens to enter the waters of the Jordan, cosmic in extension. "It [the Jordan] does not have its source in Palestine in order to pour into the neighboring sea."[43] Unlike other rivers in the Holy Land, the Jordan empties into the Dead Sea but has its source someplace outside of Palestine. If its source were in Palestine, the Jordan would be like all other rivers, limited in its source, limited in its extension. "Rather it encompasses the whole world."[44] Its source is the universalism of paradise. (Gregory may be using the Greek Homeric cosmic ocean one meets in Hippolytus to speak of the cosmic Jordan.) "It [the Jordan] flows into Paradise."[45] So the Jordan flows out of paradise and into paradise.

To exalt the Jordan, Gregory then expands on the contrast between it and the four rivers in paradise: "It [the Jordan] flows opposite to the four rivers that flow out of there [paradise past], and it carries along things much more precious into paradise [future] than those which were brought out from there [paradise past—by the four rivers]."[46] The Jordan brings into paradise future what is more priceless than what the four rivers bring out of paradise past. The four rivers bring out "sweet spices, things that grow in the land, and the produce of the earth."[47] Unlike other rivers, "the Jordan brings men, begotten of the Spirit, [into paradise]."[48] The paradise past and paradise

41 Ibid.
42 Ibid.
43 Ibid.
44 Ibid.
45 Ibid.
46 Ibid.
47 Ibid.
48 Ibid.

future must not be pressed, because the paradise future is already now.

This can be seen when Gregory introduces the image of a person drawing off water from the Jordan, as in irrigation, to water the land. "Wherever you might drain [the Jordan], it irrigates the whole earth."[49] To break into the flow of the Jordan does not limit its expanse. The cosmic Jordan waters the whole world. "It does not exhaust the flow by being divided into parts."[50] This practice of draining the Jordan into irrigation channels to irrigate the great expanse of the world also does not stem or deplete the flow of the waters. Why? "For it [the Jordan] has a rich source, Christ, and it flows from him."[51] The universal Christ is the source of the universal Jordan. Here is the identification of the Jordan with the Word made flesh that is met with in Origen.[52] "It [the Jordan] makes the whole world a sea."[53] If the cosmic Jordan is universal in its source in paradise and in the universal Christ, it is again universal because it spreads over the whole earth and empties into the universal paradise. The Jordan is a cosmic sea making salvation available to all.

In another homily, *On the Baptism of Christ*, Gregory returns to these themes. Like Origen he singles out the Jordan. Both "the excellency of Carmel" and "the glory of Lebanon" are transferred to the river Jordan.[54] The Jordan is an instrument of universalism. "For the Jordan alone of all rivers, receiving in itself the first-fruits of sanctification and benediction, conveyed in its channel to the whole world, as in a self-contained source, the grace of baptism."[55] Because the Jordan is cosmic, any water can become baptismal water. The cosmic Jordan in its relationship to the baptism of Christ moves the Christian life to an ultimate fulfillment.

---

[49] Ibid.
[50] Ibid.
[51] Ibid. I thank Knute Anderson for help with this text.
[52] *Commentary on John* 6:42; SC 157:296, 298.
[53] *Against Those Who Baptize in a Different Manner*; PG 46:420.
[54] *On the Baptism of Christ*; PG 46:593.
[55] Ibid.; PG 46:592.

Chapter Eleven

The Descent into the Jordan and the Descent into Hell

A not very extensive tradition exists associating the baptism of Jesus with the belief that Christ after his death descended into the lower regions of the earth, or "descended into hell," as the Apostles' Creed puts it. Belief in the *descensus* evidently surfaced in various places, possibly independently of one another. In Asia Minor and especially in Syria it appeared very early, but is also found in Rome.[1]

Before commenting on the relation of the two mysteries to one another, it is important to understand first what the purpose of the descent of the risen Christ into hell or Sheol is. Many understand it as referring to the liberating of Adam, the patriarchs and prophets, and the just of the Old Testament. Or as one of the Christian traditions has it, the victorious Christ invades the kingdom of evil. In this tradition the purpose of Christ's *descensus* is to enter the lair of Satan and overthrow him, the Lord of Death, in his own domain. A variety of motives were assigned to the *descensus*.[2]

The Old Testament understanding of Sheol is broad. Sheol is the name most commonly used to refer to the abode of the

---

[1] W. Bieder, *Die Vorstellung von der Höllenfahrt Jesu Christi* (Zürich: Zwingli, 1949) 198, 199.

[2] Bieder sums up the research on the motives for the descent. Ibid., 198–209.

dead, occurring some sixty-six times in the Hebrew Scriptures, though the word is not found in any of the cognate languages. Typically it is somewhere to which one "goes down" or "descends" (Num 16:30: Job 7:9), and represents the lowest place imaginable (Deut 32:22; Isa 7:11). Often it is associated with water images (Jonah 2:36). Darkness is a key characteristic (Job 17:13), but both the righteous and unrighteous dwell there. In a word, the good and evil of life cease; what continues is shadowy non-specific existence.[3]

In the New Testament there are still remnants of the Old Testament conviction that "the abyss," the depths of the waters, are the abode of demonic forces (Luke 8:31; Rev 9:1; 17:8; 20:1). Some in the early Church thought that Jesus himself hinted at the existence of Sheol in his prophecy that the Son of Man would spend three days and three nights in the heart of the earth (Matt 12:39). In the early reflections on the biblical text, Peter's transference of Psalm 16:8 ("For you do not give me up to Sheol, or let your faithful one see the Pit") to Christ (Acts 2:27-31) was taken to refer to Sheol.[4] In modern times Ernst Käsemann recognizes that in Romans 10:6, 7, Paul for the first time in the New Testament joins Christ's ascension to his descent into "the abyss."[5]

Why Did Christ Descend into Sheol?

As J. Chaine, Friedrich Loofs, and J.N.D. Kelly have pointed out that by the second century, the descent of Christ into Sheol is a

---

[3] J. H. Bernard, "The Baptism of Christ and the Descent into Hades," in *The Odes of Solomon* (Cambridge: Cambridge University, 1912) 32-39 (Texts and Studies 3).

[4] Kelly, *Early Christian Creeds*, 379.

[5] Käsemann, *Commentary on Romans*, 288. A comprehensive study of the history of exegesis of 1 Peter 3:19 is Reicke, *The Disobedient Spirits and Christian Baptism*. Regarding the earliest interpretation, he concludes: "If any theory is to be regarded as specially strong because of being relatively older and of its greater frequency, it is probably the one that presumes the conversion of the 'spirits' in the time before the coming of Christ, for this theory can . . . be found already in Hippolytus and the Latin and Syrian translations of the Bible, and it distinguishes in general the interpretation of the modern Roman Catholic Church. But this circumstance alone does not in any way convince us that this theory expresses the original meaning of the text." Ibid., 51.

well-attested belief.[6] Among others it is referred to by Ignatius of Antioch (twice),[7] Polycarp,[8] Justin,[9] Irenaeus (four times),[10] and Tertullian (once, but extensively).[11] In the earliest days it was not associated with the text of 1 Peter 3:19 (Christ "went and made a proclamation to the spirits in prison") but arose independently of this text.[12] Scholars today are not in agreement that this verse in 1 Peter refers to the *descensus* of Christ, or to what in the Western world is often referred to as "the Harrowing of Hell."[13] But from the time of Clement of Alexandria (he expands on the theme)[14] and Origen,[15] the connection between Sheol and 1 Peter has been established.

Evidence indicates that Christ descended in order to overthrow the kingdom of darkness and to preach to the Jews and pagans who had died since the beginning of time. This belief belonged to the central theological tradition of East and West and was not a piece of esoterica. When giving what Cyril of Jerusalem calls "a short summary of the necessary doctrines," Cyril devotes a whole paragraph to Sheol, though the *descensus* was not included in the Jerusalem creed.[16] He presents the descent as a deliverance of "those imprisoned from Adam onwards," specifically naming David, Samuel, all the prophets,

---

[6] J. Chaine, "Descente du Christ aux enfers," in *Supplément au Dictionnaire de la Bible* (Paris: Letouzey et Ané, 1934) 2:395–431; F. Loofs, "Descent to Hades," in *Encyclopedia of Religion and Ethics* (New York: Scribner, 1912) 4:654–663; Kelly, *Early Christian Creeds*, 378–383.

[7] *To the Magnesians* 9:2; *To the Trallians* 9:1; SC 10:88, 101.

[8] *To the Philippians* 1:2; SC 10:178.

[9] *Dialogue with Trypho* 72; PG 6:645.

[10] *Against Heresies* 3, 20, 4; 4, 22, 1; 4, 27, 2; 5, 31, 1; SC 211:396; SC 100:686, 688, 738; SC 153:390.

[11] *On the Soul* 55; CCh 2:862. E. G. Selwyn, *The First Epistle of St. Peter* (London: Macmillan, 1949) 340, 341; Kelly, *Early Christian Creeds*, 379. See J. H. Waszink, *De Anima* (Amsterdam: Meulenhoff, 1947) 553–558.

[12] Selwyn, *The First Epistle of St. Peter,* 340.

[13] W. J. Dalton contends that it does not refer to Christ's descent in "The First Epistle of Peter," in *The New Jerome Biblical Commentary,* 907; Spicq thinks that it does in *Les Épîtres de Saint Pierre,* 136–139, as does D. Senior in *1 & 2 Peter* (Wilmington: Glazier, 1973) 70.

[14] *Stromata* 6:6; PG 9:265–275.

[15] *On John* 6:35; SC 157:260.

[16] *Catechetical Lectures* 4:11; Reischl 1:102.

and John the Baptist.[17] Very often the patriarchs are among the delivered. The belief was sure enough in the tradition for Cyril to insist upon it in instructing catechumens, not the occasion for proposing speculative doctrine. In any case, Cyril was essentially a pastor rather than one given to theoretical elaborations. It is still preserved in the *Roman Catechism* of the Council of Trent,[18] and Loofs found it in all the main Christian traditions.[19]

The medieval West draws on a document known variously as the *Gospel of Nicodemus, Acts of Pilate,* or *Christ's Descent into Hell.*[20] This text brings together the image of light along with the baptism of Jesus, his passion, and his descent into Sheol. Behind the belief in the *descensus* of Christ into "hell" is the conviction that Christ's redemptive work is effective not only in the present and future but also among dead of the past ages. The mythical expression of this theological insight is the *descensus* of Christ into Sheol, where the dead, both just and unjust, dwell.[21]

The Martyrdom and Ascension of Isaiah is a Jewish work of the second century B.C.E., with Christian additions dating from the

[17] Ibid., Kelly, *Early Christian Creeds,* 379.

[18] 1:5, 1–6; *Catechismus ex Decreto Concilii Tridentini ad Parochus* (Regensburg: Mainz, 1905) 49–52.

[19] Loofs, "Descent to Hades," in *Encyclopedia of Religion and Ethics,* 4:654.

[20] Three Galilean rabbis who had witnessed the ascension of Jesus meet a great multitude of men "clothed in white, who had died before this time." When asked to identify themselves, they reply: "We rose with Christ from hell, and he himself raised us from the dead. And from this you may know that the gates of death and darkness are destroyed, and the souls of the saints are set free and have ascended to heaven with Christ the Lord." Latin version of *Christ's Descent into Hell* 2; Schneemelcher, *New Testament Apocrypha,* 1:528. Those who had risen ask for paper and record their experience: "We, then, were in Hades with all who have died since the beginning of the world. And at the hour of midnight there rose upon the darkness something like the light of the sun and shone, and light fell upon us all, and we said to one another: 'This shining comes from a great light.' " John the Baptist enters and recounts the baptism of Jesus in the Jordan, and concludes, "for this reason he sent me to you [here in Sheol], to preach that the only begotten Son of God comes here, in order that whoever believes in him should be saved. . . ." *Acts of Pilate,* 2:18; ibid., 522.

[21] S. Brock, *The Harp of the Spirit,* in Studies Supplementary to *Sobornost* no. 4 (Fellowship of St. Alban and St. Sergius, 1983) 39.

end of the first century to the fourth century of the Christian era. This text has God send Jesus into Sheol (without specific reference to his baptism), where the angels and lights of heaven are also present. He is to destroy "the gods of death," after which he ascends in glory.[22] Cyril of Jerusalem takes up the tradition and links it to the baptism of Jesus. What are the reasons behind Jesus' baptism? They have to do with participation or communion. At the Jordan a divine exchange takes place, a mutuality in *koinonia*, a reciprocity in sharing. As Jesus shares in our flesh and blood, so we participate in his divine life lived in the flesh. The reason for his baptism is that we might have *koinonia*, communion in his dignity and salvation. For this to come about, Jesus goes down into the water, thereby crushing "the heads of the dragon."[23]

Cosmos as Instrument of Salvation

The same themes can be found in a Christian, second-century (C.E.) interpolation of the second-century (B.C.E.) *Testament of Asher:* ". . . you shall be regarded as worthless like useless water, until such time as the Most High visits the earth. [He shall come as a man eating and drinking with human beings,] crushing the dragon's head in the water."[24] Christ descends into the Jordan to bind the strong one in his own territory. The notion of *descensus* to give battle is fundamental to this mythological view.[25] Jesus' going down into the water of the Jordan is merged with Jesus' *descensus* into Sheol.[26] By going down into

[22] 10:7-16; Charlesworth, *Old Testament Pseudepigrapha*, 2:173.

[23] *Catechetical Lectures*, 3:11; Reischl, 1:78.

[24] Charlesworth, *The Old Testament Pseudepigrapha*, 1:88.

[25] Lundberg, *La Typologie Baptismale dans l'Ancienne Église*, 226.

[26] O. Rousseau, "La descente aux enfers, fondement sotériologique du baptême chrétien," in *Recherches de Science Religieuse* 40 (1951–1952) 283–297; J. Daniélou, *The Theology of Jewish Christianity*, 225, 227. This theme is enshrined in the Greek liturgy of the Blessing of Baptismal Water, which understands that the depths of the water are inhabited by demonic powers. A. Baumstark, *Comparative Liturgy* (Westminster: Newman, 1958) 138. A similar conception is found in Clement of Alexandria in *Selections from the Prophets (Eclogae Propheticae)* 7; PG 9:702: "The Lord had himself baptized, not because he needed it himself, but so that he might make holy all water for those that are brought to new birth in it. Thus our souls,

the Jordan, Jesus cleanses all water of evil forces so that these waters can purify and sanctify those who go down into the waters of baptism.[27] Cosmos is caught up into salvation.[28]

In Christian iconography the descent is depicted as a bold, triumphal entry, the crucified and risen Lord breaking down the portals, forcing the evil one into submission, leading Adam and Eve by the hand out of the abyss. Incorporated in the iconography is the blood and the water that come forth from the side of Christ on the cross. The blood comes first in order to give life to Adam. Then the water comes, in which Adam is baptized.[29] In medieval iconography the blood and water flow down the wood over the skull of Adam at the base of the cross. The earliest written source in Syriac for this conception is the *Cave of Treasures*, a compendium of biblical history, possibly written in the sixth century, probably from the school of Ephrem.[30]

Though the Christian belief in Sheol is very old, it did not find its way into the Old Roman Creed, a baptismal creed dating from the closing decades of the second century. Neither is it in any of the creeds of the first three centuries, nor the Nicene Creed. Only in the fourth century, May 359 to be precise, was it inserted for the first time in what is technically known as the Fourth Formula of Sirmium,[31] and found its way into the so-called Athanasian Creed, a Western fifth- or sixth-century composition, and into the *Exultet* of the Easter Vigil. In the credal tradition the *descensus* is not associated with the baptism of

---

and not only our bodies, are cleansed and the sanctification of the unseen parts of our being is signified in that even the unclean spirits who cleave to our soul, are taken away from the time of our new spiritual birth."

[27] For the counterpart in Christian baptism of this struggle with evil powers, see J. Daniélou, *The Bible and Liturgy*, 20–22, 58, 59, 61–63, 89, 96, 97.

[28] Daniélou, *The Theology of Jewish Christianity*, 213.

[29] *The Book of the Cave of Treasures*, E.A.W. Budge, ed. (London: Religious Tract Society, 1927) 231.

[30] Brock, *The Harp of the Spirit*, 40.

[31] Kelly, *Early Christian Creeds*, 102, 289, 290, 378–383. It does appear in a doxology having a credal character in the Syrian *Didascalia* 64. Connolly, *Didascalia Apostolorum: The Syriac Version Translated and Accompanied by the Verona Latin Fragments* 259.

Jesus. Possibly because of the design difficulties inherent in combining two "events," Christian iconography rarely depicts Christ's baptism in its relation to the descent into hell.[32] But elsewhere the link is made, also in the liturgy.[33]

The Symbolic Journey Through Sheol

Ephrem has an extended exposition of the mystery of Sheol at the beginning of his *Sermon on Our Lord*, indicating its importance in his theology.[34] He sees Sheol as part of a salvific journey. "The Only-Begotten journeyed from the Godhead [that is, the Father] and resided in a virgin, so that through physical birth, the Only-Begotten would become a brother to many. [Having descend into Sheol] he journeyed from Sheol and resided in the [heavenly] kingdom, to make a path from Sheol, which cheats everyone, to the kingdom, which rewards everyone [according to their due]."[35] The purpose, then, of the journey to Sheol, and from Sheol to the heavenly kingdom and his Father, is to open up the path for the journey of those who had died. In *The Hymns Against Heresies*, Ephrem has Christ break-

---

[32] J. Strzygowski mentions only a cover of a Gospel book dating between 1051 and 1053, designed by a certain Ellenhardus, on which are depicted, side by side, four scenes: annunciation, birth, baptism, visitation, presentation in the Temple, and Christ in Sheol. *Iconographie der Taufe Christi* (Munich: Riedel, 1885) 21. In the monastery of Nea Moni on the Greek island of Chios, the squinches (a quarter-spherical segment of masonry vaulting giving space for decoration) in the church, dating from between 1042 and 1054, parallel the baptism of Jesus on one side with the descent into Sheol on the other. D. T. Rice, *Art of the Byzantine Era* (Oxford: Oxford University, 1963) 96.

[33] A. De Meester gives the liturgical sources. "Descente du Christ aux enfers," in *Dictionnaire d'Archéologie Chrétienne*, 4/1:682–696. In the older form of the *Exultet*, the rising victorious from Sheol is more explicit. "This is the night in which Christ snapped the chains of death and rose conqueror from hell." O. B. Hardison, Jr., *Christian Rite and Christian Drama in the Middle Ages* (Baltimore: Johns Hopkins, 1965) 148. The present English translation of the *Exultet* reads: "This is the night when Jesus Christ broke the chains of death and rose triumphant from the grave."

[34] 1–4; CSCO 271:1–5.

[35] Ibid., 1; CSCO 271:1. The English translation of the text is that *The Fathers of the Church* by E. G. Matthews, Jr. and J. P. Amar (Washington, D.C.; The Catholic University of America, 1994).

ing the bars that block the way out of Sheol and impede access to the heavenly Eden.[36]

The passage in the *Sermon on Our Lord* goes on to use the episode of Simon the Pharisee and the sinful woman (Luke 7:36-50). Simon, who failed in the courtesies due Jesus, is likened to Sheol because there is no discrimination in Sheol between the just and the unjust. The heavenly kingdom, where guests are received according to their due, is symbolized by the sinful woman.[37] In short, Sheol does not discriminate, but heaven does. Though a repentant woman gains entry into heaven, others are barred. The passage continues: "For our Lord gave His resurrection as a guarantee to mortals that He would lead them out of Sheol, which takes the departed, without discrimination, to the kingdom, which welcomes guests with discrimination, so that we might journey from where everyone's bodies are treated the same, to where everyone's efforts are treated with discrimination."[38]

Ephrem places Sheol in relation to the baptism of Jesus. Here Ephrem is speaking of the begetting of the Son from the Father eternally, in the flesh of the Virgin in time, in baptism in the Jordan, and in Sheol. The text reads:

"The Father begot Him, and through Him He made all
      creation.
Flesh begot Him, and in His flesh He put passions to death
Baptism begot Him, that through Him it might make [our]
      stains white.
Sheol begot Him to have her treasuries despoiled by Him."

The baptism of the Son is redemptive, removing our sins. The meaning of the begetting in Sheol should not be pressed. What is significant is the circular, symbolic journey: the journey takes its point of departure from the Father and Eden past, and passes through Sheol, leading back to Eden future and the Father. The milestones along the way are "the names, Father, Son, and Holy Spirit, the symbols of the anointing and bap-

---

[36] 26 6; CSCO 170:97
[37] McVey, *Ephrem the Syrian*, 274 n. 8.
[38] *Sermon on Our Lord* 1; CSCO 271:1.

tism, the breaking of the bread and the cup of salvation, and the scriptures. Blessed be the King, for the milestones of his way are mountains that cannot he hidden."[39] The journey is specifically trinitarian in character. The way leads through the sacramental mysteries to the heavenly kingdom, to the king and his gifts.[40]

The Waters Were in Dread

The last half of Ephrem's *Nisibis Hymns* also gives attention to Christ's descent into Sheol.[41] Ephrem and Syriac liturgical texts, base themselves on the conceptuality found in Psalm 29:3 ("the voice of the LORD is over the waters; the God of glory thunders, the LORD, over mighty waters), Psalm 77:16 ("when the waters saw you, they were afraid"), and Psalm 114:3 ("the sea looked and fled"). The Syriacs speak of the dread the waters themselves had of Jesus stepping into the Jordan.[42] At least five of the *Odes of Solomon* mention Sheol.[43] The *Odes* (dating from approximately the second half of the second century) sing of the fear and awe that the inhabitants of the deep had for Jesus' baptism.[44] Possibly referring to the baptism, the text reads: "Sheol saw me and was shattered."[45]

Ode 24 is clearly about the baptism of Jesus. It begins with a reference to the descent of the Spirit: "The dove fluttered over the head of our Lord Messiah." Then there is an allusion to the fright of those in Sheol: "Then the inhabitants were afraid . . . and the chasms were opened and closed." The inhabitants of the deep from the time of Adam were looking forward to the

[39] *Hymns Against Heresies* 27:3; CSCO 170:99.
[40] *Hymns Against Heresies* 26:4, 9; CSCO 170:96-98. Murray, *Symbols of Church and Kingdom* 246-249.
[41] CSCO 219, 241. Brock, *The Harp of the Spirit*, 39.
[42] *Carmina Sogyâtâ* 5:25-31; CSCO 187:204. Bernard, *The Odes of Solomon*, 33, 34.
[43] 17, 22, 24, 39, 42.
[44] *Ode* 22 and 24; Charlesworth, *The Odes of Solomon*, 89-91, 97, 98. "The theme here is the Baptism of Christ and the terrors which it inspired among the dwellers in the Abyss, the Underworld which is the abode of evil spirits, and the story is told in terms of the story of the Flood, when the waters destroyed the wicked." Bernard, *The Odes of Solomon*, 103.
[45] *Ode* 42:11; Charlesworth, *Odes*, 145.

time of deliverance as those looking expectantly for birth: "They were seeking the Lord as those who are about to give birth." This is possibly drawing on the same tradition that Philoxenus draws on when he has the cosmos in labor until the baptism of Jesus.

The depths of Sheol are then overwhelmed by the waters of the Jordan: "But the chasms were submerged in the submersion of the Lord." The author next returns to the birth image of baptism: "For they travailed from the beginning, and the end of their travail was life."[46] The cosmic travail ends in producing life; the baptismal travail produces new life, a new creation. The descent into Sheol is merged with Jesus' descent into the Jordan.[47] Indeed, the author(s) combine the baptism of Jesus, his death, the descent into Sheol, and the expansion of the way of salvation ("the Lord . . . spread widely His grace").[48]

The Combined Descent into the Jordan/Sheol

Sebastian Brock has shown how Jacob of Serugh overlays the baptism of Jesus with his descent into Sheol. When John the Baptist resists Jesus' request for baptism, Jesus explains to John why he must be baptized: "I am trying to find the lost Adam; let me go down and look for Adam, the fair image."[49] The framework here is what Gabriele Winkler calls "Adam mysticism," so strong in Syriac sources.[50] Jacob views Adam as a lost

[46] Ibid., 98. D. Plooij thinks that *Ode* 22 (which in his numbering is 21) possibly merges Sheol and the baptism of Jesus. "Der Descensus ad infernos in Aphrahat und den Oden Solomos," in *Zeitschrift für die neutestamentliche Wissenschaft und die Kunde des Urchristentums* 14 (1913) 229.

[47] Reicke, *The Disobedient Spirits and Christian Baptism*, 245. There may be elements of the Flood story, but the primary analog is the baptism of Jesus.

[48] Bieder, *Die Vorstellung von der Höllenfahrt Jesu Christi*, 174; *Ode* 24:13; Charlesworth, *Odes*, 99.

[49] Bedjan, 1:177. I thank Columba Stewart for verifying the citations. Sebastian Brock gathered the research, and the translations are his. They are found in "Baptismal Themes in the Writings of Jacob of Serugh," in *Symposium Syriacum 1976*, 328.

[50] Also found in Greek texts, as in Irenaeus: "Adam never really escaped from the hands of God," the hands being the Son and the Spirit. *AH* 5, 1, 3; SC 153:28.

pearl that Jesus goes down into the Jordan/Sheol to rescue: "He [Christ] was baptized in the sea of sufferings and brought up the pearl, because of the great image depicted on it, so that it should not be lost."[51] He relates the theme more specifically to Sheol:

"Christ was baptized in the pit, and feeling around Sheol,
    he drew out Adam;
he groped in the mud of the dead, and sought out the pearl
    [Adam]."[52]

Or more expansively:

"He went down to the sea of the dead to be baptized like
    those who bathe;
he brought up from thence the pearl [Adam], depicted
    in his own image.
He spent three days in the pit, and found there
    the image that the serpent had stolen and hidden away
    in the bottom of Sheol."[53]

Sheol and Jordan are merged. Jesus descends for three days into Sheol/Jordan to search out the lost Adam who bears his image, groping for him in the mud of the dead where the Serpent had hidden him, and finding him, as one finds a precious pearl, leads him out.

The Armenians carry the tradition further in their ancient baptismal liturgies: "By thy dread command, thou didst close up the abysses and make them fast . . . though didst bruise the head of the dragon upon the waters."[54] Other liturgies took over the tradition, depicting the waters as terrified at Christ's descent into the Jordan, also based on Psalms 29, 76, and 114:55.[55] Not only the waters, but the evil spirits were afraid and fled in

---

[51] Bedjan, 1:697.
[52] Ibid., 2:599.
[53] Ibid., 3:423.
[54] Conybeare, *Rituale Armenorum*, 101.
[55] Bernard, *The Odes of Solomon*, 33.

the liturgies attributed to Severus of Antioch and Jacob of Edessa (ca. 640–708).[56]

Jordan: A Prophecy of Calvary

A different but related association is that of Jesus' baptism with the passion. Christ's baptism is prophetic of his passion. Jesus is baptized in view of his death. He is the ultimate reconciler because he takes on himself all the sins that the Jews bring to the Jordan. In his baptism in the Jordan, the whole plan of salvation that he has to realize is openly laid before him.[57] What took place at the Jordan is completely unfolded only at Calvary. When Luke reports Jesus saying "I have a baptism with which to be baptized, and what stress I am under until it is completed" (Luke 12:50), this does not necessarily come from the post-Easter community.[58] The events of Calvary are only to be understood as the full realization of what was begun at his baptism in the Jordan.[59] D. Plooij thinks that Jesus received baptism from the hands of John as "an initiation to His passion and death."[60] That this is so should not be a matter of surprise, since there exists the conviction that the baptism of Jesus foreshadows and symbolically sums up Jesus' mission as son and servant, including his death, resurrection, and ascension.[61]

[56] "The abyss is frenzied at your sight." *Baptismal and Confirmation Ordo of Jacob of Edessa; Ritus Orientalium*, H. Denzinger, ed., 2 vols. (Würzburg: Staehlan, 1863–1864) 1:313. "The waters have seen you, God. The waters have seen you, Lord, and they tremble: the abyss is in confusion. . . . They saw him and fled." *Baptismal and Confirmation Ordo of Severus of Antioch*; ibid., 1:282.

[57] O. Cullmann, *The Christology of the New Testament*, rev. ed. (Philadelphia: Westminster, 1963) 67.

[58] H. Schürmann, *Traditionsgeschichtliche Untersuchungen zu den synoptischen Evangelien* (Düsseldorf: Patmos, 1968) 53.

[59] J.A.T. Robinson, *Twelve New Testament Studies* (Naperville: Allenson, 1962) 22.

[60] "The Baptism of Jesus," in *Amicitiae Corolla* 241. I. de la Potterie thinks that both Mark 10:38 and Luke 12:50 are "without doubt" references to his passion in the context of his baptism in the Jordan. "L'onction du Christ," in *Nouvelle Revue Théologique* 80 (1958) 247, n. 61.

[61] B.W.H. Lampe, *The Seal of the Spirit*, 2nd ed. (London: SPCK, 1967) 33; W. F. Flemington, *The New Testament Doctrine of Baptism* (London: SPCK, 1953) 32, 39, 40.

The association between baptism and passion is found in Ignatius of Antioch, who says of Jesus that "he was born and baptized that by his suffering he might purify the water."[62] The Jordan event announces his passion. Ignatius is using very old confessional material. Even though the formulation may be colored by his own views, it still preserves the conviction of the ancient Church that there is a connection between his baptism in the Jordan and his atoning suffering.[63]

Justin Martyr joins baptism to passion in a loose fashion, saying that just as Jesus did not need baptism but nonetheless submitted to baptism "solely for the sake of man," so also he had "no need to be begotten or crucified."[64] Justin, therefore, singles out incarnation, baptism, and the crucifixion. Irenaeus also presupposes that the baptism is related to the passion. After writing of the death and resurrection, he turns his attention to the anointing with the Spirit that took place at the Jordan.[65]

In speaking of the relation between the baptism of John the Baptist and that of Jesus, Tertullian asserts that even after Jesus instituted baptism, "the apostles were not able to confer it because the Lord had not yet consummated his glory, nor had he established the efficacious nature of baptism by his passion and resurrection."[66] So closely are baptism and passion linked that the apostles are restrained from administering Jesus' baptism until after the death and resurrection of Jesus.[67]

The Four Bridges to the Kingdom

Ephrem is also explicit. He mentions "four bridges" that lead to the kingdom: incarnation, baptism, death, and resurrection:

---

[62] *Ephesians* 18:2; SC 10:74. See n. 3. See also Lundberg, *La Typologie Baptismale dans l'Ancienne Église*, 189. The relation of baptism to passion is also found in the baptismal doctrine of the Gnostics. E. Fabbri, "Le bautismo de Jesús y la unción del Espíritu en la teología de Ireneo," 14, 15.

[63] Cullmann, *The Christology of the New Testament*, 68.

[64] *Dialogue with Trypho* 88; PG 6:685.

[65] *Against Heresies* 3, 18, 3; SC 211:350, 352.

[66] *On Baptism* 11:4; SC 35:81.

[67] Tertullian is not alone is this opinion. A number of early authors, not all, followed him. A. d'Alès, "Baptême," in *Supplément au Dictionnaire de la Bible*, 1:858.

"His birth is followed by his baptism, and it is tied to his baptism. Then, his baptism hurries on to his death; his death without a break attains to his resurrection. There are four bridges that lead to his kingdom. Behold his flock follows his footsteps."[68] The four bridges bind together the mysteries that move to the consummation. The one who passes over a single bridge is moved on to the other bridges with some urgency. The baptism, therefore, is an anticipation of his death and resurrection. This is further articulated in his conviction that there are two baptisms: one of water, the other of the cross. But the passion contains the meaning of the water: "There are two baptisms of our Lord: the one is the baptism of water; the other is the baptism of the cross. The passion explains for us the nature of the baptism of water."[69]

What this baptism/passion tradition shares with the more specific Sheol tradition is the redemptive quality of the mysteries of Christ. Both *descensus* and baptism are related to the passion. Neither is an isolated act but a mystery belonging to the great drama of salvation. However, the tradition failed to expand on the combined theme of the *descensus* into the Jordan and the *descensus* into the passion.

The descent into hell is a mythological way of stating a profound theological insight. The geographical dimension is not the issue. Christ's triumphant victory and the extent of salvation is. The theological perspective here goes beyond spiritual experience and spiritual redemption. The range is cosmic. The tradition sees fire and light and water as part of the witness of the created universe to the baptism of Jesus. Jesus' descent into the Jordan is merged with his *descensus* into Sheol, with the waters in terror and the inhabitants of the deep in dread, an attempt to bring the cosmos to testify that the baptism of Jesus is not naked sign but redemptive symbol. Life enters into the very domain of death and conquers the gods of death. With divine freedom Jesus extends his victory to the just from the days of

---

[68] *Hymns on Epiphany* 10:9; CSCO 187:167.

[69] I quote the text from Saber, *La Théologie Baptismale de Saint Éphrem*, 133. After many hours of search, I have been unable to locate the text. Saber gives the reference as CSCO, 2, c. 21, 32, p. 230.

Adam—patriarchs, prophets, and the holy ones—living a shadowy, neutered existence in Sheol.

While the incarnation takes place in linear time, within the temporal sequence, the *descensus* into Sheol takes place in sacred, or liturgical, time, where there is no measure of motion, no sequence from past to future. Here, past and future are one. Sacred time is preoccupied with the saving content, the ultimate meaning, of what transpired in historical time.

Not a religious abstraction, the Jordan/*descensus* ruptures the space-time bonds, proclaiming that the power of Christ transforms those living in the present, grasps those still in the far reaches of the future, but, triumph of triumph, overthrows sequence and succession to enter the past, there to bring the good news not as a hope but as a realized salvation. The Lord of the Cosmos, the Sovereign of the Universe, claims his universal dominion.

Chapter Twelve

Contemplation and Initiation— Institution of Christian Baptism

When dealing with questions of the beginnings of the Christian sacrament of baptism, and of the relation of the sacrament to the baptism of Jesus, several categories are relevant: origin, institution, source, and paradigm. The search for the origin of the sacrament of baptism and questions of institution are related but not identical. And neither origin nor institution is synonymous with paradigm. Origin refers more specifically to antecedents. Where did it come from? Institution is more the constitutional question, a legal matter of established forms, of the organized structures of the faith and sacramental life. Thus, who started it and when? Source also corresponds to the question of who and when. Paradigm has to do with the interior substance and even with causation. Where does the content of baptism come from? Is there a causal relationship between the baptism of Jesus and the sacrament of baptism? Paradigm is not just an exterior prototype but has to do with the interior principle of life.

There is overlap between these categories, but not strict equivalency. In the literature they are not always distinguished. While in more historically oriented studies origin refers to antecedents, in many theological texts origin refers also to institution; source and paradigm are also used interchangeably. In these pages I generally follow the freer theological usage.

I am not attempting to give an exhaustive account of institution. Though I will treat of foot-washing in Aphrahat, my principal focus is the baptism of Jesus and the Romans 6:4 text. Except in Jacob of Serugh, I am only peripherally looking at the pierced side because it never attained the major significance that the events at the Jordan and Calvary did.

While there is a consensus on the origins, that is, antecedents, of the Eucharist, no such consensus exists among scholars on the origin of the sacrament of baptism, and the matter is still under dispute.[1] No one suggests that Jesus invented baptism. Rather the contention is that he more radically reinterpreted the going down into the waters than John the Baptist interpreted the many water baths in the history of Israel. The baptism to be found in the Christian community is indeed John's baptism, but given new content and a new teleology, in fact, completely changed and transformed. The new content is a new mode of God's presence as expressed in the voice of the Father and the descent of the Spirit in the form of the dove, a participation in the giving of the Spirit to Jesus without measure, and the first light of the new day of the Lord, the move to God's future consummation in the parousia.[2]

What Are the Criteria?

In his commentary *Matthew*, John P. Meier takes the position that Matthew probably understands the baptism narrative as ''a lesson on what baptism means for Christians (the Father grants sonship by bestowing his Spirit), especially since Matthew, alone among the gospels, attaches a 'Trinitarian' formula to baptism (28:19).''[3] In *A Marginal Jew*, Meier points out that no New Testament author ''directly and explicitly'' links Christian

---

[1] A. Y. Collins, "The Origin of Christian Baptism," in *Studia Liturgica* 19 (1984) 28f; P. F. Bradshaw, *The Search for the Origins of Christian Worship* (New York: Oxford University, 1992) 45–47.

[2] G. W. Lathrop, "The Origins and Early Meanings of Christian Baptism: A Proposal," in *Worship* 68 (1994) 516.

[3] *Matthew* (Wilmingtom: Glazier, 1980) 28.

baptism with the Jordan event; nor is Jesus' baptism ever explicitly proposed as the cause, archetype, or model of Christian baptism.[4] The difference between the two positions is not great. Meier believes that Christian baptism is related to the baptism of Jesus, but the relationship is not direct and explicit.

Others take a less nuanced position, among them Rhyndholm, Légasse, and Marsh. Légasse, the latest author to take up a strong position against any relationship, contends that "the New Testament does not offer the least support."[5] Marsh offers as corroboration "the strange lack of interest in this event which the earliest Christian literature reveals."[6]

One will certainly support the position asserting the want of explicit linkage between Jesus' baptism and Christian baptism within the New Testament. One must, further, leave open the possibility that the narrative of Jesus' baptism has been influenced by the practice of baptism in the infant Church, instead of Jesus' baptism giving structure to Christian baptism.[7] But it is

[4] 105. Because of the specific purpose of the whole book, Meier takes no account of the early post-biblical witness.

G. R. Beasely-Murray, *Baptism in the New Testament* (London: Macmillan, 1963) 64: "Despite attempts to prove the contrary, it would seem that *no writer of the New Testament brings the baptism of Jesus into relation with Christian baptism.*" (Emphasis is in the text.) Likewise P. Ryndholm: "The institution of Christian baptism is not a momentary action but a history." Quoted in Beasely-Murray, 64.

[5] *Naissance du Baptême* 69. In referring to the Markan account, Légasse contends that "when it is a question of 'baptize' or of 'baptism,' nothing in the text permits one to establish, either directly or indirectly, the least reference to Christian baptism." Ibid., 65. Légasse later expands: "The preceding examination of the synoptic pericopes leads to the negative verification, corroborating the ensemble of the New Testament: no indication exists which would permit that the Christians of the first century had established some relationship between the baptism of Jesus by John and the rite of initiation practiced in the church." Ibid., 68.

[6] *The Origin and Significance of the New Testament Baptism*, 107.

[7] "Allowance must be made for the probability that the description of Christ's baptism has been assimilated in certain details to the rite of Christian baptism which was practiced in the early Church." Marsh, *The Origin and Significance of the New Testament Baptism*, 106. While granting that the narration of Jesus' baptism probably served as an institution narrative, which the Church otherwise lacked, Benoit notes the possibility that "the narration of the baptism of Jesus had been influenced by the practice of

only a possibility. It seems improbable that the priority of Christian baptism and its influence on the baptismal account of the Jordan event would have completely disappeared in all New Testament documents.[8] With the evidence at hand, we cannot determine whether the actual practice of Christian baptism began with Jesus himself or only after the resurrection.

One is forced to contest Marsh's suggestion that the early post-biblical literature was disinterested in the relation between the two. As early as Ignatius of Antioch and Tertullian, Jesus' baptism is seen as the model and source of Christian baptism, to be followed immediately, as we have seen, by a number of early authors (Clement of Alexandria, Origen, Aphrahat, Ephrem, etc.).[9]

Does the New Testament Link Jordan and Christian Baptism?

How much is one to trust early post-biblical authors who look upon the baptism of Jesus as the institution of Christian baptism? Raymond Brown notes that often they are not engaging in exegesis but in catechetics, and in a rather free metaphorical use of Scripture, a species of spiritual exegesis. One can indeed ap-

---

Christian baptism, the evangelists attributing to Jesus the rite such as it was found in the practice of their epoch." Benoit, Le Baptême Chrétien au Second Siècle, 180; R. Bultmann, The History of the Synoptic Tradition, 2nd ed. (New York: Harper & Row, 1968) 251*–252*, suggests that the baptismal legend (he does not deny historicity) was influenced by Christian cult. Vincent Taylor believes that those who hold that Christian baptism formed the narrative of Jesus' baptism have some probability in their favor, but it is more credible to see the baptism of Jesus as the primary analogue of Christian baptism. "The Baptism of Jesus," The Gospel According to St. Mark, 2nd ed. (New York: St. Martin, 1966) 618. J. Denney is apodictic in his rejection of Christian baptismal practice influencing the narrative: "It is literally preposterous to argue that Christian baptism set the type for that of Jesus; it is the baptism of Jesus which sets the type for the sacrament of the church." Jesus and the Gospel (London: Hodder, 1909) 202. See also E. Schlink, "The Historical Problem of the Origin of Christian Baptism," in The Doctrine of Baptism (St. Louis: Concordia, 1972) 26–31.

[8] Meier, A Marginal Jew, 105.

[9] Ignatius of Antioch, Ephesians 18:2; SC 10:74; Tertullian, On Baptism 9:2; SC 35:78.

peal to the early authors, but it must be done with caution. The mere presence of a sacramental interpretation of biblical texts in these early post-biblical texts is not enough to justify a sacramental reading of the New Testament. There must be some positive indication of a sacramental meaning in the biblical text itself. This need not exclude symbolism. We are less inclined to use symbolism than were the biblical writers and we may therefore miss the subtle symbolic meaning. Who would have seen the lifting up of the bronze serpent as a symbol of the crucified Jesus if this had not been pointed out by the evangelist (John 3:14)? The biblical, symbolic mentality is not our mentality, and the symbolic may elude us. To justify a sacramental understanding of a biblical text, there must be, in addition to the post-biblical witness of the early authors, some evidence in the biblical text itself.[10]

Exegetes differ whether these indications are present in the text. Beasley-Murray and Rhyndholm find no such indications. But a number of exegetes do contend there are indicators that the baptism of Jesus in the Jordan is the institution of Christian baptism, among them D'Alès, Lagrange, Flemington, White, Cullmann, and Schierse.[11] Oscar Cullmann holds that "[Jesus'

---

[10] Brown, The Gospel According to John I-XII, cxiii.

[11] The baptism of Jesus marks "the decisive instant" in the institution of the sacrament of baptism. A. D'Alès, "Baptême," in Supplément du Dictionnaire de la Bible, L. Pirot, ed. (Paris: Letouzey et Ané, 1928) 1:856. "The first step of a Christian corresponds to the first step of Christ. In a certain manner, the gospel begins here." M. J. Lagrange, Évangile selon Saint Marc, 4th ed. (Paris: Gabalda, 1935) 5; ". . . in our attempt to describe the antecedents of Christian baptism we do well to give conspicuous place to the baptism of our Lord. It may be that this event has exercised a more considerable influence than has hitherto been recognized upon the origin of the Christian rite." Flemington, The New Testament Doctrine of Baptism, 29; R.E.O. White enumerates five elements in Jesus' baptism that affect the meaning of Christian baptism, namely: 1) he lends his personal authority to the practices; 2) dominance of positive elements (sonship, Spirit, theophany) over negative renunciations; 3) linking of imitatio Christi to baptism; 4) overtones of filial relationship and privileges; 5) rite linked to reception of Spirit. White concludes: "Taken together these five new elements in the baptismal conceptions deriving almost wholly from the baptismal experience of Jesus, abundantly justify the contention that it is to His act we must look for the main origin of the Christian rite." "The Baptism of Jesus" in

baptism] is in fact the historical origin of Christian baptism. . . .
There stands right at the beginning of John's Gospel the reference to the *institution* of *Christian Baptism* by him who as 'Lamb'
has removed the sin of the world and has therefore fulfilled the
meaning of all Baptism and brought Baptism with the Spirit.[12]
Hartwig Thyen maintains that in the account of the Jordan
event Matthew wanted to tell his readers about the institution
of Christian baptism. More specifically, it proceeds from the
baptismal practice of the Church, yet treating the baptism of
Jesus as a cult legend, proposing the Jordan event as the cause
and origin of Christian baptism. Matthew's insistence on "we
must fulfill all righteousness" (3:15) shows the beginning way of
Christian righteousness in Christian baptism.[13] The baptism of
Jesus is the *Urbild* of Christian baptism.

The linkage between the Jordan event and Christian baptism,
though never explicit, is not fanciful. Baptism involves a relationship with the Father (Matt 28:19), becoming children of God
(John 7:37-39; and possibly John 3:5; Titus 3:5), and receiving the
abundant gift of the Spirit in power (Mark 1:8; Acts 1:5, 11:16;

Christian Baptism, A. Gilmore, ed. (Chicago: Judson, 1959) 97; "It is clear
. . . that when the evangelists tell us about this baptism (of Jesus) they are
thinking of the baptism of Christians; the visible manifestation of the Spirit
foreshadows baptism in the Spirit, and the Father's designation of the Son
points toward the adoption of the baptized as sons." A. George et al.,
Baptism in the New Testament (Baltimore: Helicon, 1964) 16; "It is not a case
of a report of a biographical experience, but is part of a baptismal catechesis, that wants to teach about the theological meaning of the Christian
sacrament." Basing himself on the biblical evidence and on the witness of
Tertullian, Schierse concludes that texts (Mark 1:9-11 and parallels) constitute the institution and foundation of Christian baptism. F. J. Schierse,
"Die neutestamentliche Trinitätsoffenbarung," *Mysterium Salutis*, 5 vols.
(Einsiedeln: Benziger, 1965-1976) 2:100. R. E. Brown simply says: "John
says that the Spirit came to rest . . . on Jesus; and since Jesus permanently possesses the Spirit, he will dispense this Spirit to others in Baptism." *The Gospel According to John (I–XII)*, 66.

[12] Emphasis in the text. O. Cullmann, *Early Christian Worship* (London:
SCM, 1953) 60, 65. This does not mean that all themes of the passion are
excluded from the baptismal narrative and texts. Idem, *Baptism in the New
Testament* (London: SCM, 1950) 16–18.

[13] H. Thyen, *Studien zur Sundenvergebung* (Göttingen: Vandenhoeck &
Ruprecht, 1970) 214, n. 2.

John 7:37-39); baptism is the source of eternal life (John 4:13, 14).[14] Also, as Etienne Nodet points out, there is an internal coherence between the baptism of John, the baptism Jesus received, and Christian baptism, namely, the forgiveness of sins. For this reason, the primitive community places forgiveness at the center of its preaching. This is also the reason for the obligatory nature of Christian baptism. Who is without sin?[15]

There is another indication within the New Testament that Jesus' baptism is the paradigm for Christian baptism. That the earliest Christian communities practiced baptism from the beginning is very likely best explained by Jesus telling his disciples how important his baptism was for him.[16] "Jesus' baptism by John was probably the occasion for an experience of God that had epochal significance for Jesus."[17] The most striking features of this experience are sonship and Spirit, in other words, God as Father and the power of God. Is it an accident that sonship and Spirit are closely associated with the sacrament of baptism in Acts (2:38; 10:44-48; 1 Cor 6:11; 12:13) and in the epistles (Gal 3:26, 27; Eph 4:4, 5)? These are not characteristics of John's baptism.[18] The authority that Jesus exercised in his ministry is rooted in his relation to the Father, and in his being Spirit-empowered, two aspects of one reality. These are the sources of his identity. From these he lived and ministered.[19] They also define Christian baptism. Whatever the problems involved in peeling back the layers to expose the original meaning of Jesus' baptism, these two mysteries are how the narrative of the theo-

[14] Schnackenburg, *The Gospel According to St. John,* 1:305, says that in the Fourth Gospel, Jesus' reference to "birth from water and the Spirit" (John 3:5), "the evangelist certainly has in mind the Christian notion . . . as in the sacrament of baptism, which makes men children of God through the power of the Holy Spirit."

[15] E. Nodet, in a review of Légasse's *Naissance du Baptême* in *Revue Biblique* 102 (1995) 600–611. I thank Etienne Nodet for allowing me to see an advance copy of this review and Justin Taylor for sending it to me.

[16] Flemington, *The New Testament Doctrine of Baptism,* 31; Dunn, *Jesus and the Spirit,* 65.

[17] Ibid.

[18] Flemington, *The New Testament Doctrine of Baptism,* 29.

[19] Dunn, *Jesus and the Spirit,* 65.

phany, a Christian composition, seems to present the Jordan event.

However, Légasse contends that the link between Christian baptism and the imparting of the Spirit, which is so important a part of the biblical narration of Jesus' baptism, is far from being either clear or general in the New Testament.[20] He further contends that Jesus' baptism in water at the Jordan is water baptism, in contrast to a baptism in the Holy Spirit. Légasse suggests that those who propose baptism in water as the model of Christian baptism should know that there is no basis in the Scriptures for this conviction. But can one distinguish so easily between water baptism at the Jordan and Spirit baptism? Whether or not John the Baptist imparted the Spirit through his baptism, at the very least, in this case, the Spirit sovereignly descends on Jesus. Is it advisable to divide the Jordan event into discrete segments, and then to segregate them from the entire Jordan experience? Is not the descent of the Spirit, resting upon Jesus (Mark 1:10; John 1:32), integral to the whole event, though chronologically after the ascent out of the Jordan? The one who is baptized in the Jordan is the one who will baptize in the Holy Spirit according to the Baptist (John 1:33) and to the risen Christ (Acts 1:5). Légasse's only objection is to Jesus' baptism *in water* being the model of Christian baptism.[21]

In a long, critical review of Légasse's book, Etienne Nodet takes issue with his rejection of the baptism of Jesus in the Jordan as the model for Christian baptism.[22] According to Nodet, Légasse presents the baptism of Jesus as "a simple accident without a definite signification"; indeed, Légasse suggests that the biblical texts attest a discontinuity between Jesus' baptism and Christian baptism.[23] Nodet questions this position. The Christians at Ephesus (Acts 19) were not troubled with the question of institution, but passed immediately from John's baptism to that given in the name of the risen Christ. Regarding the hypothesis that Jesus created nothing new, Nodet notes that Jesus enters into the rite of John, appropriating and trans-

[20] *Naissance du Baptême*, 64, 118–120.
[21] Ibid., 69.
[22] *Revue Biblique* 102 (1995) 600–611.
[23] Ibid.

forming its meaning, orienting it to the resurrection. The discretion of the biblical text with regard to institution is explained by a continuity between John's and Jesus' baptism, a continuity that is not discussed in the Scriptures.

The Witness of Luke and the Fourth Gospel

In Luke, the Baptist distinguishes between the baptism he administers and the baptism Jesus will give (Luke 3:16 par Matt 3:11). In Luke, the "fire" associated with the Spirit seems to find its accomplishment with Pentecost (Acts 2:2-4). Christian baptism enters only at the end of Peter's discourse (Acts 2:38).[24]

With the fourth evangelist the situation is different. We know from John 4:2 that during his lifetime the disciples were baptizing, but is this the same as the post-resurrectional baptism? Exegetes tend to believe that Acts 1:5 (". . . you will be baptized with the Holy Spirit not many days from now") refers to a periodization between the time of Jesus and the time of the Church.[25] The Syrian authors of antiquity go beyond periodization and generally believe that the Pentecost event of Acts 2 also marks the origin of Christian baptism.[26] If baptism imparts the Spirit, then it must follow the outpouring of the Spirit at Pentecost and not come before, so the Syrians argue. The outpouring of the Spirit is a baptism in the Holy Spirit (Acts 1:5), imparting not only the Spirit but forgiveness of sins (Acts 2:38).

The fourth evangelist presents baptism as a birth event (". . . being born of water and the Spirit . . ."), the new creation by the Spirit of God (John 3:5). Also, one must mention the pierced side of John 19:34 ("and at once blood and water came out"). Rudolf Bultmann thinks the Johannine passage is an ecclesiastical redaction intended to show that the sacraments of baptism and the Lord's Supper have their foundation in the death of Jesus.[27] Eduard Schweizer ascribes the passage of the pierced side to the evangelist, who intends an allusion to the

[24] Légasse, *Naissance du Baptême* 65, 66.

[25] R. Pesch, *Die Apostelgeschichte (Apg 1–12)* (Zurich: Benziger, 1986) 67; H. Conzelmann, *Acts of the Apostles* (Philadelphia: Fortress, 1987) 6.

[26] Brock, "The Epiklesis in the Antiochene Baptismal Ordines," in *Symposium Syriacum 1972*, 204.

[27] *The Gospel of John* (Philadelphia: Westminster, 1971) 666, 677, 678.

sacraments.[28] Augustine favored this interpretation,[29] and, with many variations, it dominated the exegesis of the early Church and the Middle Ages.[30] Both John 3:5 and 19:34 have a long history of sacramental interpretation in the tradition.

The argument for the baptism of Jesus being the institution of Christian baptism need not mean that in all respects the Jordan event and Christian baptism are the same. This would fly in the face of the New Testament evidence, which emphasizes the uniqueness of Jesus' baptism (his relationship to the Father and his role as primary carrier of the Spirit).[31]

Nonetheless, if one takes the witness of the early post-biblical authors cited above, that is, those who stand nearest the New Testament and the apostolic age, their reading of the biblical text carries some authority because of their proximity. Already at the end of the first and the beginning of the second century, the relationship between the baptism of Jesus and Christian baptism was established in the writings of Ignatius of Antioch. He is no ordinary authority. If the conjecture that he was born around 35 C.E. and died about 107 C.E. is even approximately correct, he lived through the formative years of the apostolic Church, possibly in one of the centers of the new faith, Antioch. Ephrem speaks for Ignatius and for the way the earliest ages read the Scriptures when he says that Jesus "took baptism out of the Jordan."[32] The exegetical question remains open.

Does the Command to Baptize Come from Jesus?

But the question is not finished when one has cited the evidence concerning the baptism of Jesus in the Jordan. The post-

[28] "Das johanneische Zeugnis vom Herrenmahl," in *Evangelische Theologie* 12 (1952/1953) 349, 350.

[29] *On John*, Tract 120:2; CCh 36:661.

[30] B. F. Westcott, *The Gospel According to St. John* (Grand Rapids: Baker, 1908/1980) 328–333. The witnesses include the Greek authors Apollinaris, Eusebius, Chrysostom, Cyril of Alexandria, Macarius the Greater, John of Damascus, Euthymius, Theophylact. The Latins include Tertullian, Cyprian, Novatian, Ambrose, Jerome, Rufinus, Prudentius, Rupert of Deutz.

[31] A. Kavanagh, *The Shape of Baptism: The Rite of Christian Initiation* (New York: Pueblo, 1978) 13.

[32] *Sermon on Our Lord* 56; CSCO 271:53.

resurrection words of the risen Christ are widely looked upon as the institution of the sacrament of baptism (Matt 28:19 and Mark 16:16). These two texts are the only ones in the New Testament that attribute the command to baptize to Jesus himself. Both texts are problematic from a strictly exegetical point of view.[33]

The Markan command to baptize is in an appendix (16:15, 16), and is not a part of the text of Mark with him as its author. Though there is a suggestion that the appendix is simply a mosaic of elements borrowed from the other Gospels, this has been contested. Rather, it seems, the author of the appendix, writing in the first half of the second century (the First Gospel seems to have been written at the end of the first century), knows the traditions that the evangelists have collected and reshaped. The Markan appendix goes back to what is given in the ecclesial tradition.[34]

As for Matthew, nothing in the text raises the suspicion that the command to make disciples of all nations, baptizing them in the trinitarian formula, is a creation of Matthew. However, the question remains: Does the command go back to Jesus? Légasse remarks that though Paul speaks many times of baptism, he receives it as a practice already in force before he appeared on the scene. While he attributes the institution of the Eucharist to Jesus (1 Cor 11:23-25), he does not make the same claim for baptism.[35] In a liturgical portion of the *Didache*, the text instructs

---

[33] We know from Acts 2:38; 8:16; 10:48; 19:5, as well from Galatians 3:27 and Romans 6:3, that the trinitarian formula commanded by Jesus in Matthew 28:19 and Mark 16:16 was not universally part of the liturgical rite. Matthew seems to incorporate the liturgical practice of the Matthaean community into his gospel; nonetheless, the triadic formula "has a strong probability of being authentic." B. J. Hubbard, *The Matthean Redaction of a Primitive Apostolic Commissioning: An Exegesis of Matthew 28:16-20* (Missoula: Scholars, 1974) 171. The text of Mark 16:9-20 is most likely a second-century compendium of appearance stories from Luke and John, and is therefore not authentically Markan. Although a later addition to the Gospel, it is considered canonical by Roman Catholics. D. Harrington, "The Gospel According to Mark," in *The New Jerome Biblical Commentary*, R. E. Brown et al., eds. (Englewood Cliffs: Prentice Hall, 1990) 629.

[34] Légasse, *Naissance du Baptême*, 12.

[35] Ibid., 11.

one to baptize in the trinitarian formula[36] but does not attribute the practice to Jesus, as it does for the Our Father.[37] If one is looking for a pattern which, though very late, might be in the biblical tradition, there is 2 Peter 1:17 with its mention of the transfiguration, which seemingly contains "echoes of the baptismal theophany."[38] If transfiguration is linked with the baptism of Jesus at the Jordan—so the argument goes—why would not some such linking be found in the New Testament between the Jordan event and Christian baptism?[39] In opposition to Légasse, Nodet holds that the difference regarding the institution of the Eucharist and baptism does not go back to Jesus.[40]

Does Matthew want to establish a relationship between, on the one hand, the beginning of Jesus' public life with the Jordan event and, on the other, the command of the risen Christ at the other end of the Gospel to the eleven disciples on the mountain to baptize all nations (Matt 28:19)? Or is the use of *baptizein* different in the two instances? If Jesus is giving an example to be followed at the Jordan, is the paradigm necessarily the baptism itself? Why not the obedience of Christ as the paradigm?[41] Or can the two easily be separated?

If Légasse is correct, the exegetical conclusion seems to be that the attribution to Jesus of the command to baptize—with possible links to the institution of Christian baptism—is limited and late in the New Testament. The attribution appears in compositions characterized by theological and christological elaboration. Nonetheless, they are susceptible of being interpreted as the carriers of an echo of the authentic words of Jesus. No one should suggest that the two authors, Mark and Matthew, are deprived of all relationship to the historical Jesus.[42]

[36] 7:1; SC 248:170.

[37] 8:2; SC 248:172.

[38] J. H. Neyrey, *2 Peter, Jude* (New York: Doubleday, 1993) 173.

[39] Légasse, *Naissance du Baptême*, 66.

[40] *Revue Biblique* 102 (1995) 600–611. The command "do this in memory of me" of Luke 22:19b-20 is missing from the Western text, and appears to be an import into Luke from 1 Corinthians 11:24, 25. Nodet's position is supported by J. Jeremias, *The Eucharistic Words of Jesus* (Philadelphia: Fortress, 1977) 145.

[41] Légasse, *Naissance du Baptême*, 66.

[42] Ibid.

Paul represents yet another biblical tradition: "Therefore we have been buried with him by baptism into death, so that, just as Christ was raised from the dead by the glory of the Father, so we too might walk in newness of life" (Rom 6:4). This text gives us no information on the origin or institution of baptism. Also missing from it are important theologoumena in the primitive and even Pauline view of baptism, namely, the imparting of the Spirit and the sacramental incorporation into the body of Christ.[43] One needs to keep in mind that the Paul who wrote of being baptized into the death of Jesus also wrote "by one Spirit we are all baptized into one body" (1 Cor 12:13). This is not clear in Romans 6:4, which is, nonetheless, a major baptismal paradigm.

Given the considerable variety of baptismal traditions in the New Testament, one cannot be surprised that attempts to harmonize and incorporate them into the post-biblical tradition, especially in the liturgies, were so diverse.[44] What is a matter of surprise is that in the immediate post-biblical period, the second century, the Pauline paradigm of death and resurrection fell out of Christian consciousness so completely. As was said, the Pauline paradigm seemingly had fallen through a hole in the memory of the early Church.[45] To be specific, in the second century the Pauline baptismal paradigm of Romans 6:4 is found neither in the *Didache,* nor in the *Epistle of Barnabas,* nor in the letters of Ignatius of Antioch, nor of Clement, nor in *Pastor Hermas,* nor in Justin or the other apologists, nor in Irenaeus. "The Pauline baptismal themes are totally absent."[46] No echo is heard of this major paradigm, though people like Justin and Irenaeus know Romans and cite it.

---

[43] Käsemann, *Commentary on Romans,* 163, 164. Käsemann believes that the participation in the resurrection is not present, but only future.

[44] Bradshaw, *The Search for the Origins of Christian Worship,* 46.

[45] Kelly, *Early Christian Doctrines,* 194.

[46] Benoit, *Le Baptême au Second Siècle,* 227.

No completely satisfying explanation can be found for this. Walter Bauer thought that Paulinism had come under suspicion because Paul was so highly venerated in heterodox circles. Paul, in fact, enjoyed the favor of the heretics,[47] especially Marcion, who rejected the Old Testament, along with Matthew, Mark, and John. Marcion taught there were two Gods, one expressed in Law, the other in Gospel. He preached an ascetic rigorism, rejecting marriage and procreation. Paul absorbed his religious imagination. "Paul commands papal authority. He is the sole infallible teacher."[48] The rest of the apostles were considered Judaizers. In the broader Church there was not much interest in Romans and the two letters to the Corinthians.[49] More than any other single person, it was due to Marcion that the significance of Paul was not overlooked in the second century.[50] Before Marcion there was no canon: "this idea came into existence at one stroke with Marcion and only with Marcion," with Galatians being the canon within the canon for him. Marcionism is a kind of "dogmatic Paulinism."[51] His canon included ten letters of Paul and an edited recension of Luke. Though Marcion and his followers stand somewhat apart from Gnosticism, they also share certain common features of the Gnostic movement that came to prominence in the second century.

Marcion and his followers were the chief danger to the larger Church in the second century. Tertullian devoted the longest of his extant works, the five books *Against Marcion,* to this important threat to the Church, and Marcion is the principal adversary in *On the Flesh of Christ.* The use Marcion and the Gnostics make of Paul prompted Tertullian's characterization of Paul as

[47] W. Bauer, *Orthodoxy and Heresy in the Earliest Christianity*, R. Kraft and G. Krodel, eds., (Philadelphia: Fortress, 1971) 224, 227, 228, 236.

[48] R. J. Hoffmann, *Marcion: On the Restitution of Christianity* (Chico: Scholars, 1984) 308.

[49] Bauer, *Orthodoxy and Heresy in Earliest Christianity*, 219.

[50] E. C. Blackman, *Marcion and His Influence* (London: SPCK, 1948) 110.

[51] H. von Campenhausen, *The Formation of the Christian Bible* (London: Black, 1972) 148, 153.

"the apostle of heretics,"[52] but Tertullian also recognized Paul as the "common master" for both the Marcionites and the Church.[53] An older opinion, represented by Bauer and Benoit,[54] that second-century writers were ignorant of Paul's teaching, has had to be modified.[55] Some leaders in the early Church might have been hesitant about Paul because of the role he played in heterodox thought, but in the earliest written documents we possess—up to Irenaeus—there is no evidence of widespread mistrust.[56]

This history might have played a role in the absence of the Pauline baptismal paradigm of Romans 6:4 in the second century.[57] The first to use the Romans' baptismal text and write of a symbolic participation in the death and resurrection of Jesus is Origen, to whom I will return.[58] He may have rescued the baptismal appeal to Romans 6:4 from heterodox circles.[59]

Though the absence of the Romans text is very likely not the sole reason for the emergence of the baptism of Jesus, what is clear is that in the first two post-biblical centuries the baptism

[52] *Against Marcion* 3:5; CSEL 47:382; E. Dassmann, *Der Stachel im Fleisch: Paulus in der frühchristlichen Literatur bis Irenäus* (Münster: Aschendorff, 1979) 193–200.

[53] *Against Marcion* 3:14; CSEL 47:394. R. D. Sider, "Literary Artifice and the Figure of Paul in the Writings of Tertullian," in *Paul and the Legacies of Paul*, W. S. Babcock, ed. (Dallas: Southern Methodist University, 1990) 99–120.

[54] *Orthodoxy and Heresy in Earliest Christianity*, 225. *Le Baptême au Second Siècle*, 227, 228.

[55] A. Lindemann, *Paulus im ältesten Christentum* (Tübingen: Mohr [Siebeck], 1979) 396–403; Dassmann, *Der Stachel im Fleisch*, 316–320. When early authors are silent on Paul, this does not necessarily mean hostility. Ibid., 318. Opposition to Paul could also be found in Gnostic writings. Ibid., 319. I am indebted to K. Froehlich, "Which Paul? The Image of the Apostle in the History of Biblical Interpretation," in *Essays in Honor of John Meyendorff*, B. Nassif, ed. (Grand Rapids: Eerdmans, 1995).

[56] Dassman, *Der Stachel im Fleisch*, 318.

[57] Brock notes that the Pauline baptismal paradigm of Romans 6:4 made little impression on the Antiochene baptismal texts. "The Epiklesis in the Antiochene Baptismal *Ordines*," in *Symposium Syriacum 1972*, 207. These texts are much later, and other factors are undoubtedly at work.

[58] *On Romans*; PG 14:1018.

[59] 5:10; PL 14:1018. Finn, "General Introduction," in *Early Christian Baptism and the Catechumenate*, 9.

of Jesus was the dominant model for addressing questions of origin, institution, and paradigm of the sacrament of baptism.

Institution by Efficacy

However one interprets the biblical text, the belief that the baptism of Jesus is the foundation of Christian baptism goes back at least to the earliest post-biblical period, to the beginnings of the second century in the witness of Ignatius of Antioch. He writes: "He [Jesus Christ] was born, and he submitted to baptism, so that by his passion he might sanctify the water."[60] The larger context is Ignatius' polemic against those who deny the reality of Jesus Christ's humanity. Here Jesus' baptism in the Jordan is a symbol anticipating the redeeming death of Jesus, which is real because his humanity is not a phantom but is full and complete. In some way the water is penetrated with the efficacy of that death, an efficacy touching the future candidates of baptism. Already at this early date there is evidence of the institution of Christian baptism by the efficacy of Jesus' death anticipated in the baptism of Jesus.[61] This is not a reference, however, to Romans 6:4.

Speaking of the origins of Christian baptism in a more general context, institution may be too precise, too legal a term, though all constitutional notions should not be excluded. What is more typical is the tendency to argue from efficacy, that is, from source to effects. In this case the argument proceeds from the baptism of Jesus to Christians receiving the Spirit and the gifts of the Spirit in sacramental baptism, being led into the source of divine knowing, being initiated into the beginnings of glory, and becoming children of God. This is to establish institution by efficacy.[62] The baptism of Jesus is the institution of Christian baptism because therein is found the effective content of the sacrament. In almost the same terms as in Ignatius, Tertullian writes: "Christ was baptized, that is, he sanctified the waters by his baptism."[63] Again, the efficacy of Christian baptism is found in the baptism of Christ.

[60] *Ephesians* 18:2; SC 10:74.
[61] Légasse, *Naissance du Baptême*, 57.
[62] Finn, *Early Christian Baptism and Catechumenate*, 11.
[63] *Against the Jews* 8:14; CCh 2:1362.

The locating of the institution of baptism is not a critical process nor strictly an historical one. The argument does not proceed by demonstration but by contemplation and initiation. One arrives not by analysis from outside the mystery but by participation from within. This is a species of symbolic logic that goes beyond conceptualization. The experience of the mystery of Christ's baptism cannot be taught. This does not mean that knowledge of the relevant biblical texts is unimportant. They occasion the mystery, as do the rites of Christian initiation. This contemplative approach is strong in Origen and the Syrian authors, such as Aphrahat, Ephrem, and Jacob of Serugh.

One should not oppose this more reflective participatory approach to the institution of sacramental baptism to the great commission ("Go therefore and make disciples of all nations, baptizing . . ."—Matt 28:19; Mark 16:15, 16), or to references to the death of Jesus (Rom 6:4), or to the pierced side ("at once blood and water came out"—John 19:34), as the source of Christian baptism. In this symbolic framework various texts can occupy the same space, even if, in particular cases, one text carries more weight.

Chapter Thirteen

The Principle:
Jesus' Baptism Constitutes
Our Baptism—Institution

In the closing years of the second century, Tertullian proposed
a view that some modern exegetes, Beasley-Murray and Ryndholm
among them, have taken up again in somewhat modified form,
namely, that a whole series of mysteries of Christ's life go into
the fashioning of baptism, not just the baptism of Jesus.[1] Tertullian elaborates on the Old Testament mysteries, all involving
water, that led up to Christ's baptism in the Jordan and to
Christian baptism: the escape of the Israelites through the
waters of the Red Sea (Exod 14:21-29), the bitter fountain waters
at Marah made sweet by Moses (Exod 15:24, 25), the rock from
which water flowed (Exod 17:6), the rock following the Israelites
being Christ (1 Cor 10:4). This leads Tertullian to exclaim: "We
see in this water flowing from Christ the consecration of baptism; what privilege water has in the sight of God and his
Christ."[2]

Then Tertullian proceeds to enumerate the New Testament
mysteries in which water is associated with salvation. First, Ter-

---

[1] *Baptism in the New Testament*, 64. Beasley-Murray quotes P. Ryndholm.
[2] *On Baptism* 9:3, 4; SC 35:78.

tullian enunciates the principle in one of those lapidary phrases for which he is so justly famous: "Christ is never without water!" (numquam sine aqua Christus!).[3] First, "he himself is baptized in water" (Matt 3:13), then, at the wedding feast at Cana (John 2:7), he "inaugurates the beginnings of his power," a reference to the beginning of his ministry of signs.[4] "If he proclaims the Word, he invites the thirsty to drink his eternal water (John 4:14). If he speaks of charity, he recognizes the giving of a glass of water to a neighbor as an act of love."[5] At a well of water he regains his strength (John 4:6). He walks on water (Matt 14:25) and he washes the feet of his disciples with water (John 13:5-10). Tertullian interrupts the list of mysteries that in the New Testament began with the baptism of Jesus to comment on the span: "The witness to baptism [as a sacrament] lasts up to the passion." Water, he notes, played a role in Pilate's washing of his hands (Matt 27:24). And water bursts forth from Christ's side when he is pierced by the soldier's lance (John 19:34).[6]

So Tertullian places the baptism of Jesus at the conjunction of the Old Testament and New Testament witnesses to Christian baptism, but he does not expand on it. The baptism of Jesus is the first in a series of mysteries that pour content into the sacrament. This appears to account for institution of the sacrament, but institution without immediate efficacy. During Jesus' life the apostles, Tertullian believes, could not administer baptism because "the Lord had not yet fully attained his glory and the efficacy of baptism had not been founded by his passion and resurrection."[7] Therefore the whole history of the mysteries in Jesus' life, with the baptism of Jesus as its beginning, went into the institution of Christian baptism, but the passion and death constitute the inner efficacy making the content operative and effective. Here again we have institution by contemplation and initiation. Though a certain mystery may have dominance, one cannot isolate a given mystery to the exclusion of others.

[3] Ibid; SC 35:79.
[4] Ibid.
[5] Ibid.
[6] Ibid.
[7] Ibid., 11:4; SC 35:82.

Ephrem will propose a similar teaching, namely, the whole of Christ's incarnate life: the full range of mysteries, from conception through nativity, on through death and resurrection to the ascension, are all concentrated in the mystery of his baptism.[8] Or as the modern exegete Beasley-Murray puts it, Christian baptism appropriates "the total redemptive action which the baptism of Jesus set in motion."[9]

Images of Extravagance at the Jordan

The main focus of these pages is a kind of guarded equivalency between the baptism of Jesus and our baptism in the post-biblical period. An early statement of the principle is a text from the Rome of the 250s by Novatian, the leader of a rigorist schismatic group, who wrote a completely orthodox work, *On the Trinity*. Novatian has been writing of the difference between the modest outpouring of the Spirit on the prophets, in contrast to the whole treasury of the Spirit being poured out on Jesus: "It is he [the Holy Spirit] who after the baptism of the Lord came upon him, and remained on him under the form of a dove, fully and wholly dwelling on Christ alone, without being measured or diminished by sharing [with us]. [The Spirit] was distributed and sent with an overflowing abundance in order that others might receive something of an advance taste of these graces. The whole source of the Holy Spirit dwells in Christ in order that from him might flow the channels of gifts and works, the Holy Spirit dwelling superabundantly in Christ."[10] The Spirit who brings such divine bounty in the baptism of Jesus "brings about the second birth, from water," namely Christian baptism.[11]

One should notice the central role the Spirit has as the link between Christ's baptism and ours. Novatian repeats images of extravagance: plenitude, without measure, superabundance,

---

[8] *Hymns on the Church* 36:3; CSCO 199:88; S. Brock, "St. Ephrem on Christ as Light in Mary and in the Jordan: *Hymni de Ecclesia* 36," in *Eastern Churches Review* 7 (1975) 140.

[9] *Baptism in the New Testament*, 64.

[10] *On the Trinity* 29; CCh 4:70.

[11] Ibid.; CCh 4:71.

whole source. That the Spirit, the whole source, came upon and rested on Jesus as a symbol of divine fullness (there is a resemblance to the formulation in the *Gospel of the Hebrews*) is the assurance that the same abundance flows from Christ to us in our baptism. Here is an early statement of the principle.

In briefer form, Clement of Alexandria enunciates the principle: "That which happened at the Jordan happens to us also, for Christ is our model. . . . Baptized we are illumined; illumined, we are adopted as sons; adopted, we are made perfect; made perfect, we receive immortality.[12] Ambrose hands on the tradition, saying that Christ was baptized in the Jordan and there instituted the form of the saving bath."[13] Clearer still is the mysterious work known as the *Incomplete Commentary on Matthew*, a text by a sixth-century author, Pseudo-Chrysostom, that enjoyed a great reputation during the Middle Ages: "All that happened to Christ at his baptism, happened with regard to the *mysterion* of all those who will be baptized in ages to come."[14] The baptism of Jesus is the interior sum of Christian baptism.

A much later Syrian text of Anthony of Tagrit (d. ca. 850) establishes this relationship in terms of the anointing. "[The Father] anoints him [Jesus] with the Spirit at his baptism in the Jordan in order that this [anointing] might be the origin [of baptism/anointing] of our race. The divine Spirit rests on us [also] so that from now on we might be shown to be sons of God and children of the spiritual mother [baptism]."[15]

With these statements of the principle, we can look at a series of witnesses without claims of completeness.

Aphrahat—The Two-Source Theory

Aphrahat (ca. 270–ca. 345), first Father of the Syrian Church, is a significant witness because he considered himself "a disciple of

[12] *Teacher* 1, 6, 25; SC 70:158.
[13] *On the Interpellation of Job and David* 4; PL 14:816.
[14] PG 56:659. I am indebted to T. Camelot, *Spiritualité du Baptême* (Paris: Cerf, 1960) 257–281, for some texts.
[15] *Treatise on Myron*, manuscript in the British Museum. Quoted by Varghese, *Les Onctions Baptismales dans la Tradition Syrienne*, 220.

the Scriptures,"[16] a boast that is amply justified by the exclusive reliance on the biblical text without any trace of Greek philosophical influence. His theological world is wholly biblical, wholly symbolic, enriched with Targumic traditions.[17]

Without a doubt Aphrahat saw the Jordan as the source of Christian baptism. He writes: "Many prophets came and were unable to reveal baptism, until the great prophet [Christ] came, and he alone opened it, and was baptized in it."[18] Christ not only opened baptism; he opened it by himself being baptized. Nonetheless, Aphrahat demonstrates the fluidity of the contemplative approach to questions of the institution of sacraments. He has another perspective, which in no way cancels out the Jordan as the source of Christian baptism.

In an extended reflection, Aphrahat orchestrates a symphony of symbols. Typical of his profoundly Old Testament orientation, he begins with Israel being "plunged into the middle of the sea—in this night of the Passover," which is for Israel "the day of salvation."[19] The Christian pasch is also the day of salvation. This passing through the waters of the sea is a type of Christian baptism: "Our Savior has washed the feet of his disciples," be it noted, also in "the night of the Passover," thus constituting "the mystery of baptism."[20] As the Jews were saved by passing through water on the Passover, so the disciples are saved by having their feet washed during the Christian pasch. Referring to the night Christ washed the feet of the disciples, Aphrahat continues: "For you ought to know, my friend, that it is during that night [of the pasch] that our Savior gave the true baptism."[21]

He then repeats the relation of foot-washing to the institution of baptism, and introduces Romans 6:4, a rare exception at this early date: "For it was in that very night that he showed them [the disciples] the mystery of baptism—which is the passion of

---

[16] Demonstration 22:26; SC 349:39.

[17] R. Lavenant, "Aphraates," in Encyclopedia of the Early Church, 54.

[18] Homily 4:5; Aphrahat's des Persischen Weisen Homilien, G. Bert, ed. (Leipzig: Hinrich, 1888) (Texte und Untersuchungen 3/3-4) 56.

[19] Demonstration 12:10; SC 359:582.

[20] Ibid.

[21] Ibid.

his death, as the Apostle says: 'You have been buried with him by baptism for the death—and we rise with him by the power of God.' "[22] Of the disciples at Ephesus, Aphrahat says that "they were baptized with a true baptism—the mystery of the passion of our Lord."[23] Christ points to this baptism when he says "You will baptize [sic] in the Holy Spirit."[24]

At this point Aphrahat narrates the washing of the disciples' feet by Christ, which is followed by a eucharistic reference: "For it is after he had washed their feet that he goes to the table and gives them his body and his blood."[25] In a summary way Aphrahat says that after instituting baptism by washing the disciples' feet, Christ sits at the table and institutes the Eucharist. Both baptism and the Eucharist are instituted at the Last Supper.[26] The origin and institution of Christian baptism is the passion and resurrection to which the Last Supper belongs. Though he mentions Romans 6:4, it does not play a significant role in his baptismal theology.

Aphrahat was not innovating when he has baptism instituted at the washing of the feet but reflects a tradition well known to the Syrian Church.[27] Cyrillona, a fourth-century Syrian poet of whose life we know nothing, seems to presuppose that baptism was instituted at the washing of the feet.[28] This tradition seems reflected in the liturgical practice of foot-washing as part of the sacrament of baptism, evidenced in Tertullian, Tatian, Ephrem, Ambrose, and Augustine, to name a few.[29]

[22] Ibid.

[23] Ibid.; SC 359:583.

[24] Ibid.

[25] Ibid.; SC 359:584.

[26] It is possible that Aphrahat has the risen Christ promulgating the baptism he instituted at the Last Supper. "When our Lord gave the mystery of baptism to his apostles, he said to them, 'the one who believes and is baptized will live' " (Mark 16:16). *Demonstration* 1:17; SC 249:231.

[27] Brock, *The Holy Spirit in the Syrian Baptismal Tradition*, 79.

[28] Quoted in Duncan, *Baptism in the Demonstrations of Aphraates the Persian Sage*, 70, 71. Duncan, 67–81, treats of the washing of the feet in Aphrahat as the institution of Christian baptism.

[29] A. Jaubert, "Une Lecture du Lavement des Pieds au Mardi-Mercredi Saint," in *Muséon* 79 (1966) 257–286; G. Richter, *Die Fusswashung im Johannesevangelium* (Regensburg: Pustet, 1967); J. Michl, "Der Sinn der Fuss-

Aphrahat is significant because he demonstrates the fluidity of the contemplative approach to the origin of Christian baptism. Moving in a cosmos where one symbol does not displace another, he names without embarrassment both the baptism of Jesus and the death and resurrection of Jesus (washing of the feet) as the origin and institution of Christian baptism.

As we shall see, there was a view that baptism originated out of the side of Christ on the cross. This is not the same as the Pauline view that baptism is a communion in the death and resurrection of Jesus (Rom 6:4). But it shares the link to the death of Jesus. Clearly the process of becoming a Christian was expressed in a variety of ways.[30]

Ephrem—"The Aesthetic Truth of Symbols"

With this background it is understandable that the ancient Church, in general, and the Syrian tradition, in particular, tied the institution of the sacrament of baptism more to the baptism of Jesus than to the words of the risen Christ in Matthew 28:18-20.[31] Ephrem takes up and develops the theme Aphrahat announces about Christ opening up baptism by himself being baptized. Ephrem writes: "Our Lord opened our baptism in the blessed river Jordan."[32] *The Teaching of St. Gregory* also establishes Christian baptism by the baptism of Jesus and likewise has Jesus' baptism opening Christian baptism: "The Son of

---

washung," in *Biblica* 40 (1959) 697–708. Especially good in the early witnesses is N. M. Haring, "Historical Notes on the Interpretation of John 13:10," in *Catholic Biblical Quarterly* 13 (1951) 355–380.

[30] Bradshaw, *The Search for the Origins of Christian Worship*, 46.

[31] Ignatius of Antioch, *Ephesians* 18:2; SC 10:74; Clement of Alexandria, *The Teacher* 1:6.26.1; SC 70:158; Tertullian, *On Baptism* 9:2; SC 35:78. See F. M. Braun, "Le baptême d'après le quatrième évangile," in *Revue Thomiste* 48 [1948] 358, 362. The baptism of Jesus as the institution of the sacrament of baptism became enshrined in Aquinas' *Summa Theologica* III, q.66, a.2: ". . . it seems that a sacrament is then instituted, when it receives the power of producing its effect. Now baptism received this power when Christ was baptized. Consequently baptism was truly instituted then, if we consider it as a sacrament. But the obligation of receiving this sacrament was proclaimed to mankind after the passion and resurrection."

[32] *Hymns on Epiphany* 11:2; CSCO 187:170.

God, therefore, came and was baptized, to establish the baptism of all who would be baptized, that handing on this tradition, He might reveal salvation to all, and be understood and known, and that by this He might open his life-giving teaching of truth to be revealed to the world."[33] The Son of God institutes baptism by being baptized, thus establishing his own baptismal tradition, in which salvation is revealed, making manifest the transforming teaching of the gospel. The baptism of Jesus closes his hidden life, opens up Christian baptism, and is the beginning of Christ's public ministry.

Though the vocabulary is different, the conception of Christ's baptism opening Christian baptism is also found in Cyril of Jerusalem,[34] Gregory Nazianzus,[35] and John Chrysostom,[36] among others. This would indicate that the idea of Christ opening baptism by his baptism was extensive in the East.

For Ephrem it is not enough that Jesus' baptism is the model of Christian baptism. Jesus' baptism is the effective cause: "the Spirit is given by his baptism,"[37] indicating that the baptism of Christ is the origin and source of Christian baptism through the imparting of the Spirit first at Christ's baptism and then at ours.[38] Ephrem says that by his baptism Jesus "bound the invisible Spirit with simple water" so that anyone who is wet with this water "should perceive [in one's spirit] the gift of the Spirit."[39] Christ's baptism is the efficacious source of Christian baptism because the interior reality of the first is made effective in the second.

The Teaching of St. Gregory, which comes out of the related Armenian tradition, is even more specific: "The Son of God, therefore, came and was baptized, to establish the baptism of all who would be baptized."[40] In the words of Jacob of Serugh,

---

[33] *Teaching of St. Gregory* 420; Thomson, 91.
[34] *Catechetical Lecture* 3:11; Reischl, 1:78, 80.
[35] *Discourse* 39:15, 16, SC 358:182–186.
[36] *On Matthew* 12:3; PG 57:205, 206.
[37] *Commentary on the Diatessaron* 4:3; SC 121:95.
[38] This is a major preoccupation of the research of both Winkler and Brock. See also Braun, "Le baptême d'après le quatrième évangile."
[39] *Sermon on Our Lord* 55; CSCO 271:52.
[40] 420; Thomson, 91. Aphrahat tied the formal institution of the sacrament of baptism to the washing of feet, the first of the oriental fathers to

Jesus' baptism is "the perfect baptism," and thus is the source of Christian baptism. In part this explains why catechumens wanted to be baptized in the actual waters of the Jordan. Not surprisingly, each baptism of a Christian was considered a reenactment of Jesus' baptism effected by the Holy Spirit.[41] This is reflected in both East and West in the decoration of early baptisteries.[42]

With Ephrem the contemplative approach to institution is intensified. No contemplation is possible without awe and wonder. Essentially biblical and Semitic in his thought, he has nothing of the dogmatizing tendency of Greek theology, or philosophically inspired definitions.[43] What Jean Pierre Mahe calls the "aesthetic truth of symbols" well describes what Ephrem seeks to penetrate.[44] Ephrem looks upon John the Baptist as the "Treasurer of Baptism," who mediates to Jesus in the Jordan the prophetic/sacerdotal tradition of the Old Testament.[45] Jesus takes John's baptism, perfects it by his own baptism at John's hands, thus transforming John's baptism from a purification rite to a sacrament conferring the Spirit—in a word, instituting Christian baptism. Without the baptism of Jesus in the Jordan, "the order [of succession]" might be lost, coming as it does from the Old Testament and passing through the Jordan event on into the New Testament.[46] "Praise be God who gave us his order."[47] In this elevation of John's baptism in his own baptism, Christ reveals himself as more than a link in the order of

---

make such an association. *Demonstrations* 12:10; SC 359:583. See Duncan, *Baptism in the Demonstrations of Aphraates the Persian Sage*, 68, 70.

[41] Brock, "St. Ephrem on Christ as Light in Mary and in the Jordan: *Hymni De Ecclesia 36*," 140.

[42] H. Leclercq, "Baptistère," in *Dictionnaire d'Archéologie Chrétienne et de Liturgie*, 2:397; A. Khatchatrian, *Les Baptistères Paléochrétiens: Plans, Notices et Bibliographie* (Paris: Centre National de la Recherche Scientifique, 1962).

[43] S. Brock, *St. Ephrem the Syrian: Hymns on Paradise* (Crestwood: St. Vladimir, 1990) 40; idem, *The Luminous Eye*, 29–31.

[44] "Introduction," in *La Caverne des Trésors*; CSCO 527:XVII. Mahe is describing the theological approach of *The Cave of Treasures*.

[45] *Sermon on Our Lord* 55; CSCO 271:52.

[46] *Hymns Against Heresies* 22:19; CSCO 170:81, 82.

[47] Ibid.

succession. He is the "Lord of the Economy,"[48] master of the plan of salvation. Also at the Jordan Jesus shows himself a pastor, and, in fact, enters into his pastoral charge.[49] About a hundred years later the Armenian document *The Teaching of St. Gregory* has similar ideas, as we have seen.

To make an equivalency between the baptism of Jesus and Christian baptism, Ephrem has a number of instruments at hand. The garment image, already familiar, makes this type of identification possible. Christ put off his garment in the Jordan. Even so "every garment is forever bound up with the garment of the one who put it off."[50] No real alienation of the garment exists, even if the candidate descends into the waters and puts it on. It remains the garment of Christ, "which will clothe its bearer in eternity."[51]

Another image serving the identification between Christ's baptism and ours is the sanctifying of the waters: "Blessed little river Jordan, into which descends the sea of purity in order to be baptized by your waves; your waters have been purified by the descent of the Holy One who institutes the baptism of the justification of souls."[52] His baptism sanctifies the waters, thus instituting Christian baptism.

A hymn ascribed to Ephrem combines the sanctifying of the waters with the most graphic image of identification, Fire and Spirit.

"By my baptism the waters are sanctified,
and they receive from me the Fire and the Spirit.
And if I had not been baptized,
they [the waters] would not have been made perfect."[53]

---

[48] *Sermon on Our Lord* 55; CSCO 271:52. In the *Hymns Against Heresies* 22:19, John invests Jesus with the prophetic and priestly office. In the *Sermon on Our Lord* 53; CSCO 271:50, 51, it is Simeon at the presentation in the Temple who performs the same function.

[49] Saber, *La Théologie Baptismale de Saint Éphrem*, 70.

[50] *Hymns on Epiphany* 4:2, 3; CSCO 187:142.

[51] Ibid.

[52] *Sermon on Our Lord* 55; CSCO 270:52.

[53] Sogita, 5:32; CSCO 187:204. For the authenticity of these Sogita hymns, see E. Beck, "Vorwort," in *Ephraem des Syrers: Hymnen de Nativitate (Epiphania)*; CSCO 187:XI.

In a text we have already met, Jesus himself puts into Christian baptism the Fire and the Spirit manifest in his own baptism, the same Fire and Spirit present in Mary at the incarnation, in his own baptism in the Jordan, and in the Eucharist:

"Fire and Spirit are in the womb of her who bore You,
Fire and Spirit are in the river in which You were baptized
Fire and Spirit are in our baptism,
and in the Bread and Cup is Fire and Holy Spirit."[54]

A consistent pneumatology binds together this history of holy mysteries. Ephrem goes on to combine this theme with the image of clothing: "The children of baptism, children without spot, have clothed themselves in Fire and Spirit."[55]

Jesus Wraps Our Baptism in His Baptism

As is evident, the identity of Jesus' baptism in the Jordan with Christian baptism is carried mostly by the Spirit. Ephrem has the Spirit at the Jordan isolate Jesus from the other penitents: "In the baptism of John he [the Spirit] left all the others and let himself come down upon only One."[56] Then Ephrem moves to Christian baptism: "But now [at the baptism of Christians] he alights and rests upon each one who is born out of the water."[57]

In a similar formulation in his *Commentary on the Diatessaron*, Ephrem first points to the unique character of the Jordan event in terms of the Spirit: "Many were baptized on that day, but the Spirit descended and rested on one single person, in order to distinguish by a sign the one who, by his appearance, is not distinguished from other men."[58] Then he uses the Spirit to be the constitutive link with Christian baptism: "As the Spirit

---

[54] *Hymns on Faith* 10:17; CSCO 155:35, 36.

[55] *Hymns on Epiphany* 4:19; CSCO 187:144.

[56] Ibid., 6:2; CSCO 187:147. In his *Commentary on the Diatessaron* 4:3; SC 121:95, Ephrem repeats this idea.

[57] *Hymns on Epiphany* 6:1; CSCO 187:147.

[58] 4:3; SC 121:95.

descended on him during his baptism, so the Spirit is given by his baptism."[59] Again the Jordan event is efficacious.

The descent of the Spirit on Jesus is more than a proof for Ephrem of the presence and action of the Spirit at Jesus' baptism in the Jordan. It demonstrates the presence and action of the Spirit also in the baptism that Christ gives, namely, the sacrament of baptism.[60] "The Lord opened baptism in the blessed Jordan river."[61] "The Holy One, descending and washing in you [Jordan], has gone down by his baptism to open baptism and reconcile souls."[62] Ephrem uses the image of wrapping. After the Jordan event, Jesus wraps Christian baptism in his baptism, and this Christ carries away from the Jordan to give to the community of believers in the sacrament: "After his baptism our Lord enveloped in the baptism [he received] the baptism he carried away."[63] In a word, Christ "took baptism out of the Jordan."[64]

Ephrem gives little attention to the Pauline teaching on baptism as participation in the death and resurrection of Jesus, *pace* Saber.[65] In this he is one with Aphrahat and the Syrian tradition, at least to a fairly late date.[66] Nonetheless, Ephrem wishes to relate the mysteries of Jesus to one another, and that includes relating baptism to the paschal events: "The birth hastens to his baptism and joins it; the baptism hastens until it comes to the death. Without a break, your death arrives at the resurrection. So as we have seen, a fourfold bridge [exists] to his kingdom—

---

[59] Ibid. A similar conception is found elsewhere: "The Spirit rested on him in the form of a dove during his baptism in order to show without doubt that he will baptize in fire." *Hymns of Faith* 7:8; CSCO 155:24, 25.

[60] Beck, "Le Baptême chez Saint Éphrem" 114; Saber, *La Théologie Baptismale de Saint Éphrem* 87, 88.

[61] *Hymns on Epiphany* 9:2; CSCO 187:170.

[62] *Hymns on Virginity* 15:3; CSCO 224:51. "Christ, immortal in nature, clothes himself in a mortal body, and plunges under the waters and brings out of the water the treasure of life of our first parents." Ibid., 7:10: CSCO 224:27. Christ's baptism, the source of Christian baptism, restores believers to the life of Adam and Eve.

[63] *Sermon on Our Lord* 55; CSCO 271:52.

[64] Ibid., 56; CSCO 271:53.

[65] *La Théologie Baptismale de Saint Éphrem*, 133.

[66] Brock, *The Holy Spirit in the Syrian Baptismal Tradition*, 79.

and see! his flock follows in his tracks."[67] The four bridges to Christ's kingdom are incarnation, baptism in the Jordan, death, and resurrection. The last bridge is not an appeal to participation in the death and resurrection of Jesus of Romans 6:4, but to the pierced side of John 19:34. In part the small notice given to the Pauline conception may be due to the dominant role the womb plays as an image of the font.[68]

Though Ephrem moves in a symbolic world that is often without theological precision, his meaning regarding the relation of the Jordan event to Christian baptism is clear. The baptism of Jesus is more than a prototype that defines from the outside. The baptism of Jesus is also efficacious, "its principle and its institution."[69] In this Ephrem is very likely handing on the tradition of the Church of Edessa.[70]

[67] *Hymns on Epiphany* 10:9; CSCO 187:167.

[68] Brock, *The Holy Spirit in the Syrian Baptismal Tradition*, 79.

[69] Beck, *Le Baptême chez Saint Éphrem*, 112; Saber, *La Théologie Baptismale de Saint Éphrem*, 70; Varghese, *Les Onctions Baptismales dans la Tradition Syrienne*, 43.

[70] Saber, *La Théologie Baptismale de Saint Éphrem*, 70.

Chapter Fourteen

Calvary Threatens the Dominance of Jordan—Institution

We must go back chronologically to look at Origen, who introduces a substantial witness to the Pauline theology of Romans 6:4, a significant moment in the development of baptismal theology. He wants to be faithful to the full biblical witness, including the Pauline biblical theology. Because of the dearth of references to Romans 6:4 in the second century, it is important to identify the location and extent of the Romans text in Origen's works at the beginning of the third century. For he is the first to call attention to Romans 6:4. A quick survey shows he refers to this Pauline baptismal theology in the following works: *Commentary on John* (his first published work),[1] *Homilies on Luke*,[2] *Homilies on Exodus*,[3] *Homilies on Samuel*,[4] *Commentary on the Canticle of Canticles*,[5] *Homilies on Ezekiel*,[6] *Homilies on Genesis*,[7]

---

[1] *Commentary on John* 1:27; 2:32; 2:33; 10:35; 20:12; 20:25; SC 120:150, 342, 342; SC 157:522; SC 290:206, 268, 270. *On First Principles* is also an early work. There is a possible reference in 1, 3, 7; SC 252:156, 158.

[2] 17:3; SC 87:255.

[3] 5:2; SC 321:154.

[4] 1:19; SC 328:152.

[5] 1, 3, 7; SC 375:212.

[6] 2:5; SC 352:116.

[7] 3:7: SC 7:140.

Homilies on Leviticus,[8] *Homilies on Jeremiah,*[9] *Commentary on Romans,*[10] *Commentary on Matthew,*[11] *Against Celsus,*[12] *Homilies on Joshua* (among his last works).[13]

Several things need to be noted. The use of the Pauline baptismal theology enshrined in the Romans 6 text is to be found at the beginning of his theological development, *Commentary on John* (begun between 226–229, before he left Alexandria in 231), and in every other period, including his last works *Homilies on Joshua* (ca. 249 or 250). Within his professional life, this represents a constant. If the *Commentary on John* was begun sometime before 231, then his awareness of the baptismal import of Romans 6:4 predates the *Commentary on the Romans*, written sometime before 244. Except for the *Commentary on Romans*, the references are generally made in passing, but the number of times the text surfaces, and the variety of contexts, would indicate a firm conviction of the relevance of Paul's baptismal theology.[14]

Origen associates Romans 6:4 with the imparting of the Spirit, as also the remission of sins and the giving of life. Origen recalls that Jesus himself called his passion "baptism" (Mark 10:39).[15] Baptism in the Jordan is the beginning of a first resurrection, imperfect, but directed toward the second resurrection, the perfect resurrection after the death on the cross.[16]

---

[8] 2:4; SC 286:110.

[9] 1:16; SC 232:234; 19:15; SC 238:238.

[10] 5:10; PG 14:1018.

[11] 16:6; PG 13:1381, 1384.

[12] 2:69; SC 132:448.

[13] 4:2; SC 71:150. This overview is not meant to be exhaustive.

[14] H. Windisch points out that Origen uses Romans 6 to teach the ascetic approach to baptism, namely, that only those who are dead to sin are truly baptized in the death of Jesus. *Taufe und Sünde im ältesten Christentum bis auf Origenes* (Tübingen: Mohr [Siebeck], 1908) 475.

[15] *Commentary on Matthew* 16:6; PG 13:1381, 1384.

[16] *On Romans* 5:9; PG 14:1047. This is in the Latin translation of Rufinus, sometimes thought to be too free, but Rufinus' fidelity to the main lines of Origen's thought is supported by Henry Chadwick and Caroline P. Hammond Bammel. The Romans 6:4 text is also preserved in a Greek fragment, no. 29. A. Ramsbotham, ed., *The Commentary of Origen on the Epistle to the Romans II*, in *Journal of Theological Studies* 13 (1912) 363. H. Crouzel, "La 'première' et la 'second' resurrection des hommes d'après Origène," in *Didaskalia* 3 (1973) 3–19. See Bammel's magisterial *Der Römerbrieftext des Rufin*

Given the absence of the Romans text from second-century authors, this is a surprising development. The surprise is heightened by the relative absence of the Pauline baptismal theology from the subsequent tradition until the fourth century. However, Origen's stance is in keeping with his relation to the previous tradition. If one compares his theology to that of his predecessor, Clement of Alexandria, one is struck by the gain in precision.[17] Also, his devotion to the word would not allow him to let a passage like Romans 6:4 go unexploited.

The Cosmos of Symbols and the Jordan Event

Origen's interest in the baptismal theology of Romans 6 does not mean that he has abandoned the previous tradition that took the baptism of Jesus as its primary paradigm. Origen illustrates how difficult it is to stake out exclusive claims of any one text as grounding the institution of baptism. He has a revolving symbolic world, with symbolic wheels turning within symbolic wheels. Therefore isolation of a given symbol like the Jordan event as alone establishing the institution of the sacrament of baptism is untrue to Origen's thought. Yet the baptism of Jesus is a major image in this symbolic cosmos. Using an etymology found in Philo, which allows him to relate Jordan to "descent," Origen plays on the descent of the Word at the incarnation and the descent of Christ into the Jordan. He says: "The Jordan means 'descent.' The river of God 'which descends' with the power of a mighty current, is our Savior and Lord, in whom we are baptized in the true water, the water of salvation.'"[18]

Without concern for overlapping images, Origen joins the candidate for baptism to the descent of Jesus into the Jordan, which river is itself Christ. In a separate Lukan fragment, Origen again presents Christ as the river that is descending. The Jordan equals Christ. Origen then indicates that this river which is Christ is the source of Christian baptism: "The baptism of

---

and Seine Origenes-Übersetzung (Freiburg: Herder, 1985) and her *Der Römer-briefkommentar des Origenes* (Freiburg: Herder, 1990).

[17] R.P.C. Hanson, *Origen's Doctrine of Tradition* (London: SPCK, 1954) 183.

[18] Origen, *Homilies on Luke* 21:4; SC 87:294.

Christ contains in its perfection the remission of sins [for believers] by the sole act of [his] receiving it."[19]

For Origen, the sacrament of baptism is located in a series of symbols corresponding to a three-leveled perspective in which the Old Testament is shadow, the temporal gospel is image, and the eternal gospel is reality.[20] The Scriptures are filled with the mysteries of God into which one enters; and entering, one is initiated into divine knowing. In writing of baptism his main focus is on the mystical dimension, the call to ascetic life and perfection.[21] He is not greatly concerned with institutional questions. Origen wants to present the Christian mysteries as demanding an interior transformation, in contrast to the pagan rites, which leave the moral structure of the person unchanged.[22] This ascetic dimension is of great importance for Origen. He also desires to be a faithful dispenser of the divine mysteries.[23]

The Jordan that cleanses Naaman the Syrian is "of sovereign virtue and very good to drink. Just as no man is good save God the Father, so no river is good except the Jordan."[24] It was necessary for Naaman "to grasp the great mystery of the Jordan."[25] As Naaman was cleansed in the Jordan, so we can receive baptism only in the Jordan, where Christ was baptized; only from it can we draw those great benefits in the measure of our need.[26] Those who deposit their uncleanness in the Jordan will be purer than the foulest leper, "capable of receiving twice-over the graces (charismata) of the Spirit and ready to welcome the Spirit. The dove of the Spirit does not fly over any other river."[27]

The Spirit resting on Jesus in the Jordan means that the Spirit

---

[19] Fragment 51; *On Luke* 3:3; SC 87:498, 500.
[20] H. Crouzel, *Origen* (San Francisco: Harper & Row, 1989) 223.
[21] C. Blanc, "Le Baptême d'après Origène," in *Studia Patristica* 11 (1972) 113.
[22] *Homilies on Ezekiel* 6:5; SC 352:224, 226; *Homilies on Numbers* 3:1; SC 29:89–91.
[23] *Commentary on John* 20:2; SC 290:160.
[24] Ibid., 6:47; SC 157:314.
[25] Ibid., 6:47; SC 157:312.
[26] Ibid., 6:48; SC 157:318.
[27] Ibid.

will never be taken away.[28] The dove remains attached to Jesus, and "it is not able to fly far from him," for the Spirit is given to be imparted.[29] "The Lord received baptism, the heavens were rent, the Holy Spirit descends on him, and the voice from heaven like thunder says: 'Here is my beloved Son, in whom I am well pleased.' Likewise one ought to say, thanks to the baptism of Jesus, the heaven is opened [upon us] and the Spirit descends . . . the Lord communicating the Spirit who had come upon him."[30] The Spirit received at the Jordan is the Spirit imparted after the resurrection.[31]

I repeat several texts mentioned earlier. Origen speaks of "the great mystery of the Jordan,"[32] likening the unique character of the Jordan to the unique Father: "Just as no one is good, except the one only God, the Father, so, among the rivers, no river is good except the Jordan."[33] One needs to interpret "Jordan" in a manner "worthy of God," Origen suggests.[34] By this he means a series of baptismal realities: the baptism in the Jordan (it is not clear whether he is referring to John's ministry of baptism or to Christian baptism), the fact that Jesus is baptized there, and a mysterious "house of preparation," which might be the baptism of Jesus as the content of Christian baptism.[35] Origen explicitly identifies the Jordan with Jesus Christ three times. The Jordan is "the Word of God made flesh and dwelling among us."[36] As we have seen, Origen bases himself on an etymology he took from Philo. Origen explains: "Jordan means 'to descend.' The river of God descending with the power of a mighty current is our Savior and Lord in whom we are baptized in the true water, the water of salvation."[37] He returns again to this etymology: "Above all the Jordan means

---

[28] *Homilies on Numbers* 18:4; SC 29:370.
[29] *Commentary on John* 6:42; SC 157:296, 298.
[30] *Homilies on Luke* 27:5; SC 87:348.
[31] Ibid.
[32] *Commentary on John* 6:47; SC 157:312.
[33] Ibid.; SC 157:314.
[34] Ibid., 6:48; SC 157:318.
[35] Ibid.
[36] Ibid., 6:42; SC 157:296.
[37] *Homilies on Luke* 21:4; SC 87:294.

'descent,' and it is there [at the Jordan] that Christ, the river of God, the true drink, the water of God, descends.''[38]

How are these two paradigms, the mystery of the Jordan and the paschal mystery, related in Origen? Hugo Rahner thinks that the baptism in the Jordan is the primary exemplar for the new life, while the death on the cross and the resurrection are the power of the new creation.[39] In any case, Origen, like Aphrahat, working with a contemplative, participatory model of locating the origin of the sacrament of baptism, maintains the two sources, the Jordan and the paschal mystery.

Philoxenus—"He Was Baptized and Immediately He Gave It to Us"

One could continue to look at the Greek tradition, which has its own history of interest in the baptism of Jesus, but I have chosen to look at the Syrians, both Syriac- and Greek-speaking, where the Jordan tradition is the strongest. Who were the players and what were the changes?

Philoxenus of Mabbug and Severus of Antioch are among the most important monophysite, anti-Chalcedonian theologians of the fifth and sixth centuries. The bishop of Mabbug was trained in Edessa, where Ephrem had long lived. Philoxenus stands in the Syrian tradition, indeed, is a faithful example of the indigenous Syrian culture, but he is in a different position than Ephrem. Even though Philoxenus gives pride of preference to Ephrem, who is adverse to the Greek philosophical style, he openly proclaims the Greek text of the Old Testament superior to the Syriac, and is moved to apologize for Ephrem's lack of philosophical precision.[40] In the face of bitter christological con-

---

[38] Fragment 51; *On Luke* 3:3; SC 87:498, 500. This may be a variant reading of *Homilies on Luke* 21:4; SC 87:294.

[39] "Taufe und geistliches Leben bei Origenes," in *Zeitschrift für Aszese und Mystik* 7 (1932) 212.

[40] He sponsored two important revisions of early Syriac translations from the Greek and gave his rationale in his *Commentary on the Prologue of John*, CSCO 381:52, 53, that the Syriac translators "have sinned against many [words]," translating them "in other senses." Brock, "From Antagonism to Assimilation: Syriac Attitudes to Greek Learning," in *Syriac Perspectives on Late Antiquity* V:20; Varghese, *Les Onctions Baptismales dans la Tradition Syrienne*, 163.

troversies demanding philosophical rigor and finely tuned tools, Philoxenus and other Syriac writers feel obliged to abandon the symbolic theology of their predecessors—Ephrem among them—and opt for Greek philosophical exactitude. Ephrem perceives as "venom" the "wisdom of the Greeks," that is, philosophical logic applied to theology. Now in Philoxenus that poison becomes the ideal medicine. Other ages, other needs.

Philoxenus takes up the Syrian tradition of the baptism of Jesus as the principle and source of Christian baptism; for him the baptism of Jesus plays a central role.[41] He establishes the role of the Jordan event in the constitution of Christian baptism in various ways. Of Jesus' baptism in the Jordan, Philoxenus says: "Jesus has been born anew by baptism."[42] As Jesus undergoes "new birth" at the Jordan, so Christians are born again at baptism. Philoxenus has Jesus praying to the Father: "O Father, through my prayer, open heaven and send thy Holy Spirit upon this new womb of baptism."[43] This is not a generic reference but is related specifically to Jesus' baptism in the Jordan: "I have been baptized and have prepared baptism that it may become the spiritual womb which gives birth to men anew."[44] Like Ephrem, the Spirit that was sent on Jesus is sent on those going down into the font, linking baptism to baptism: "Whenever they baptize and pray to you and ask, send the Holy Spirit upon the baptism by which they are baptized."[45] In fact, when Jesus went down into the Jordan, he intended to give his baptism to us to be our baptism.

This role of the Spirit in Christ's baptism and in ours is given further specification in Philoxenus' teaching on baptismal anointing. The anointing of candidates in baptism is itself a participation in the anointing of Christ by the Spirit at the Jordan. Commenting on the Jordan event, Philoxenus says: "He was

[41] Ibid., 167.

[42] *Homilies* 9; SC 44:246; *Commentary on the Prologue of John* 93; CSCO 381:213. In fact, there are three births: eternally from the Father, temporally from the virgin, spiritually from the Jordan. Ibid., 13: CSCO 381:35.

[43] Fragment 50, *Fragments of the Commentary on Matthew and Luke* 50; CSCO 393:59.

[44] Ibid.

[45] Ibid.

anointed with us in the economy, and he received [what is] ours, because he became as us."[46] The anointing of Jesus is not simply the eternal anointing by the Father, but is in the economy, that is, at the Jordan and in our history.

In the most explicit text he writes: "He was baptized [of] our baptism, because he was going to give it to us, because it is a type of his death and of his resurrection. And just as he died and rose and became for us the first-fruits from the dead, so he was baptized sacredly for our baptism."[47] Jesus had no need of baptism, but he approached John the Baptist to be baptized because he wanted to take his baptism and give it to us as the first-fruits of his new public life.[48] Philoxenus then combines the Jordan event with the mystery of the cross. We know from elsewhere that this refers specifically to participation in the paschal mystery as envisioned by Paul in Romans 6:4.[49] No suggestion here that the death and resurrection displace the mystery of Jesus' baptism as the content of Christian baptism, but the two mysteries are communicated simultaneously, with the baptism of Jesus being the primary carrier.[50] Our baptism is Jesus' baptism because "he was baptized sacredly for our baptism, and immediately he gave it to us."[51]

---

[46] The Second Letter of Philoxenus to the Monasteries at Beit Gaugal 36; A. de Halleux, "La Deuxième Lettre de Philoxène aux Monastères du Beit Gaugal," in Muséon 96 (1983) 59; Varghese, Les Onctions Baptismales dans la Tradition Syrienne, 167.

[47] Fragment 13, On Matthew 3:1; Fragments of the Commentary on Matthew and Luke; CSCO 393:16, 17.

[48] De Halleux, Philoxène de Mabbog: Sa Vie, Ses Écrits, Sa Théologie, 454.

[49] Ten Dissertations on One from the Holy Trinity Made Flesh and Suffered 13, 21; Patrologia Orientalis 39:669, 673, 675.

[50] I differ from A. Grillmeier, "Die Taufe Christi," in Fides Sacramenti: Sacramentum Fidei 144. Grillmeier believes that the Pauline baptismal theology of Romans 6:4 has displaced the baptism of Jesus as the primary theological motif. Though Romans 6:4 has a very significant role in Philoxenus' baptismal theology, there is no indication that he wants to abandon the baptism of Jesus from its role in constituting Christian baptism. K. McDonnell and G. Montague, Christian Initiation and Baptism in the Holy Spirit: Evidence from the First Eight Centuries (Collegeville: A Michael Glazier Book/The Liturgical Press, 1995) 299–338.

[51] Fragment 13; On Matthew; Fragments of the Commentary on Matthew and Luke; CSCO 393:16, 17.

As early as the beginning of the second century, Ignatius of Antioch places the Jordan event in relation to the cross: Jesus was baptized so that by his passion he might cleanse the water."[52] His baptism is, therefore, the image and proclamation of his death and resurrection, the water participating in the power of his passion.[53] The perspective continues in representatives of Greek and Latin traditions; among the authors are Chrysostom,[54] Cyril of Alexandria,[55] Augustine,[56] and Aquinas.[57]

But it is especially among the Syrians that the passion, in the image of the pierced side as the source of baptism, flourished. Indeed, John 19:34 ("one of the soldiers pierced his side with a spear, and at once blood and water came out") is a point from which early Syrian exegesis looks back to the old paradise of Genesis, and forward to the new paradise of the Church's sacraments.[58] It has a two-directional perspective. Though the pierced side is not a major preoccupation of Ephrem, he does refer to it.[59] Ephrem specifically calls baptismal water "the well which flows out of the side of the Son of God.'"[60] He places

[52] *Ephesians* 18:2; SC 10:74.

[53] Lundberg, *La Typologie Baptismale dans l'Ancienne Église*, 187–189; Camelot, *Spiritualité du Baptême*, 263–281.

[54] *In Praise of Maximus;* PG 51:229; *On Ephesians* 20:3; PG 62:139.

[55] "They pierced his side with a lance; and from it burst forth blood and water, as if God wished to give us an image and first fruits of the eucharistic mystery and baptism." *On John* 12; PG 74:677.

[56] "His side was pierced with a lance, blood and water flowing on to the earth. Without doubt these are the sacraments by which the church is formed." *Sermon* 218; PL 38:1087. Also *On John* 120:2; PL 35:1953.

[57] "Water flowed from the side of Christ for the purpose of washing; blood for redeeming. Therefore blood is fitting for the sacrament of the Eucharist, but water for baptism. However, the latter's power to cleanse comes from the power of Christ's blood." *Summa theologica* 3, 66, 3, ad 3.

[58] S. Brock, "The Mysteries Hidden in the Side of Christ," in *Sobornost* 7 (1978) 462. In these pages I am especially indebted to this article of Brock's as well as his "Baptismal Themes in the Writings of Jacob of Serugh," in *Symposium Syriacum 1976,* 325–347. See also R. Murray, "The Lance Which Re-opened Paradise: A Mysterious Reading in the Early Syriac Fathers," in *Orientalia Christiana Periodica* 39 (1973) 224–234.

[59] *Commentary on the Diatessaron* 21:10; SC 121:379, 380.

[60] *Hymns on Epiphany* 13:13; CSCO 187:177.

the pierced side in relation to Adam: "Water and blood came forth. Adam washed, revived, and returned to paradise."[61] Adam therefore washes in the water that flowed from the side of Christ on the cross.

However, it was Jacob of Serugh, a contemporary of Philoxenus', who develops the pierced side more extensively. Jacob, one of the greatest Syrian doctors, wrote in Syriac, but he knew Greek and tended to see Greek theology through the eyes of the school of Edessa. He remained more symbolic in his theology than the Christian Platonism of Philoxenus and especially Severus of Antioch.[62]

Jacob sees the water flowing from the side of Christ on the cross as the main source of Christian baptism:

"Christ came and opened up baptism by his cross
so that it might be a mother of life for the world in the
    place of Eve;
water and blood for the fashioning of spiritual babes
flowed forth from it, and baptism became the mother of life.
No previous baptism [i.e., of Moses or John] ever gave the
    Holy Spirit,
only the baptism which was opened up by the Son of God
    on the cross.
It gives birth to children spiritually with 'water and the
    blood.' "[63]

He spells out this relationship more clearly still:

"Christ came and opened up baptism on his cross
so that it should be the 'mother of living things,' in
    place of Eve.
Water and blood, for the fashioning of spiritual children,
flowed, and baptism became the mother of living things."[64]

[61] *Hymns of Nisibis* 39:7; CSCO 241:18.

[62] R. C. Chesnut, *Three Monophysite Christologies* (Oxford: Oxford University, 1976) 113.

[63] Bedjan, 1:162. The translations in this section come from Brock, "Baptismal Themes in the Writings of Jacob of Serugh," in *Symposium Syriacum 1976*, 325–347. I thank Columba Stewart for verifying the texts.

[64] Bedjan, 1:162.

Or Jacob will make a comparison between the deep sleep of Adam, during which a rib was taken from his side to form Eve, and the death of Christ on the cross, a death that is for Jacob a kind of sleep. From the side of the sleeping Christ flows the water and the blood, which constitute "the second mother," that is, "baptism."

"He painted the whole image of the cross in Adam.
And [God] made him to fall asleep and he took a rib from
     him. . . .
And from his side flows the second mother: baptism."[65]

Or more explicitly:

"[Christ] slept on the cross, and baptism came forth from him.
The Bridegroom slept, and his side was pierced in his sleep."[66]

The same ideas can be found in the sixth-century *Cave of Treasures*, also of Syrian provenance.[67]

Blood and Water or Water and Blood?

The text of John 19:34 reads: "blood and water came out." But in Jacob it is "water and blood." The reversing of the order, with water coming before blood, is more in keeping with the sacramental sequence of baptism and Eucharist. In one of his letters he seems to indicate that this was the only order of which he was aware. He writes: "He [author of Fourth Gospel] did not write that there came from him 'blood and water,' but he testified that there came first water."[68] In fact, this reading has also been adopted in many Greek Gospel manuscripts,[69]

[65] Ibid.
[66] Bedjan, 2:589.
[67] 48:20; CSCO 527:92. Brock, "The Epiklesis in the Antiochene Baptismal *Ordines*," in *Symposium Syriacum 1972*, 212.
[68] G. Olinder, *Iacobi Sarugensis Epistulae quotquot supersunt*; CSCO 110:263–264; quoted from Brock, "Baptismal Themes in the Writings of Jacob of Serugh," in *Symposium Syriacum 1976*, 330, n. 23.
[69] Ibid. The gloss to Matthew 27:49 reads "water and blood," though it is probably a harmonization with 1 John 5:6, 7. But M. E. Boismard, "Problèmes de Critique Textuelle concernant le Quatrième Évangile," in

and among others is repeated by John Chrysostom.[70] But the text may have been influenced by 1 John 5:6 ("This is the one who came by water and blood, Jesus Christ, not with the water only but with the water and the blood").[71]

Jacob's conception is essentially ecclesiological: "The Bridegroom's side has been pierced and from it the Bride (the Church) has come forth."[72] The Church flows from the pierced side. But Jacob's perspective is also cosmic.

"A new well was opened on Golgotha;
this is the blessed fountain of Eden,
which divided itself up as a great river [flowing]
towards the four quarters [of the earth],
so that the whole of afflicted creation might drink of it."[73]

The four rivers covering the whole of creation represent the cosmic river we have already met. The four rivers are an image of the superabundance of water, the instrument of salvation, proffered to all.

Jacob exploits the pierced side of Jesus, but there is no allusion to our participation in his anointing. In fact, he never

---

Revue Biblique 60 (1953) 348–350, contends that "water and blood" may be the original order. R. E. Brown, *The Death of the Messiah*, 2 vols. (New York: Doubleday, 1994) 2:1178, n. 93.

[70] *Baptismal Catechesis* 3:17; SC 50bis:161. Varghese, *Les Onctions Baptismales dans la Tradition Syrienne*, 141. *In Praise of Maximus* 3; PG 51:22, Chrysostom cites the order given in John 19:34, but then immediately turns the order around.

[71] Though as early as Tertullian (*On Baptism* 16:1–2; SC 35:89), this text was given a sacramental interpretation, but the text cannot well support that meaning. While very likely not referring to the sacraments of baptism and Eucharist, the text offers no obstacle to interpreting water as the Jordan event, and blood as Jesus' death on the cross. Jesus Christ came to save us by a humble baptism at the hands of a prophet of lesser stature, and by a bloody death. However, 1 John 5:7-8 may have sacramental content. R. E. Brown, *The Epistles of John* (Garden City: Doubleday, 1982) 575, 577.

[72] Bedjan, 3:299.

[73] Ibid., 2:588, 589.

refers to any anointing that Christ may have received in the Jordan.[74]

Jacob of Serugh, therefore, seeks the origin of Christian baptism in Christ's baptism in the Jordan and in the pierced side of Christ on the cross. These two salvific moments constitute Christian baptism. While in Jacob the pierced side has a kind of dominance, the two moments are joined in sacred time, that is, two historic events separated in chronological time become one in sacred time, constituting the principle and source of Christian baptism.[75] Like Aphrahat, Jacob sees no reason why one symbol must displace another.

Theodore of Mopsuestia—
The Move Away from the Ancient Tradition

Theodore of Mopsuestia (ca. 350–428) is earlier than Philoxenus and Jacob; though he was born and raised in Antioch, the capital of Syria, he is Greek in his cultural and theological formation. He was a student, together with John Chrysostom and Amphilochius of Iconium (the cousin of Gregory Nazianzus), of the pagan Libanius, rhetor and sophist, one of the great teachers of the fourth century. Quite justly Theodore is regarded as a major exegete, making critical analyses of the texts. Three catecheses treating of baptism are among the sixteen discovered in 1932 in a Syriac translation. Behind the catecheses is essentially the same liturgy as John Chrysostom used, which is Syrian in its basic form.

For Theodore, the imparting of the Spirit takes place during baptism proper, or more precisely, during a post-baptismal anointing, not at the pre-baptismal anointing. The conferring of the Spirit at the pre-baptismal anointing belongs to the Syrian tradition, from which Theodore is departing. Like Chrysostom, he is more concerned with the Pauline theology of Romans 6:4,

---

[74] Varghese, *Les Onctions Baptismales dans la Tradition Syrienne*, 145.

[75] Brock, "The Mysteries Hidden in the Side of Christ," 466. While Jacob presents Christian baptism as a participation in the baptism of Jesus, he does not exploit the relationship between Christ's anointing at the Jordan and the anointing in Christian baptism. Jacob was more concerned with immersion than with anointing. Brock, "Baptismal Themes in the Writings of Jacob of Serugh," in *Symposium Syriacum 1976*, 329, 330.

than with the baptism of Jesus as the primary paradigm. Three times he comes back to Romans 6:4.[76] Referring to Paul, Theodore writes: "He clearly taught here that we are baptized so that we might imitate in ourselves the death and resurrection of our Lord."[77] However, this interest in Romans 6 needs to be nuanced. Theodore was mostly interested in Christ's resurrection as a pledge of ours.[78]

Though causes are usually multiple, the emergence of the Pauline theology is very likely among the reasons why the imparting of the Spirit is moved forward from the pre-baptismal anointing, the usual Syrian position, to post-baptismal anointing.[79] In baptism proper, one goes down into the waters, participating in the death and resurrection of Christ. In Theodore's framework, this participation in the paschal mystery should come before the conferral of the Spirit, as Calvary comes before Pentecost. Therefore, in the liturgical rite, the transfer forward, away from the pre-baptismal anointing to the post-baptismal anointing, alters the interior dynamics of the sacrament. Nonetheless, Theodore is more Johannine—with an emphasis on new birth—than Pauline—with an emphasis on death and resurrection.[80]

He also retains elements of the older tradition in which the baptism of Jesus is the paradigm. He writes: "He was baptized in our [baptism] for us, and he represented in it [his baptism] the model (tupos) of it [our baptism]."[81] He specifies in what sense Jesus' baptism is the paradigm of ours, namely, the descent of the Spirit. Then he continues: "It behooves you to know you were baptized in the same baptism as that in which Christ our Lord in the flesh was baptized. This is why you are baptized in the name of the Father, and of the Son, and of the

[76] Catechesis on Baptism 1 (Homily 12):7; 2 (Homily 13):14; 3 (Homily 14) 5; Les Homélies catéchétiques de Théodore de Mopsueste, R. Tonneau and R. Devreesse, eds. (Vatican City: Apostolic Vatican Library, 1949) (Studi e Testi 145) 333, 393, 411. Hereafter cited as Tonneau.

[77] Catechesis on Baptism 1:7; Tonneau, 332.

[78] Brock, The Holy Spirit in the Syrian Baptismal Tradition, 79.

[79] Ibid., 38.

[80] Varghese, Les Onctions Baptismales dans la Tradition Syrienne, 100.

[81] 3 (Homily 14):23; Tonneau, 451.

Holy Spirit. This [baptism of Christ in the Jordan] is portrayed in the deed itself, in a type. In effect, the Father, speaking in a loud voice, says: 'This is my beloved Son in whom I am well pleased.' "[82] Referring to the descent of the Spirit on Jesus coming up out of the Jordan as an anointing with the Spirit, Theodore says "the Holy Spirit comes also upon you, and you also are anointed with the Spirit."[83] Christian baptism is the same baptism as the Jordan event because the same voice, the same message, the same anointing with the Spirit are effective in each.

While the death and resurrection have moved to the forefront, the baptism of Jesus is still one of the sources of Christian baptism. As a matter of curiosity, the pierced side, found in Ephrem and Jacob of Serugh, is entirely absent from Theodore, as it is from his enthusiastic, subservient, Syrian disciple Narsai.[84]

Narsai—The King Walks the Road to Jordan for Us

The long-lived Narsai (399–503), the theologian of the "Nestorian" Church, studied in the school of Edessa, greatly influenced by Ephrem, which school Narsai displaced when he became the effective founder of the school of Nisibis, the center of East Syrian Christianity. His 103 years were often filled with tumult, and among his targets are Cyril of Alexandria and Jacob of Serugh.[85] Not an original thinker, he was a faithful purveyor of the thought of Theodore of Mopsuestia.

He presents John the Baptist as the treasurer, as had Ephrem, who "opened the treasury that was hidden from all generations."[86] After John, Jesus himself opens the mystery: "Our Lord has opened up for us the sweet spring of Baptism, and

---

[82] 3 (*Homily 14*):24; Tonneau, 451.

[83] *Baptismal Catechesis* 3:27; Tonneau, 457.

[84] Brock, "The Epiklesis in the Antiochene Baptismal *Ordines*," in *Symposium Syriacum 1972*, 211, 212. It seems that the East Syrian writers make special effort to avoid John 19:34.

[85] *Histoire Nestorienne (Chronique de Séert)*, A. Scher, ed.; PO 7:115; A. Voobus, *History of the School of Nisibis* 65, 66; CSCO 226.

[86] *A Homily on the Epiphany of Our Lord*; PO 40:88.

has given our race to drink of the sweetness of life immortal."[87]
As "the high priest," Christ "descended into the water and
bathed and sanctified it, and conferred upon it the power of the
Spirit to give life. The holy one drew near to the weak and inanimate element and made it a womb which begets men
spiritually. He descended and was plunged into the womb of
water as in a grave; and he rose and was raised [to life] and
raised Adam in mystery."[88] Like his master, Narsai relates the
Jordan to the paschal mysteries. He also joins the coming of the
Spirit to the coming of freedom: "In water he fixed the new
goal of spiritual birth, because everyone who willingly does
likewise receives freedom. . . . Come! Let us strive to receive
gratis the wealth of the Spirit. . . . This [is] the road [that] the
King has traversed for us in his own person. Come! Let us
travel on it to the end as long as there is light. Behold! There is
opened the womb which begets men spiritually. Bury mortality
in baptism and acquire life!"[89] These traditional themes are
combined with a number of references to Romans 6:4.[90] In fact,
he speaks of Jesus opening baptism in the Jordan, and then immediately relates this to the death and resurrection.[91]

---

[87] Connolly, On the Mysteries of the Church and on Baptism; The Liturgical
Homilies of Narsai, 46.

[88] A Homily on the Epiphany of Our Lord; PO 40:88.

[89] Ibid.; PO 40:102, 104.

[90] "Come, let us examine discerningly the hand of flesh that buries bodies
and raises them up swiftly." On Baptism; Connolly, 35. "Come, let us examine the mystery of our dying in the midst of the waters; and let us look
upon the wonder that is mystically achieved in us." Ibid.; Connolly, 41;
"The grievous thirst of death had slain our body; and He buried it in the
water, and life teemed in its mortality." On the Mysteries of the Church and
On Baptism; Connolly, 46; "The Evil One and Death are undone by Baptism; and the resurrection of the body and the redemption of the soul are
preached therein. In it, as in a tomb, body and soul are buried and they
die and live [again] with a type of the resurrection that is to be at the
end." Ibid.; Connolly, 50, 51. "Mystically he [the candidate] dies and is
raised and is adorned." Ibid.; Connolly, 52. "His death and His life men
depict in Baptism." Ibid.; Connolly, 54. "A mystery of death he shows
first to mortal man; and then he reveals the power of life that is hidden in
his words." Ibid.; Connolly, 55.

[91] On the Mysteries of the Church and On Baptism; Connolly, 46.

After the complete absence of interest in Romans 6:4 during the second century, Origen shows a surprising flash of preoccupation, citing the passage at least thirteen times. But he does not abandon the Jordan. In fact, it remains his primary paradigm. For him, however, both Jordan and Calvary are the sources of Christian baptism. In Philoxenus, the baptism of Jesus is the primary carrier, but he combines it with the death and resurrection. Using the image of the pierced side, Jacob of Serugh focuses on the paschal mysteries. While the pierced side has a kind of dominance, he sees both the Jordan and Calvary as the two constituting moments of Christian baptism. Theodore of Mopsuestia is convinced that sacramentally Calvary had to precede Pentecost. Romans 6:4 is his primary paradigm, but he retains the old tradition. The baptism of Jesus is still one of the sources of Christian baptism. Narsai retains the Jordan as his dominant model, but follows Theodore in relating it to paschal themes.

Chapter Fifteen

The Threat of Sacramental Imagination and the Jordan's Tenacity—Institution

Cyril of Jerusalem (ca. 315–386) is important for a number of reasons, but especially so in our present context because, in Cyril, one sees how great a hold the Jordan event had on the religious consciousness. This is demonstrated by Cyril's appeal to "sacramental imagination," the dangerous and glorious memories of Jerusalem embedded in the geographically immediate places, especially Calvary and the tomb.[1] Speaking of the Pentecost event, he says "this honor belongs to *us*, and we speak, not about the good things that have happened to others but *among us.*"[2] Place becomes the sacrament of mystery and the closer the place the easier a busy pastor can fire the religious imagination. In spatial terms the Jordan was not that immediate, and for this, among other reasons, the baptism of Christ was pastorally and sacramentally in a position of weakness in

[1] F. Cardman, "The Rhetoric of Holy Places," in *Studia Patristica* 17 (1982) 1, 23.

[2] CL 17:13, also 16:4; Reischl, 2:266, 208–210. Emphasis mine. "The prerogative of all good things is in Jerusalem." CL 3:7; Reischl, 1:74. R. L. Wilken, "At the Very Spot," in *The Land Called Holy: Palestine in Christian History and Thought* (New Haven: Yale University, 1992) 101–125.

comparison with the death and resurrection whose place was close to the walls of Jerusalem. How did the baptism of Christ fare under the threat of a sacramental takeover by the death and resurrection?

Cyril is one of the surprises in the history of baptismal paradigms. First, he seems to be of two minds on the primary paradigm for Christian baptism. The basic baptismal rite of Cyril, linguistically a Greek, was probably the old Syrian rite, which he modified.[3] This would indicate, if not a basic commitment to the Syrian tradition, at least familiarity with it. In the *Catechetical Lectures (CL)* he appears devoted to ancient Syrian tradition of the Jordan event as the normative event for Christian baptism. He writes: "Jesus sanctified baptism when he himself was baptized. . . . So Jesus was baptized that we, in our turn, might be made partakers in it with him, and thus we receive not only salvation, but also the dignity [as children of God]."[4]

Cyril goes on to specify the descent of the Holy Spirit. "The Holy Spirit descended when Christ was baptized, to make sure that the dignity of him who was baptized was not hidden."[5] The descent of the Spirit on Jesus is a manifestation of his identity. But there is another reason why the Spirit descends on Jesus. The operative principle: the one who receives the Spirit, imparts the Spirit. Jesus Christ is the one who baptizes in the Holy Spirit. "It was fitting, as some have explained it, that the first fruits and the first gifts of the Holy Spirit, who is imparted to the baptized, should be conferred on the manhood of the Savior, who bestows such grace."[6] Cyril is conscious of handing on the tradition ("as some have explained it").[7] While the

[3] E. J. Cutrone, "Cyril's Mystagogical Catecheses and the Evolution of the Jerusalem Anaphora," in *Orientalia Christiana Periodica* 44 (1978) 53, 54.

[4] CL 3:11; Reischl, 1:78. Cyril also portrays Jesus as descending into the waters in order to triumph over the dragon of the deep, thus empowering us to trample on the serpents and scorpions. Ibid. See also 3:14; Reischl, 1:82.

[5] CL 17:9; Reischl, 2:261.

[6] Ibid.

[7] In relating the Pentecost event, Cyril builds not only on the promise of Jesus ("you will be baptized with the Holy Spirit not many days from now" [Acts 1:5]), but on experience of baptism. "For just as one immersed

descent of the Spirit on Jesus in the Jordan is an important element in Cyril's baptismal theology in the *CL*, in these lectures he makes no reference to Jesus' having been anointed with the Holy Spirit in the Jordan, and consequently no reference to Christian baptism being a participation in that anointing. In this he resembles Jacob of Serugh. The only anointing Cyril mentions is the Father anointing Christ, an anointing from all eternity that does not cease.[8]

The role of Romans 6:4 in the *CL* has been underestimated,[9] yet it is true that the baptism of Jesus is still the dominant paradigm of Christian baptism. The baptism of Jesus constitutes the sacrament of baptism.

Cyril—Jerusalem Becomes the Place of "Seeing and Feeling"

One can express surprise, even astonishment, at the tenacity of the Jordan event in the presence of a clear threat. The menace to the baptism of Jesus is the geographical proximity of Calvary and Cyril's pastoral determination to exploit the sites of the passion, death, and resurrection in Jerusalem itself.

The *CL* were delivered in the Martyrium of the Holy Sepulcher, that is, in the body of the church, which if it did not contain Calvary in the mid-fourth century, is in proximity to it.[10] So baptismal instructions on the mysteries were given within a short distance of the place where Christ died, was buried, and rose. Secondly, Cyril, not a speculative theologian but a talented pastor, determined to turn these holy places to spiritual advantage, built on the powerful memories the stones

---

in the waters of baptism is completely encompassed by the water, so they too were completely baptized by the Spirit. The water encompasses the body externally, but the Holy Spirit baptizes the soul perfectly within." *CL* 17:14; Reischl, 2:268. This is probably a reference to the experience of Christian baptism rather than to the Jordan event.

[8] *CL* 10:14; Reischl, 1:278.

[9] Varghese, *Les Onctions Baptismales dans la Tradition Syrienne*, 69, contends that there is only one reference to Romans 6:4 in the *CL*, namely in 3:12, but the Romans text is cited in full also at the beginning of *CL* 3; Reischl, 1:64.

[10] R. E. Brown gives a brief summary of the confusing architectural history of the Sepulcher. *The Death of the Messiah*, 2:1279–1283.

evoked. He was conscious of proclaiming the mysteries in the very "theater of salvation."[11] He wrote: "The most honored privileges are ours. Here Christ descended from heaven; here the Holy Spirit descended from heaven. It is particularly fitting that as we speak of Christ and Golgotha here on Golgotha, so also we should speak of the Holy Spirit in the Upper Church."[12] Place is the sacrament of mystery. In a word, Cyril would lead the catechumens into the depths of the mystery of Christ by the experience of place.

Jerusalem was low on the ecclesiastical hierarchy. It did not rank as an equal alongside Rome, Alexandria, and Antioch, nor even a near equal. It was subject to Caesarea, which in turn was subject to Antioch. Pilgrimages to Jerusalem are so much a part of our religious awareness that we have a difficult time imagining an age in which Jerusalem was not a mighty magnet. Pilgrims had come before the age of Constantine and Cyril, but in comparison to the deluge which was to follow, it was a trickle. About the middle of the fourth century, pilgrims were drawn by the new glory created by Constantine, Helena, and Eutropia (Constantine's mother-in-law). The royal family engaged in a "massive building program," with glittering basilicas on the Mount of Olives, at Mamre, in Bethlehem.[13] The Holy Sepulcher, completed about 335, was conceived as a "mystery-site connected with the death of Christ."[14] Egeria, the lady from Spain who came to Jerusalem in the late fourth century (381–384), therefore when Cyril was still alive, left an account of the brilliance of the churches, the splendor of the ornaments, the grandeur of the liturgies, attracting pilgrims in large numbers.[15]

The Sepulcher's most prized possession was what Christians thought to be the true cross. Whether or not it was found by Helena (most probably not), it fired the imagination of Christendom and gave Jerusalem a new way of knowing. In a brief space, almost in the same breath, Cyril mentions "the holy

---

[11] G. Dix, *The Shape of the Liturgy* (New York: Seabury, 1945) 352.
[12] *CL* 16:4; Reischl, 2:208, 210.
[13] L. M. Barth, "Jerusalem," in *Theologische Realenzyklopädie* 16:613.
[14] E. Yarnold, "Baptism and the Pagan Mysteries in the Fourth Century," in *Heythrop Journal* 13 (1972) 265.
[15] Egeria, *Journal of a Journey* 25:8; 37:1; 37:3; SC 296:252, 284, 286.

cross seen among us even to this day,'' Gethsemane, the
Sepulcher, the Mount of Olives, Jordan, the Sea of Tiberias.[16]
Cyril boasts "others can hear, but we can also see and feel.''[17]

To respond to these new possibilities, Cyril developed the
Holy Week and Easter cycle that became the model for both
East and West. He gave the broad outlines of how the Divine
Office was to be celebrated publicly. He developed the proper
of the seasons as well as of the saints. More than to any other
single individual, the eucharistic doctrine of transubstantiation
is traceable to Cyril.[18] In the churches of Jerusalem one meets
for the first time liturgical vestments, the carrying of candles,
the use of incense at the Gospel, the *lavabo*, the placing of the
Lord's Prayer after the canon or anaphora. For better or worse,
he turned the liturgy away from an eschatological interpretation
of redemption, that is, oriented toward the parousia. In its
place he proposed a historical understanding, centered on the
events of Jesus' life.[19] Through his ritual innovations he
changed Jerusalem from not being a liturgical center to the city
determining the liturgies of East and West in the latter part of
the fourth and the fifth centuries.[20] The influence of Jerusalem
became "permanent.''[21]

Given the distance between Jerusalem and the Jordan, given
the proximity of sacred sites concerned with the death and
resurrection in the environs of the Sepulcher, given the practice
of celebrating the rites of initiation within the paschal liturgies,
given the greater symbolic power of death and resurrection in
contrast to the Jordan event, given the creative genius of Cyril
in exploiting the pastoral possibilities of sacred places within
the walls of Jerusalem, it is surprising that the *Catechetical Lec-*

[16] *CL* 10:19; Reischl, 1:284–286.

[17] *CL* 13:22; Reischl, 2:80.

[18] *MC* 4:2; SC 126:136.

[19] The caveat of J. F. Baldovin should be noted: "Many authors have too
quickly accepted historicization as the unique motive in the development of
Jerusalem's worship." *The Urban Character of Christian Worship* (Rome:
Oriental Institute, 1987) 87–90.

[20] H. Wegman, *Christian Worship in East and West* (New York: Pueblo,
1976) 76.

[21] J. F. Baldovin, *Liturgy in Ancient Jerusalem* (Bramcote: Grove, 1989) 5.

tures still give pride of place to the Jordan event as the norm of Christian baptism. This would indicate symbolic strength and symbolic resistance in the presence of a "threat."

The Remarkable Resistance of the Jordan Under Threat

But there is a shift when one moves from the CL on to the *Mystagogical Catecheses (MC)*, delivered not in the Martyrium or body of the church, as were the CL, but in a building slightly set aside from the Sepulcher, yet architecturally related.[22] The CL and the MC are of different theological genres. The first are catechetical instructions given before the celebration of the water bath, the anointing and/or imposing of hands, and the celebration of the Eucharist. The CL are concerned primarily with knowledge. The MC are mystagogy, given after the rites of initiation to recapture the sacramental encounter and expand on the meaning. They are principally concerned with experience. The move from the CL to the MC is a move from outside the mystery to inside.

The differences between the CL and the MC have sparked a long debate whether Cyril is the author of both, or John of Jerusalem the author of the MC.[23] If Edward Yarnold has not completely vindicated Cyril's authorship also of MC, at least he has established a strong presumption in the favor of it.[24] In a significant study, combining multiple critical approaches, Alexis J. Doval has gone beyond the research of Yarnold and seems to

---

[22] A. Grabar, *Martyrium: Recherches sur le Culte des Reliques et l'Art Chrétien Antique*, 3 vols. (Paris: College de France, 1946); *Egeria's Travels*, J. Wilkinson, ed. (London: SPCK, 1971) 36-53. A. A. Stephenson raises some doubts as to where the MC were delivered. *The Works of Saint Cyril of Jerusalem*, 2 vols., L. P. McCauley and A. A. Stephenson, eds. (Washington, D.C.: The Catholic University of America, 1970) 2:150, 151.

[23] I have briefly reviewed this debate in *Christian Initiation and Baptism in the Holy Spirit*, 229-230.

[24] "The Authorship of the Mystagogic Catecheses Attributed to Cyril of Jerusalem," in *Heythrop Journal* 19 (1978) 143-161. Yarnold thinks that the differences between the CL and the MC can be accounted for by the theological development of Cyril over a period of some thirty or forty years. See also F. Young, *From Nicaea to Chalcedon* (Philadelphia: Fortress, 1983) 128-130.

have established the question of the authorship of the *MC* in favor of Cyril.[25]

What difference do the two series manifest in relation to the baptism of Jesus and the Romans 6:4 theology? The author of *MC* states his principle: "Your salvation began from him who was anointed by the Holy Spirit in truth [at the Jordan]."[26] Unlike the *CL*, the *MC* recognize that Jesus was anointed at the Jordan by the Holy Spirit, of which the anointing of Christians is an imitation: "He bathed in the river Jordan and, after imparting the fragrance of His Godhead to the waters, came up from them. Him the Holy Spirit visited [at the Jordan] in essential presence, like resting upon like. Similarly for you, after you had ascended from the sacred streams, there was an anointing with chrism, that is of the Holy Spirit."[27] Then Cyril cites the words of Jesus in the synagogue at Nazareth when Jesus recalls his baptism in the Jordan by citing the words of Isaiah: "The Spirit of the Lord is upon me, because he has anointed me . . ." (Luke 4:18).[28] This anointing, the author reminds us, was not with material oil, but with the Holy Spirit, the author citing Peter's words referring to the baptism of Jesus, "God anointed [him] with the Holy Spirit."[29] The essential gift of the Spirit in Christian baptism is effected by the anointing in imitation of Christ's baptism.

Though retaining anointing from the Jordan event, he links it to the theology of Romans 6:4, that is, becoming "companions

[25] A number of partial studies have been done in the past (W. J. Swaan, W. Telfer, E. Bihain, G. Kretschmar, A. A. Stephenson, A. Renoux, F. L. Cross, A. Piédagnel, J. Quasten), but Doval is the first to subject the texts to a combination of textual, literary, and computer analyses. He has examined the manuscript and literary traditions, presented an extensive comparative analysis of the contents (never before attempted in a systematic way), for the first time subjected the texts to a stylometric analysis (a computer-based statistical analysis of literary style). Doval concludes that the *MC* are rightly attributed to Cyril of Jerusalem. A. J. Doval, "The Authorship of the Mystagogic Catecheses Attributed to St. Cyril of Jerusalem" (D. Phil dissertation, Oxford University, 1992).

[26] *MC* 3:6; SC 126:128, 130.

[27] *MC* 3:1; SC 126:120, 122.

[28] Ibid.

[29] *MC* 3:2; SC 126:122.

and partakers of Christ'' in his crucifixion, burial and resurrection.[30] The *MC* repeatedly returns to the Pauline theology of Romans 6:4,[31] marking a new prominence that did not obtain in the *CL*. However, there is no retreating from the Jordan event as being normative for the sacrament of initiation. The two mysteries, the baptism of Jesus and the death/resurrection, share the honors as the origin of Christian baptism, with Romans 6:4 clearly gaining ground.[32] Very likely the demise of the baptism of Jesus as the primary model was in process by the time of Cyril of Jerusalem, about the last quarter of the fourth century. Nonetheless, if Cyril wrote *MC* thirty or forty years after writing the *CL*, as Yarnold contends, and if Romans 6:4 gained in significance during that period, the staying power of the baptism of Jesus as a paradigm of Christian baptism, in the face of the threats named above, is impressive in both the *CL* and the *MC*.[33]

John Chrysostom—The Turn to Calvary

The *Baptismal Catecheses* of John Chrysostom must rank with Cyril of Jerusalem and Theodore of Mopsuestia in theological

[30] Ibid.

[31] 2:4, 5, 6.

[32] Varghese, *Les Onctions Baptismales dans la Tradition Syrienne*, 79, 80, exaggerates, in my judgment, the differences between *CL* and *MC*. He says that in conformity with the Syrian tradition, the *CL* 3:14; 4:16 and 17:9 have the Spirit descend on Jesus while he is still in the Jordan, this descent being the *raison d'être* of the Spirit's descent in Christian baptism. According to the *MC*, the Spirit descends on Christ only when he ascended from the Jordan. But as Brock has pointed out, there is in the Syrian tradition, in the person of Jacob of Serugh, the insistence that the Holy Spirit appeared after the baptism in the Jordan, the role of the Spirit being merely to witness, along with the voice of the Father. Jacob wrote more than a century after Cyril's death, but this may have already been in the tradition. ''Baptismal Themes in the Writings of Jacob of Serugh,'' in *Symposium Syriacum 1976*, 327. Therefore, the differences between the two series are not that significant, and, in my view, do not militate against Cyril being the author of both. The differences can be accounted for by Cyril's development over a period of thirty or forty years, as Yarnold asserts.

[33] G. Kretschmar, ''Recent Research on Christian Initiation,'' in *Studia Liturgica 92*, remarks that the demise of the baptism of Jesus as the primary model was in process by the time of Cyril of Jerusalem.

significance.[34] Chrysostom represents Greek culture, even though Antioch was the capital of Syria. He never learned Syriac, which he thought was a barbarian tongue.[35] Like Jerusalem, Antioch belonged liturgically to the Syriac family. Indeed, Chrysostom's baptismal homilies are one of the sources of Syriac rites.[36] But from the beginning, the liturgical language of Antioch was Greek. Unlike Cyril and Theodore, whose instructions were only to candidates, Chrysostom is addressing the whole congregation.

He speaks of the baptism of Jesus and its significance for Christian baptism in his *On Matthew*. In this he was only reflecting the ancient Antiochene tradition where the baptism of Jesus was the dominant model from the beginning.[37] In his *On Matthew* he contends that the heavens open over Jesus, the voice of the Father speaks so Christians can hear the voice of God calling them to their country on high. The Spirit, too, descends on Jesus to teach us that in baptism the Spirit also descends on the candidates.[38] Influenced by the baptismal practice of his age, Chrysostom has the Baptist touching Christ's head with his hand during Christ's baptism, although this is not found in any Gospel. Twice Chrysostom says that "what happened in the case of our Master's body also happens in the case of your own."[39] Chrysostom specifies that it is at the moment the bishop lays hands on the candidate that "the Spirit descends, and it is a different person who ascends [out of the water]."[40] The allusion to the Jordan event is manifest.

However, there is no allusion to the anointing of Jesus in the Jordan, and consequently no attempt to relate it to the two pre-

---

[34] P. W. Harkins, Introduction, *St. John Chrysostom: Baptismal Instructions* (Westminster: Newman, 1963) 8. (Hereafter cited as Harkins).

[35] G. Bardy, *La Question des Langues dans l'Église Ancienne* (Paris: Beauchesne, 1948) 19.

[36] L. Duchesne, *Christian Worship: Its Origin and Evolution* (London: SPCK, 1904) 55, 56; F. E. Brightman, *Liturgies Eastern and Western* (Oxford: Clarendon, 1896) xvii–lxiii.

[37] Brock, *Holy Spirit in the Syrian Baptismal Tradition*, 38.

[38] *On Matthew* 12:2; PG 57:201.

[39] *Baptismal Instructions* 11:13; Harkins, 164.

[40] *Baptismal Catecheses* 2:25; SC 50bis:147.

baptismal anointings.[41] While Chrysostom retains a remnant of Syrian interest in the baptism of Jesus, he focuses on the death and resurrection of Jesus as the primary paradigm. He cites Romans 6:4 at least thirteen times.[42] Integral to his concern for the death and resurrection is the pierced side of Christ from which flows, according to Chrysostom, water and blood (in that order), signifying baptism, Eucharist, and the Church.[43] The paschal mystery is his point of departure. He states with clarity: "Baptism is burial and resurrection."[44]

Severus of Antioch—"I See Jesus Standing in the River"

The last in this line of witnesses is Severus of Antioch, who became patriarch a little more than a hundred years after the death of Chrysostom, in the same city in which Chrysostom delivered his *Baptismal Catecheses*. A prolific Greek-language author, Severus is rightly considered the founder of Monophysitism, though he is only a Monophysite in a verbal sense—he contended against radical Monophysites on the left and Chalcedonians on the right. The unjust identification with Monophysitism proper meant that his vast output was put to the torch, his work surviving only in Syriac translations.

He adds nothing new to the issue at hand, the baptism of Jesus as the origin of Christian baptism. Nonetheless, he is important because he retains the Jordan as the central paradigm but sees the theological and pastoral possibilities in the Pauline baptismal theology of Romans 6:4. He chooses both, keeping the two in balance. He demonstrates that to proclaim the one is not to deny the other.

Though he sees Christ "as the giver of the Spirit, he (Christ) received the descent of the Spirit" in the Jordan.[45] Severus, who many times celebrated the feast of Epiphany, comes to the

[41] Varghese, *Les Onctions Baptismales dans la Tradition Syrienne*, 90.

[42] T. M. Finn, *The Liturgy of Baptism in the Baptismal Instructions of St. John Chrysostom* (Washington, D.C.; The Catholic University of America, 1967) 158.

[43] *Baptismal Catecheses* 3:161; SC 50bis:160, 161; Chrysostom, *Homily on Marriage* 3:3; PG 51:229.

[44] Ibid., 2:11; SC 50bis:139.

[45] *Hymns on Epiphany* 15; PO 6:58.

liturgical celebration a stranger each year, as though visiting for the first time, contemplating the mystery with wonder and awe: "I am struck with astonishment in my spirit, for I have been transported to the banks of the Jordan and I believe I see Jesus himself standing in the middle of the river."[46] He sees "the Source of the waters" descending toward the waters.[47] This Jesus is himself the wisdom and power of God, the very source of life, justice, holiness, and salvation. "Once he was baptized in the waves of the Jordan, he put in them—and gave them without restriction—all the things that he possesses by essence, making the waters give brilliance, bringing children to birth, vivifying, giving wisdom, power, holiness, salvation, and justice."[48] Christ himself received nothing from going down into the waters, but by that act he "imparted divine baptism."[49] He has Christ saying "I will come to the Jordan. . . . I will establish my baptism," that is the sacrament of baptism.[50] Repeatedly, Severus says that Christian baptism has its source in the Jordan.[51] The Jordan, womb and mother, "invisibly mixes the waters with the Spirit."[52] In other words: "The baptism in the Holy Spirit commenced at the Jordan, when the Spirit of adoption descended there."[53]

Baptism Is Meant for Real Life in the World

Severus orients the Jordan to the demands of Christ's larger ministry, to the trials of his public life, as does his contemporary, Philoxenus.[54] By Christ's baptism, says Severus, Christ "filled our baptism with light, life, and holiness."[55] More than

[46] *Homily 85; PO 23:25.*
[47] Ibid.; PO 23:31.
[48] Ibid.; PO 23:32.
[49] *Hymn on Epiphany 25; PO 6:67.*
[50] *Homily 46; PO 8:333.*
[51] In *Homily 88* it returns three times. PO 23:92–99.
[52] *Homily 88; PO 23:99.*
[53] *Homily 46; PO 8:341.*
[54] *Discourse 9:276–277, The Discourses of Philoxenus,* 2 vols., E.A.W. Budge, ed. (London: Asher, 1894) 2:264, 265. I have dealt with Philoxenus' teaching in this area in *Christian Initiation and Baptism in the Holy Spirit,* 314–316.
[55] *Homily 85; PO 23:25.*

that, "he makes himself the road of the coming of the Spirit to-ward us."[56] Christ is the highway by his baptism, but he is also the way because he was led into the desert: "It is for us that he is led by the Spirit [from his baptism] into the desert."[57] Christian baptism is a preparation for the struggles of life, sacred and secular. Light, life, and holiness imparted at baptism sustain us when we are led by the Spirit into our personal deserts. No reluctance is shown with regard to embracing in the same breath the Jordan event and baptism as a participation in the death and resurrection. In the same *Homily* 88 in which he speaks so eloquently of the baptism of Jesus, Severus also says "the source of the Jordan prepares itself for the adorable day of the resurrection."[58] This is a theme we have met before: eschatology begins at the Jordan. Referring to the baptistery Severus exhorts the people "Come, let us go to the Jordan in order to honor the God-befitting mystery of the resurrection, and in it [Jordan/baptistery] worship the death of God Incarnate. . . . For all of us who have been baptized in Christ have been baptized in his death, having been planted together with him in the likeness of his death and resurrection."[59] When Christ "goes to the divine bath," the believers prepare "to enter with him in the house of light on the day of the passion and resurrection of our Savior."[60] He fuses Jordan, Calvary, and resurrection.[61] The baptism of Jesus is, indeed, a preparation for death and resurrection.

Severus is a witness to the determination of the Church of Antioch at the end of the fifth and the beginning of the sixth centuries to embrace both mysteries within the rite of Christian initiation. He wants to maintain a kind of harmony between the two, to see in both the paradigm of sacramental baptism, even while reserving to the Jordan event the most explicit references to the constituting of Christian baptism. Given the dramatic,

[56] Ibid.
[57] Ibid.
[58] *Homily* 40; PO 36:9.
[59] *Hymn Sung on the Entry into the Baptistery at Dawn on Sunday* 91; PO 6:131, 132.
[60] *Homily* 121; PO 29:99.
[61] Ibid.; *Homily* 70; PO 12:45–47.

liturgical possibilities of celebrating Christian baptism during the community's celebration of the paschal mysteries, the continuing role of the baptism of Jesus is a sign of its considerable staying power.

Why the Transfer from Jordan to Calvary?

As we have seen, in both East and West there is a renewed interest in Paul in the late fourth century.[62] The greater role of Pauline baptismal theology necessitates a new understanding of the all important pre-baptismal anointing in the sacramental rite. Earlier, it had been related to Jesus being anointed with the Spirit at his baptism, an insight that seems to have its origins in the New Testament.[63] In the early tradition, the sacramental rite understood the pre-baptismal anointing as a "charismatic experience," but now it became a purely cathartic, exorcistic rite, concerned with purgation.[64]

Only at this time was it noted that in the Gospel narratives the Spirit descends on Jesus only *after* he had ascended out of the Jordan. This was now pressed in a somewhat literalist fashion. If baptism is a going down into the death and resurrection of Jesus, then the Spirit and the gifts of the Spirit cannot be imparted before that sacramental experience of dying and rising. Calvary comes before Pentecost. The Spirit and the gifts of the Spirit cannot logically be given in a pre-baptismal anointing. The imparting of the Spirit, therefore, is either transferred to later in the baptismal rite, as in Chrysostom, or to a post-baptismal anointing introduced in the Antiochene area around

[62] Brock, *The Holy Spirit in the Syrian Tradition*, 38; For Augustine's rediscovery of Paul, see Paula Fredriksen, "Beyond the Body/Soul Dichotomy: Augustine's Answer to Mani, Plotinus, and Julian," in *Paul and the Legacies of Paul*, 227–251; for the East, see Kretschmar, "Die Geschichte des Taufgottesdienstes," 148; Ratcliff, "The Old Syrian Baptismal Tradition and Its Resettlement Under the Influence of Jerusalem in the Fourth Century," in *Liturgical Studies* 142.

[63] T. W. Manson, "Entry into Membership of the Early Church," in *Journal of Theological Studies* 48 (1947) 25–32.

[64] Brock, *The Holy Spirit in the Syrian Baptismal Tradition*, 38; Winkler, "The Original Meaning and Implications of the Prebaptismal Anointing"; idem, *Das Armenische Initiationsrituale* 373–378.

the year 400, toward the end of Chrysostom's life.[65] These interior shifts were a manifestation that the Pauline theology of baptism was changing the understanding of the interior dynamics of the sacrament with the greater emphasis on catharsis, as Winkler has pointed out. The baptism of Jesus was not well suited to these changes in the rite of baptism.

Also, in the face of Arian and semi-Arian denials of the divinity of Christ, participation in the death and resurrection could be an affirmation of that divinity under threat.[66] One should recall that some Adoptionists had used the baptism of Jesus to promote a "low christology," the Spirit descending on Jesus at his baptism so that he worked miracles, but did not become divine. Other subordinationists held that Jesus became divine at this baptism, and still others, at his resurrection. The baptism of Jesus, therefore, became identified with a denial that Jesus was divine from the first moment of his existence. This contributed to the abandonment of the Jordan event as the primary paradigm, and promoted the theology of Romans 6:4.[67] Further, as elsewhere, the catechumens are prepared to be baptized during the paschal vigil, when the death and resurrection is the prime mystery. This would heighten Pauline theology.

Finally, there was "a mass accession to the Church" in the second half of the fourth century, placing the Church in a new situation.[68] To accommodate this new flood of converts, some may have thought that Romans 6:4 offered possibilities the Jordan event did not. For all—Jews, Gentiles, catechumens, Christians—death is a more primary anthropological event, a weightier universal experience, more threatening, rooted deep in the archaeology of dread, tapping unconscious forces of great power. In symbol, drama, and imagination, it makes the Jordan

---

[65] Brock, *The Holy Spirit in the Syrian Baptismal Tradition,* 38.

[66] Varghese, *Les Onctions Baptismales dans la Tradition Syrienne,* 90, 91.

[67] Winkler, "A Remarkable Shift in the 4th Century Creeds: An Analysis of the Armenian, Syrian, and Greek Evidence," 1399.

[68] Kretschmar, "Recent Research on Christian Initiation," in *Studia Liturgica* 92. H. Marrou, "The Expansion of Christianity Outside the Roman World," *The First Six Hundred Years* (New York: McGraw-Hill, 1964) 281–289; idem, "The Progress of Christianity Within the Empire," ibid., 291–299.

event seem almost decorative. The pastoral and liturgical possibilities of death and resurrection, together with the call to radical conversion implicit in it, may have been too much to resist.

John Chrysostom belongs more definitely than Cyril to the move away from the baptism of Jesus, a development still leaving references to the Jordan event in Chrysostom's own catechesis and in the pre-baptismal anointings of later liturgies that have their origin in Antioch.[69] This development in Antioch has more than local significance, for it is at this time that Antioch, like its sister Church of Jerusalem, became a liturgical force.[70] However, one should not forget that Chrysostom was not alone in his desire to retain the Jordan event. Aphrahat, Theodore of Mopsuestia, Jacob of Serugh, Narsai, and Severus of Antioch were also unwilling to simply surrender the baptism of Jesus. They tried to achieve a measure of harmony between Calvary and Jordan.

Middle Ages and Beyond: An Uncertain Tradition

The tradition of the baptism of Jesus as the source and institution of Christian baptism was mediated to the Middle Ages by Peter Lombard. The Master gives two opinions as to the institution of baptism. The first is enshrined in Jesus' words to Nicodemus ("without being born of water and Spirit" [John 3:5]), the second in the great commission of Matthew 28:19 ("Go, therefore, and make disciples of all nations . . ."). The Lombard prefers a third opinion: "It is more fitting to say that it [baptism] was instituted when John baptized Christ in the Jordan."[71]

Thomas Aquinas also transmits the tradition. In the *Summa theologica*, he quotes not Peter Lombard but Pseudo-Augustine: "From the moment that Christ was immersed in the waters,

---

[69] S. Brock, "Studies in the Early History of the Syrian Orthodox Baptismal Liturgy," in *Journal of Theological Studies* 23 (1972) 29; Kretschmar, "Recent Research on Christian Initiation," 92, 93.

[70] Ibid., 91.

[71] *Fourth Book of the Sentences* Distinctio 3, caput 5. The critical edition of Lombard is found in *Doctoris Seraphici S.Bonaventurae Opera Omnia*, B. a Porto Romatino, ed., 10 vols. (Quarrachi: Ad Claras Aquas, 1882–1902) 4:62.

from this very time water washes away the sins of all.'"[72] From this text Aquinas deduces that Christ instituted the sacrament of baptism at his own baptism because the sacrament is instituted when it receives the power (virtus) to produce the necessary effect. "This power, however, baptism receives when Christ is baptized."[73] Yet the necessity of receiving the sacrament existed only from the time after the death and resurrection because baptism configures one to the death and resurrection. Therefore it was necessary that Christ suffer and die before the necessity of receiving baptism was imposed.[74] Aquinas is trying to harmonize Jordan and Calvary, but the institution of the sacrament is clearly at the Jordan. Later he stresses baptism as "the sacrament of the death and passion of Christ insofar as a person is regenerated in Christ in virtue of his passion,"[75] but he weakens the Jordan event by saying that "baptism was already instituted in some manner (aliqualiter) in the very baptism of Christ."[76] He opens the possibility that Christ may have instituted the sacrament only after his passion. Aquinas is trying to accommodate three elements: the baptism of Jesus, the death and resurrection, and the belief that Jesus himself baptized before his death.[77] The harmonization is not smooth.

The Council of Trent itself says nothing on this topic, but the Catechism of the Council of Trent is emphatic: "It is clear that this Sacrament was instituted by our Lord when, having been baptized by John, He gave to water the power of sanctifying."[78] The baptism of Jesus is cited as an example to be followed but

---

[72] Pseudo-Augustine, Sermon 135; PL 39:2012; Summa Theologica 3, 66, 2.

[73] Ibid.

[74] Ibid.

[75] Ibid., 3, 73, 3 ad 3.

[76] Ibid., 3, 73, 5 ad 4.

[77] Ibid., 3, 73, 5 ad 4. Here Aquinas relates the baptism of Jesus to the text of John 3:22 (referring to the journey into Judea with his disciples, "and he spent some time there with them and baptized"). John 4:2, on the other hand, seems to indicate that it was not Jesus who baptized, only his disciples. But see Légasse, "Jésus Baptiste," Naissance du Baptême, 71–87.

[78] 2nd rev. ed., J. A. McHugh and C. J. Callan, eds. (New York: Wagner, 1934) 170.

is not related to the institution of baptism in German catechetical material from the last century.[79]

Cardinal Gasparri's *Catholic Catechism* omits it,[80] and it is absent from a modern German catechetical handbook.[81] The influential text of Emmanuel Doronzo gives it ample space,[82]
while the widely used manual of A. M. Diekamp has only one
sentence stating that the Jordan event "announced and prepared" Christian baptism.[83] The *Theological Library* published by
the French Dominicans after the Second World War mentions
the baptism of Jesus briefly, together with the pierced side and
the passion.[84] But the Romans 6:4 theology receives most of the
attention.[85] The so-called *Dutch Catechism* says the meaning of
baptism is found by returning to the Jordan and Calvary. It
links Jordan with Calvary: "He was baptized unto his death."[86]
However, the baptism of Jesus receives the merest mention; the
focus is on participation in the death and resurrection.

The Church's Confession of Faith: A Catholic Catechism for Adults,
largely authored by Walter Kasper under the aegis of the German Bishops' Conference, recalls that the primitive Church
"counted as fundamental Jesus' undergoing the baptism of
John, when Jesus was proclaimed Son of God and Spirit-filled
Messiah. . . . Christian baptism [is] founded in Jesus' own
baptism."[87] Though there is a broad presentation of the biblical
evidence, including the pierced side, Romans 6:4 holds un-
disputed sway.[88] The new *Catechism of the Catholic Church*

---

[79] J. Schuster, *Katechetisches Handbuch*, 4 vols. (Freiburg im Breisgau, 1857)
2:60–64.

[80] New York: Kennedy, 1932.

[81] F. Schreibmayer, K. Tilmann, H. Kahlefeld, *Handbuch zum Katholischen
Katechismus*, 3 double vols. (Basel: Freiburg, 1964).

[82] *De Baptismo et Confirmatione* (Milwaukee, Bruce, 1947) 19–34.

[83] *Theologia dogmaticae manuale*, 4 vols. (Paris: Desclée, 1934) 4:79.

[84] A. M. Henry et al., *Christ in His Sacraments* (Chicago: Fides, 1958) 60,
63. It also printed the picture of a twelfth-century baptismal vessel depicting the baptism of Jesus. Ibid., 69.

[85] Ibid., 63, 64, 71, 72.

[86] *A New Catechism: Catholic Faith for Adults* (New York: Seabury, 1973)
246.

[87] San Francisco: Ignatius Press, 1987, 271. Emphasis in the original.

[88] Ibid., 116, 214, 273, 274.

represents a retrieval of the Jordan event.[89] Both the Romans 6:4 theology and the baptism of Jesus are mentioned, as well as the pierced side, but the Jordan event receives new prominence, though not dominance.

The relationship between the baptism of Jesus and Romans 6:4 needs much more extensive examination, including the Latin sources. But from the leads given by Sebastian Brock and Gabriele Winkler, and the texts here presented, a pattern seems to be emerging by the beginning of the sixth century. The earliest tradition had the baptism of Jesus as the source of Christian baptism. After a brief upsurge of interest in Pauline theology in Origen at about the beginning of the third century, it fades again. Romans 6:4 begins to threaten the Jordan event in the fourth century. Even when the conditions were favorable to death and resurrection as the dominant paradigm, the baptism of Jesus shows remarkable tenacity. While the paschal mystery is dominant in John Chrysostom, Severus manages to keep the two mysteries in balance. The Middle Ages still honors the baptism of Jesus, but it has an unsteady history.

[89] "Christ's Baptism," *Catechism of the Catholic Church* (Washington, D.C.; United States Catholic Conference, 1994) nos. 1223–1225.

Conclusion

Trinity

The Jordan event manifests Jesus, sent by the Father, as coming in the power of the Holy Spirit, as permanently possessing the Holy Spirit and as the Messiah. The Spirit rests on Jesus and in Jesus. Later, the risen Christ dispenses the Spirit to believers out of his own fullness. And all believers are baptized in a single Spirit. In the Son and by the power of the Spirit, believers become sons and daughters of God, sharers in the divine life. The baptism constitutes a moment of christological concentration in a trinitarian context, a pneumatological event with trinitarian moorings defining the inner life of the Church, a cosmic bath catching up the universe into the trinitarian dynamic moving back to the Father.

This triadic teaching establishes the Father and the Spirit as the principle of identity of Jesus. If this is true of Jesus, is it not true of Christian identity? Does it not also establish the Christian community, as the body of Christ, as a communion in trinitarian life?

The baptism of Jesus, together with the annunciation, proclaims the pneumatological origins of Jesus, his trinitarian pedigree. It has been said that the health of pneumatology is in christology. One could also say that the health of christology is in pneumatology. Both could further be improved by saying that the health of christology (and pneumatology) is in trinity. If one says "Trinity," one is not simply affirming a divine "three-ness." Rather one is assenting to a trinitarian dynamic, a movement from the Father through the Son in the Spirit to touch, redeem, and transform the world and the Church, to lead them in the Spirit through Christ back to the Father.

Trinity rightly takes its point of departure from a christological center. Without calling into question the centrality of Jesus Christ, crucified and risen, to the proclamation of the good news, we need to recognize the fullness of the Spirit's mission. A fully trinitarian theology where the mission of the Spirit is equal to the mission of the Son does not mean "equal time" for the Spirit in our theologies and proclamation. However, if the Spirit has a diminished mission, the Trinity will collapse. Equal persons cannot have unequal missions. Nonetheless, the missions that are equal and central will manifest equality and centrality in different ways. The mission of the Son will be more visible and that of the Spirit more hidden. Unless the equality and centrality are maintained, theology will not be fully trinitarian, and liturgy and preaching and the prayer of praise will lack the power of the pneumatological dimension manifested in foundational mysteries of annunciation and the Jordan event. If christology is not truly pneumatological and trinitarian, the resulting christomonism is a truncated and impoverished view of Christ's identity and mission, with profound implications for the Church, the body of Christ, for the missionary and evangelizing outreach of the Church, and for prayer.[1]

If the Church is not caught up in this trinitarian dynamic, then ecclesiology loses its rootedness in the source and rhythms of trinitarian divine life, something Vatican II tried to correct.[2] Then the Church is in danger of becoming a structure carrying a divine blessing. Then the theologians conceive of the Church as being built up in christological categories to which they add the Holy Spirit in a second "moment," the Holy Spirit being an addendum. That is too late. The Spirit, along with the Son, belongs to the first constitutive moment of the Church's exis-

[1] K. McDonnell, "A Trinitarian Theology of the Holy Spirit?" in *Theological Studies* 46 (1985) 191–227; idem, "The Determinative Doctrine of the Holy Spirit," in *Theology Today* 39 (1982) 142–161.

[2] *Dogmatic Constitution on the Church* 1–4.

tence. When Basil says "the Church is set in order through the Holy Spirit," he is speaking specifically of a trinitarian ordering from within. If there is no movement back to the Father, then we fail to grasp an essential of liturgical worship with its *ad Patrem* intent. Then holiness is a static participation in the life of God, instead of a created participation in the inner-trinitarian movement as it enters into history in the plan of salvation through the missions of the Son and the Spirit. If there is no movement, then we are not going any place; then the Church, history, and the cosmos themselves have no goal. An eschatology without teeth is a betrayal of the biblical witness and that of the early Church.

Though the biblical mystery of Father, Son, and Holy Spirit is not the trinitarian formulation that emerged out of the christological controversies—three persons in one nature—the mystery of the Trinity came from nowhere if it did not come from the New Testament. The trinitarian thought of the biblical authors is also not that of the Cappadocian settlement in the fourth century, yet they see that sinful humanity meets its Father in heaven only through Jesus, who comes in the power of the Spirit. One can speak of this as the "original experience" of the trinitarian mystery in the New Testament.[3]

Ordo of Salvation

This trinitarian dynamic, and the sharing in divine life of Father, Son and Spirit, which is its core, is the chief element in the divine *ordo* of salvation. At the Jordan event "the order of the heavenly hidden mystery" is shown forth, manifested when the Father and the Spirit mutually show the divine self. The voice (Father) and the vision (Spirit) at the river are the principle of Jesus' identity. At the Jordan, Hilary says, "Jesus fully realized the mysteries of human salvation" and showed "the divine image of salvation." An ordering of the meaning of salvation as a process is here proclaimed.

[3] F. J. Schierse, "Die Neutestamentliche Trinitätsoffenbarung," *Mysterium Salutis* (Einsiedeln: Benziger, 1967) 2:85–131.

The image of salvation includes the created participation in divine life, or divinization. In Ephrem, cosmology in a trinitarian mode constitutes the prolegomena for Jesus' baptism and divinization. "The power of the Spirit's heat resides in everything (the whole of the created universe), with everything [the Spirit] is whole, yet entirely [whole] with the One (God), and is not cut off from the Radiance (Son), being mixed with it, [nor is the Spirit divided] from the Sun (Father), being mingled with it"—the heat of the Spirit, whole and undivided in the trinitarian communion, whole and undivided in the communion of creation.

A controlling image of divinization is the clothing of oneself in either Christ or the Spirit, and thereby putting on the divine trinitarian glory. The Jordan, a place of light and fire, is the event when the Spirit, which Adam lost for himself and for the whole of material creation, is restored to humanity and the cosmos. The Son strips off the garment of divine glory, puts on a human body, so he can clothe the naked Adam who was stripped of glory after the Fall. Christ went down into the waters of the Jordan to deposit there the robe of glory, so that Adam (both an individual and a corporate personality) can go down in baptism to recover the garment of glory. In Jacob of Serugh, all who follow Christ into the Jordan put on "a garment of living fire." As Adam's loss of the Spirit at the Fall deprived the whole of the created universe of the divine Spirit, so in the baptism of the New Adam, the restoration of the Spirit to the created order is universal.

In Jacob of Serugh, the making of the robe for the baptismal candidates is the result of the combined efforts of the Trinity: the Father preparing the robe, the Son weaving it, and the Spirit cutting it from the loom, which the candidates put on in divine fashion. In the waters of baptism the Church itself puts on Christ.

Especially in the Syrian sources, the pervasive clothing image gives coherence to the mysteries of Christ's life and the life of the Church: conception, baptism, descent into Sheol, ascension, resurrection, and informing Christian baptism, the Eucharist, anthropology, christology, Christian life, ecclesiology, and eschatology. If one can speak of "systematic" thinking in Ephrem, then the clothing image is a "systematic" umbrella. "The robe of glory" (Ephrem) is an effective way of talking about the divine life given the candidates at baptism, divinizing them, planting within them the seed to blossom into the fullness in the glory beyond. Eschatology starts at the beginning: the baptism of Jesus. The baptism of Jesus is a significant eschatological moment, where sacred history starts again.

The issue here is less the clothing image, and more what is the most effective way of speaking of the life of grace. Christ deposits the "robe of glory" Adam lost so candidates can go down and put on the robe and ascend with Christ. Both the incarnation and the baptismal event are part of the great exchange, *O! admirabile commercium*. The Church too, puts on the robe that transforms because Christ took our humanity. The Church speaks, saying, "He put us on and we put him on" (Syrian Orthodox breviary).

Preaching and Catechesis

This highly symbolic vocabulary is less appropriate to theological controversy, which is one of the reasons why Philoxenus abandoned it in an age of theological turmoil. But most of the documents using this kind of language are pastoral documents. This is a way of speaking concretely to the masses, with a depth of theological penetration. Our treatises on grace have been largely formed by theological conflict, and therefore are well adapted to theological precision. They are less adapted to liturgy, catechesis, and preaching.

These texts are an invitation to catechize and preach from within the mystery with a sense of presence, speaking in a non-abstract, graphic way about the transforming participation in the divine life and the move to the absolute future. We need to move away in preaching and catechesis from an overly conceptual, ahistorical presentation to an address speaking also in images to the imagination and to the heart. That master preacher and catechist Augustine, wrote: "There is no voice to reach the ears of God save the emotion of the heart."[4] He also mentions the necessity of repetition, because he is concerned with "the memory of your hearts."[5] Bloodless theological discourse would not reach the memory of the heart, but the personal narratives of the Scriptures proclaimed from within the mystery would. Our preaching and catechetical methods will be different from preachers and catechists in the early Church. Though our situations are vastly unlike the early centuries, we have much to learn from the methods of the early masters of preaching and catechesis.[6]

Sinless

The Sinless One, pursuing the restoration of Israel, considers himself a sinner because he belongs to a sinful people, and descends into the water asking from an inferior for a baptism of repentance of sins. The moment of self-emptying at the Jordan, like his choice for impotence, his preference for becoming the ineffective slave (Phil 2:7), continues his decision for powerlessness at the incarnation. When Christ takes off his "robe of glory" depositing it in the Jordan, he continues his choice to divest himself. This is the beginning of the gospel. The stripping of self, nakedness before God, is embodied in the rites of initiation, and has profound meaning for the nature of Christian life. It defines the first and last step in asceticism. This is the way of the Christian life from which the Church as Church is not exempt. The Church is at once holy and in continual need for purification.[7] The Church, the holy penitent, too, stands bare, exposed, uncovered, before the holiness of God, confessing the sins in the life of the Church. Without this confession of ecclesial sin, we slip into ecclesiastical arrogance.

---

[4] *On Catechizing the Unlearned in the Faith* 5:9; *De catechizandis rudibus*, J. P. Christopher, ed. (Washington, D.C.: The Catholic University of America, 1926) 44, 45.

[5] *Tract on the Gospel of John* 7:6; PL 35:1416.

[6] W. Harmless, *Augustine and the Catechumenate* (Collegeville: A Pueblo Book/The Liturgical Press, 1995).

[7] *Dogmatic Constitution on the Church* 8.

The death and resurrection paradigm of Romans 6:4 is completely absent from the second century (*Didaché*, Barnabas, Ignatius, Clement, Hermas, Justin, all the apologists, Irenaeus). Persons like Justin and Irenaeus know Romans, but they do not cite this text. Then, at the beginning of the third century, Origen, the first to mention the text, refers to it in at least thirteen of his works. Again, it fades from the memory of the Church for a hundred years, until well into the fourth century. Baptism of Jesus is the dominant paradigm in Clement of Alexandria, Novatian, Origen, Ephrem, Cyril, Philoxenus, *The Teaching of St. Gregory*, and *The Incomplete Commentary on Matthew*. Even those (John Chrysostom, Theodore of Mopsuestia) having Romans 6:4 as the dominant paradigm try to combine it with the baptism of Jesus. While the baptism of Jesus is clearly dominant in Cyril's *Catechetical Lectures*, Romans 6:4 makes some gains in the *Mystagogical Catecheses*. Nonetheless, Cyril—together with Narsai and Philoxenus—maintain the baptism as the dominant symbol, while establishing rapport between the two paradigms. Aphrahat and Jacob of Serugh, unwilling to surrender the baptism of Jesus, also keep harmony between the Jordan and Calvary.

When Romans 6:4 grasped the imagination, it did not supplant the baptism of Jesus. One paradigm does not necessarily displace another. In the symbolic world, two symbols can occupy the same space. Even Romans' most enthusiastic promoters retained the two. Even John Chrysostom, the champion of the turn to Calvary, attempted to keep the two in some kind of balance. Should not this history tell us we need to recapture the mystery of Jesus' baptism without denigrating the mystery of his death and resurrection?

Sheol

Occasionally the *descensus* into the Jordan is merged with the *descensus* into Sheol. This would indicate that the soteriological meaning of the baptism is not separated from the death and resurrection. Also, it indicates cosmic meaning of the baptism. As the *Odes of Solomon* make clear, the baptism of Jesus is the occasion of a cosmic upheaval: the waters are in terror and the inhabitants of the deep in dread, the cosmos itself testifying that the baptism of Jesus is not a naked sign. Christ goes down to destroy the gods of death for the sake of those who will live in the future. All those who have died also await the good news of their full liberation from death. Christ makes a journey through Sheol to break a path to the heavenly realm. Redemption is universal, working backwards as well as forwards. The Cosmic Lord claims and brings into subjection and glory his cosmic realm.

Cosmic

As Irenaeus points out, the cosmic dimensions of the baptism of Jesus start already in the eternal anointing the Father bestows on the Word, an anointing that is reflected in the anointing at the Jordan. No individual, no nature, no world, imagined or unimagined, is untouched by this cosmic anointing.

Gregory Nazianzus has Jesus carrying the cosmos with him as he ascends out of the water of the Jordan. The baptism makes creation witness to the mysteries of Jesus. If Melito's argument moves from the baptism of sun, moon, and stars in the ocean to the baptism of the Lord of Creation, nonetheless, the controlling principle is the Jordan event. In other contexts the new creation takes up the dynamics of first creation.

Both gospel and Genesis start with water. Again the Spirit moves over the waters. The Spirit transforms chaos into cosmos, total confusion into an ordered universe. Though effected by the Spirit, it is a trinitarian act. The Spirit present in the world at creation departs at the sin of Adam. The whole fount of the Spirit is poured out on Jesus at his baptism (*Gospel of the Hebrews*). The Spirit, thereby, is restored to the cosmos and is openly revealed at the resurrection.

The cosmic dimensions of the baptism of Jesus are part of antiquity's broader conviction, rooted in incarnation and resurrection, that the material universe, as the home of a redeemed humanity, is destined for transfiguration through the power of the Spirit manifested in the risen body of Christ.

Humanity stands within the laboring universe as it wails and cries out for the Jordan event, reaching out in hope of a joint liberation, touching visible and invisible creation, rational and irrational creatures. The goal of this cosmic birthing is to bring forth the new world where the Lordship of Jesus Christ is universal and absolute. According to Philoxenus, as Jesus steps down into the Jordan—his first step toward freedom—he takes the first step toward this ultimate cosmic freedom and transformation. This cosmic/soteriological event insures that salvation, shown forth in the baptism of Jesus, is meant also for the created universe, for the crass materiality of the cosmos, as Melito of Sardis indicates. The tainted, yet essentially good, cosmos is now touched by the baptismal waters, and receives its pledge in the resurrection of a future beyond history. The solidarity of humanity with other living and non-living creatures points to solidarity in transformation. The universe will participate in the glory revealed in the children of God.

The unity between humankind and the cosmos and their common destiny raises questions about pollution, the depletion of the ozone layer, the waste of natural resources, the denuding of our forests, the contamination of our seas, the dumping of toxic waste into our rivers, the release of harmful agents into the air. The ecological movement should have as its goal not only the preservation and restoration of the natural environment because we live and die here. Creation should be worthy of its vocation to praise. "Praise him, sun and moon. . . . Praise the LORD . . . mountains and all hills, fruit trees and all cedars! Wild animals and all cattle, creeping things and flying birds!" (Ps 148). The cosmos lives in hope. The universe is destined for God and for transformation. As the cosmos has a true historical past with God, which is part of "anamnesis," the cosmos has a real future with God.[8]

Institution

Ephrem says Christ "took baptism out of the Jordan," or again, "the Spirit is given by his baptism." Scholars disagree on

[8] K. Rahner, "The Hermeneutics of Eschatological Assertions," *Theological Investigations* (Baltimore: Helicon, 1966) 4:331; Z. Hayes, *What Are They Saying About Creation?* (New York: Paulist, 1980) 92–112.

whether the Scriptures themselves make the Jordan event the constituting moment of the sacrament of baptism. It appears to be an open question. The hermeneutical principle calls for some indication in the biblical text itself that this relationship exists; texts from the post-biblical period are not probative by themselves. The biblical arguments against the baptism of Jesus being the source of Christian baptism are strong. Yet many exegetes believe the Scriptures themselves propose the baptism of Jesus as structuring Christian baptism. They also propose arguments of weight.

The early post-biblical authors, those closest chronologically to the apostolic age, believe they are true to the biblical witness when they propose the baptism of Jesus as the source of Christian baptism. We may be impatient with the contemplative, participatory way of establishing the primary paradigm for Christian baptism because it is foreign to our scientific, critical approach. Yet, if we are not open to plural ways of knowing, we will impoverish ourselves. Truth and wisdom are not the sole preserve of the scientifically adept. This is not a plea to abandon critical ways of looking at our history.

The two references to the baptism of Jesus in the writings of Ignatius of Antioch, an author who did not have a high baptismal awareness, would indicate its importance at an early period. The absence of the Romans 6:4 text from the second century authors, its brief but significant appearance in Origen, its failure to catch on until well into the fourth century, indicates that the earliest Church's original paradigm for Christian baptism is the baptism of Jesus.

Through contemplation and participation, many arrived at institution by efficacy, sometimes with regard to Romans 6:4 (in one case to the death unrelated to the Romans text), sometimes the pierced side, sometimes the washing of the feet with mention of the Romans text, sometimes the baptism of Jesus. Many were convinced that Christ "opened up baptism" by being baptized. In Ephrem, the Jordan event is the cause of Christian baptism. Or as Philoxenus says, he was baptized and immediately gave his baptism to us. In Jacob of Serugh, Christ opened up baptism on the cross (pierced side). The Romans text emerged as a constant in the fourth century.

In Cyril of Jerusalem, we see the tenacity of the baptism of Jesus in the face of a considerable threat. Though Calvary was geographically in the environs of the city and the Jordan at some distance, the baptism of Jesus retained its dominance in the *Catechetical Lectures*, while in the *Mystagogical Catecheses* the death of Jesus makes some gains. But Cyril does not abandon the Jordan event. The two paradigms share the honors.

Theological Weight

All historical reconstruction of Jesus' history takes its point of departure from the baptism of Jesus. In the calendars followed both by the Synoptics and the fourth evangelist, the baptism of Jesus opens the liturgical year. Both among orthodox and heterodox groups, the liturgical year begins at the Jordan. The Syrians fuse Adam and Christ and have the baptism of Christ/Adam on the first day of creation. With the exception of the Easter cycle, the feast of the baptism of Jesus is the oldest feast of which we have evidence, going back to the first years of the second century. The choice of the earliest post-biblical Church of the baptism as the paradigm for Christian baptism is significant. In the early Church, the baptism of Jesus is a major mystery, ranged alongside of incarnation, death, resurrection, and ascension. Except for Easter, the baptism of the Lord is the oldest liturgical feast. The celebration of the baptism never threatened the preeminent place of the paschal mysteries in the Church's liturgical year. However, the baptism was a primary feast, celebrating the mystery that laid out the trinitarian and cosmic order of salvation.

These marks of weight and priority carry a theological and pastoral imperative. No suggestion is being made to banish or diminish the Pauline paradigm of Romans 6:4, an unthinkable impoverishment. But could we not retain both in balance, as did the fourth century? Could we not give more prominence to the baptism of Jesus in our theology, catechesis, and preaching, following the example of the new *Catechism of the Catholic Church*? Such a retrieval would give believers a sense of sharing in Christ's prophetic mission. A restoration of the baptism of Jesus might give the Christian life a deeper trinitarian awareness. The relation of the baptism of Jesus to the temptation in the desert would indicate that baptism is for real life, for struggle and trials. Christians would find more support in the stress of modern life.

Index

associating baptism and
  passion, 168
letter to the Ephesians, 26, 30, 33
letter to the Magnesians, 32
letter to the Smyrnaeans, 26, 30,
  33, 56
letter to the Trullians, 32
Incarnation, 103, 133. *See also*
  "Four Bridges"; Mary
  divinization through, 140
  three staging posts of, 139
Incomplete Commentary on Matthew
  (Pseudo-Chrysostom), 191
Institution of Christian baptism
  command to baptize, 180–182
  efficacy to establish institution,
    186
  foot-washing as, 172, 192–193.
    See also Aphrahat
  pierced side as, 213. *See also*
    Jacob of Serugh
  principle of, 188–200
Interior transformation, 138, 139,
  150
Irenaeus, 56, 57, 80, 116–118, 123,
  128 (n. 2), 158. *See also* Anointing
  (at baptism of Jesus); Soteriology
  in the apostolic tradition, 57
  relating baptism and passion, 168

Jacob of Edessa, 167
Jacob of Serugh, 41, 45, 55, 61, 67,
  102, 107–108, 135, 141, 142, 165,
  172, 187, 195, 209–211, 217, 220,
  232, 239
Jaschke, Hans-Jochen, 123
Jerome, 21, 52, 53–54. *See also*
  Gospel of the Hebrews
Jerusalem, 220–222
John of Apamea, 74, 105
John the Baptist, 1–3
  within anointing succession, 127
  Jesus and, 8–9
  in relation to descent into Sheol,
    159
  in relation to Moses, 124, 210
  "Treasurer of baptism," 196, 215
  witness of, 10–11

John Chrysostom, 73, 195, 209, 212,
  213, 225–227, 232
Jordan. *See also* Baptism of Jesus;
  Descent of the Holy Spirit;
  Voice of the Father; Water
  cosmic dimension of, 76, 145–155,
    169
  ecclesiological dimension of, 143
  as "economic perfection," 91
  establishing order, 94–95
  glorification at, 82–84
  images of extravagance at, 190–200
  as imitation, 126–127
  as instrument of universalism,
    75, 155
  knowing at, 80–81
  meaning "to descend," 205
  as point between two Edens,
    146–148
  resting at, 78–80
  and Sheol, 165–166
  soteriological significance of, 75
  "today is forever," 98–99
  as womb, 101–102
Justin Martyr, 19, 24, 26, 42, 43,
  49, 79, 80, 92, 96, 106, 107, 111,
  123, 158, 168
Juvencus, 97

Käsemann, Ernst, 15, 157
Kasper, Walter, 234
Kelly, J.N.D., 157
Key of Truth (Armeniam docu-
  ment), 80, 83
Klijn, 90
Koinonia/Communion
  between elements, 65
  between Jesus and humankind,
    160
  in trinitarian life, 115, 133

Lactantius, 22, 23, 94–95
Légasse, 173, 178, 181, 182
Legault, A., 15 (n. 3)
Leloir, Louis, 53
Lentzen-Deis, Fritzleo, 15

first used by Origen, 201–203, 242. *See also* Origen
ignored throughout second century, 183–186, 242
in John Chrysostom, 226–227
promoted by anti-Arian concerns, 231
in Severus of Antioch, 227–228
in Theodore of Mopsuestia, 213–214
in *Theological Library*, 234
well-suited to pastoral care after the Peace of the Church, 231–232
Pentecost, 79, 121, 178
Peter Lombard, 232
Philoxenus, 39, 48, 49, 55, 62, 63, 65, 66, 70, 73, 75, 102, 108, 148, 206, 217. *See also* Baptism of Jesus: as trinitarian revelation; Soteriology
Pierced side, 179, 187, 200, 209, 212, 213, 234. *See also* Jacob of Serugh
Plooij, D., 85, 167
Polycarp, 27, 56, 57, 158
Posidonius, 64–65
Preaching and catechesis, 240–241
Preaching of Paul, The, 21, 57, 106
Pre-existence. *See* Son of God: pre-existent
Proclus, 110
Prophets. *See also* Anointing (at baptism of Jesus): succession; Charisms
endowed with the Spirit, 72
not able to reveal baptism, 101
Pseudo-Athanasius, 35
Pseudo-Augustine, 232
Pseudo-Chrysostom, 191
Public life of Jesus, 13, 19
Purgation. *See* Fire

Regeneration. *See* Economy of salvation
Reinink, 90
Resurrection, 13, 51, 63, 82, 104, 133, 141, 146, 189, 202, 205. *See also* "Four Bridges"; Identity of Jesus; Origen

Robe of glory, 128–144, 145, 240, 241. *See also* Adam; Baptism of Jesus: clothing images; Divinization
"robe of the Spirit," 138
robes of glory/of light, 139
Roman Catechism (Trent), 159
Romans 6:4. *See* Pauline theology: Rom 6:4

Sacramentum. See Tertullian
Sacred (liturgical) time, 103–104, 143, 170, 213
Sacred Space, 143, 169
Salvation. *See also* Economy of salvation; Hilary of Poitiers; Universalism of redemption
baptism, "image of," 45, 238
baptism, "mystery of," 44
called "creation" in Ephesians, 63
cosmic reality, 64, 122. *See also* Philoxenus
ordo of, 29, 238
Scheizer, Eduard, 179
Schneemelcher, Wilhelm, 53
Servant of God, 3, 5, 6, 10, 11, 12, 18
Severus of Antioch, 49, 55, 76, 167, 206, 227–228, 232
Sheol, 51, 103, 104, 107, 141, 143, 156–157. *See also* Womb image
merging with Jordan, 165–166
Sinlessness of Jesus, 15–19, 22, 67, 241. *See also* Baptism of Jesus: embarrassment caused by
Son of God, 11, 13, 44, 92, 97. *See also* Anointing (at baptism of Jesus)
pre-existent, 7, 8, 9, 13
sonship and Spirit associated with baptism, 177
true divinity and true humanity of, 98
Sophronius, 77
Soteriology
of Irenaeus, 59–60
of Melito of Sardis, 50
of Philoxenus, 70
Spirit. *See also* Anointing (at bap-

tism of Jesus); Anointing (at
Christian baptism); Trinity
"autonomy" of, 123
descending on Jesus. See
Descent of the Spirit
hovering over water, 54, 103.
See also Creation story
imparting of, 219–220. See also
Christian baptism: Spirit
imparted at
mother-, 99
resting on Jesus, 11, 78–80, 83
unique bearer of, 12
Syria, 18, 36. See also Armenia
Syriac language, 37
Syrian anaphoras, 40
Syriac and Armenian sources, 26,
31, 56, 78, 81, 99. See also
Aphrahat; Ephrem; Winkler
importance of clothing images
in, 239
witness to a Semitic form of
Christianity, 131

Tatian, 93
Taylor, Vincent, 15
Teacher, The (Clement of Alexan-
dria), 116
Teaching of St. Gregory, The (oldest
Armenian catechesis), 45, 46, 47,
48, 60, 61, 80, 83, 102, 124, 127,
141, 194, 195, 196, 242. See also
Syriac and Armenian sources
Tertullian, 54, 76, 79, 114–115, 168,
184, 188–189. See also Water
Sacramentum in, 115
Testament of Asher, The, 160
Testament of Levi, The, 82, 83, 84
"Testimonia," 95
Testimonies to Quirinus (Cyprian),
95
Theodore of Mopsuestia, 39, 69,
213–215, 217, 225, 232
Theodoret, 131
Theodotus, 87
Theological Library, 234
Theophilus of Antioch, 56, 113, 114
Three births. See Baptism of Jesus:
as birth event

Thyen, Hartwig, 176
Tract on the Psalms (Hilary of
Poitiers), 98
Transfiguration, 182
Treatise on the Feasts of Christmas
and Epiphany (Ananias of
Shirak), 56
Trent, council of, 233
Trinity, 103, 141, 236
anointing set in the revelation
of, 118–119
consubstantial mystery, 47
mission of Son and Spirit,
237–238
mutual knowledge of Father
and Son, 80
trinitarian character of desert
freedom, 69
trinitarian character of journey,
164
trinitarian cosmology, 133–135.
See also Ephrem
trinitarian doctrine, 94
trinitarian dynamic, 127, 134, 238
trinitarian life of the Church, 92

Universalism of redemption, 122,
170, 239–240, 243. See also
Irenaeus; Jordan; Pentecost

Valentinus/Valentinians, 112, 114,
117
Vigne, Daniel, 35, 53, 54, 56, 85–86,
88, 90, 98
Voice of the Father, 5, 7, 46, 47,
72, 74, 80, 92, 98, 172, 204, 226.
See also Descent of the Spirit
von Rad, Gerhard, 127

Water
cosmic ocean, 149. See also Jordan
cosmic river, 212. See also Jacob
of Serugh; Jordan
cosmic waters, 61, 62. See also
The Teaching of St. Gregory
sanctification of, by Christ, 67–68
sanctification of, by fire, 107
theme of, in Tertullian, 188–189.
See also Cyril of Alexandria